IAM TWENTY-FIR

SPECIES OF SPA

CW01614147

Georges Perec was bor had moved to France in th ...eak of war in 1939, his father joined the Army and was fatally wounded in June 1940; and for the next eighteen months Perec lived with his mother in occupied Paris. He was sent south at the end of 1941 to a village near Grenoble, in the unoccupied zone, and entrusted to the care of an aunt and uncle. His mother remained in Paris, and in 1943 she was rounded up with other Jews and died in the concentration camp at Auschwitz. These tragic early experiences are echoed in his semi-autobiographical work *W or The Memory of Childhood*. Perec wanted to be a writer from an early age, but lacked confidence in his ability. After failing to complete his history degree at the Sorbonne, he got a full-time job as archivist in a science laboratory, which he gave up only four years before his death. In 1967 he became a key member of the OUvroir de LIttérature POtentielle (OuLiPo) or 'the workshop for potential literature', a group of writers and mathematicians interested in word games and in the use of formal constraints in literature. Perec's own most celebrated contribution to the work of the OuLiPo was a 300-page novel called *La Disparition* (*A Void* in its English version), which contains not a single letter 'e'. The first book Perec published, the novel *Things* (1965), won the Prix Renaudot, and *Life a User's Manual*, which appeared in 1978, received the Prix Médecis and was shortlisted for the Prix Goncourt. He also published film scripts, radio plays, book and art reviews, essays, articles and two collections of crossword puzzles. Georges Perec died of lung cancer in Paris in 1982, four days short of his forty-sixth birthday.

John Sturrock is a literary journalist, critic and translator. His other translations for Penguin include Marcel Proust's *Against Sainte-Beuve and Other Essays*, Stendhal's *The Life of Henry Brulard* and Victor Hugo's *Notre-Dame of Paris*. He is the author of *The French New Novel*; *Paper Tigers: The Ideal Fictions of Jorge Luis Borges*; *Structuralism*; and *The Language of Autobiography*.

Teesside University

This book is supported by Teesside University.

Species of Spaces and Other Pieces	*Pigeon Reader*
GEORGES PEREC	SIMON MORRIS
Edited and translated by John Sturrock	*With photographs by Susan Julia Dobson & Peter Heaton*

for Robyn,
These are questions that I ask, and I think there is some point in a writer asking them.

PENGUIN BOOKS	iam

INFORMATION AS MATERIAL

www.informationasmaterial.org
Appt 1. Harrow Court, Harrow Road, Acklam, TS5 5NY

Published by INFORMATION AS MATERIAL, 2012

ISBN 978-1-907468-15-5

The moral right of the pigeon has been asserted

Undesigned by Groundwork
Set in 11/12.25pt Monotype Walbaum
Printed in England by Henry Ling Limited, The Dorset Press, Dorchester

creative commons

This work is licensed under the Creative Commons Attribution 2.5 Licence. You are free to share or remix this work but should always attribute the work in the manner specified by the author. To view a copy of this license, visit http://creativecommons.org/licenses/by/2.5/ or send a letter to: Creative Commons, 171 Second Street, Suite 300, San Francisco, California, 94105, USA

Cataloging and publications data is available on request

Contents

Introduction

The Underwood machine at which Georges Perec did his typing was old but a survivor, and it can't often have been at rest during the twenty-odd years of his writing life. For Perec was productive: by the time of his early death in 1982, he was the author of one large book, half a dozen short, or very short, books, and a whole catalogue of sundries: radio plays, film and television scripts, book and art reviews, essays, articles and two gatherings of crossword puzzles. The large book was his vastly entertaining novel, *Life a User's Manual*, a multi-story masterpiece that launched Perec among Anglophones with an auspicious éclat when it appeared in English translation in 1987. Since then most of the short or very short books – *Things*, *A Man Asleep*, *W or The Memory of Childhood*, *A Void*, and the unfinished '*53 Days*' – have also been translated. All of these either are fiction or else contain fiction, even if there has to be something of Perec himself in the anomic anti-hero of *A Man Asleep* and rather more of him in the all-but-autobiographical *W or The Memory of Childhood*.

What has previously gone untranslated for the most part is the scatter of Perec's non-fictional and occasional writings. A selection made from what I believe to be the brightest and/or most endearing of these fills the pages which follow. It begins with the whole of a small book that he published in 1974 called *Espèces d'espaces* (Species of Spaces), which is a thoroughly Perecquian title for a thoroughly Perecquian work. He was originally contracted to write it by a friend and collaborator trained in architecture, hence the subject of the book, which is urban and domestic space and how, these days, we are made to occupy it. This is pure topography: plain to the point of obviousness at times, yet forever veering off into jolly idiosyncrasies of the kind that make Perec so entertaining to read.

After *Species of Spaces* come the Other Pieces of this volume's title – I hope and believe Perec would have liked the homophonetics of that sequence. These represent him at the length he was happiest with, of an orderly few pages at a time, written as often as not to a commission or at the prompting of others. Some of these essays and articles can safely be read as autobiographical, like the account he gives of what it was like for him to leap into the void from an aeroplane during his time as a parachutist in the French Army (p. 109), or that of an experience of psychoanalysis which he underwent at a time of depression in his mid-thirties (p. 161). Other pieces are turned at least partly away from himself and on to the material world around him, as in the impassive descriptions of the objects he can see in front of him on his work-table (p. 140), or of the changes observable over a period of time in the unhappy Rue Vilin in Paris (p. 208). Other pieces still have little or nothing to do directly with Perec, and in these he is often at his funniest: as in the splendid spoof itemizing the scientific collaboration between Léon Burp and Marcel Gotlib (p. 265). Finally, the volume also contains a delightful short story, *The Winter Journey*, the ingenious idea at the heart of which the great Borges would have been happy to find (p. 273); and a small sample – necessarily small given how hard it is to translate anything like this without ruining it – of the word games that Perec practised so attractively and with such prodigious skill.

No other recent (or not so recent) French writer can have been translated into English on quite the comprehensive scale that Perec has now achieved; and that one Perec volume should so quickly have followed another into British publication in the last few years is proof that he is being not simply translated but bought, and enjoyed, since publishers, we know, are by nature nervous about translations, looking on them as worthy ventures but all-too-likely money-losers. If Perec in English is, on the contrary, a money-maker, that is heartening. It is all the more heartening so far as I am concerned for being also a little unexpected. I remember well how I warmed to Perec the moment I first read him years ago, as an amiable and a clever writer in quite a familiar French vein; but I would not then have had him down as a writer ever likely to be taken up much abroad. He seemed the wrong sort of French writer for that.

I mean by this the sort of French writer who has things too much under control, is cool to a fault and too taken up with the formalities of writing. *Life a User's Manual* is not the sort of novel we're used to admiring in this country, for example, transparently artificial as it is, starved of 'real' people and filled with pointers to the elaborate way in which it has been organized by the novelist. It's a tremendously thought-out book, whose high popularity was not to be expected. And the same goes for what I have called the all-but-autobiographical *W or The Memory of Childhood*, inasmuch as this is an unnaturally poised attempt to come to terms with the tragic aspects of Perec's early life. These are fine, memorable books, but they go about things in ways we are normally not so friendly towards.

Georges Perec is not, then, the writer to turn to if it's the warm, uninhibited airing of serious feelings that you want. It is characteristic of him that when he writes here – in 'The Scene of a Stratagem' – about his time in psychoanalysis, he lets us know that it was in the end effective in relieving him of some intimate angst or misery, but without letting us know just what form this angst or misery took. The essay is a tease, drawing us on to feel for its author as someone we know must have been unhappy in order to become a patient in the first place, only finally to withhold the secret we have been brought to want to share. Reticence is the mark of everything Perec wrote in which the subject comes close to home.

And to reticence he may add humour, which is the most convivial way of all for a writer to keep in with his readers without letting too much of himself show. Almost all of Perec's writing has the benign, underrated quality of *lightness*, which was one of the qualities that his friend, the incomparably light Italian writer Italo Calvino (to whom one of the items here is dedicated), said belonged among the prime literary virtues. In Perec lightness and humour are all the more sociable for masking as they do a pessimistic view of his own and the human condition. The French writer he most reminds one of indeed is Raymond Queneau, who influenced the young Perec a great deal when he was starting out to write (and whose own beautifully light books have never had the popularity they deserve in English translation). Queneau, too, was a depressive man who wrote comical novels, while letting us see that the comedy was a cover, that life wasn't so very amusing once you stopped to think about it.

Like Queneau, Perec took refuge in language, as an absorbing medium with rules of its own by dalliance with which you can play consoling tricks on reality. And again like Queneau, he is a great believer in all that is most ordinary in human affairs: an unassuming laureate of the everyday, never obscure in what he writes and never in any danger of being pretentious. Perec was a Parisian and an intellectual in many of his tastes, but too nervous and too sincerely democratic ever to have wanted to start pronouncing on this and that in the megaphone role of a Paris intellectual. Jean-Paul Sartre and others were famous in their day for sitting in Left Bank cafés and laying down the ideological law; Perec, too, went to Left Bank cafés, not in his case to lay down any law (or even to sit), but rather to play the pinball machines – to the point where he used to get blistered fingers from the knobs. Which is a more human way than most of coping with *ennui*.

Behind the lightness and escapism of his writing there lay real trauma. Georges Perec was born in 1936, in Paris, the child of Polish Jews who had moved to France towards the end of the 1920s. The father did a number of very different jobs, the mother kept a hairdressing salon in Belleville, a working class quarter in the north-east of the city (see 'The Rue Vilin', a description of the street he had lived in as a very small boy, made haunting by its refusal of any explicit sentiment or nostalgia). When the war broke out in September 1939, Perec's father joined up and, because he was still a Polish citizen, was posted to the Foreign Legion; in June of the following year he was fatally wounded by shrapnel, six days before the armistice was signed with the victorious Germans. For the next eighteen months Perec lived in occupied Paris with his mother. At the end of 1941, by when the threat to French Jews was becoming more immediate, he was sent south into the Unoccupied Zone, to the village of Villard de Lans near Grenoble, to join an aunt and uncle. His mother remained behind. Early in 1943, she was rounded up along with other Jews and sent to Germany. She was never seen again, and is presumed to have died in Auschwitz. Georges Perec was subsequently brought up in Paris by the same aunt and uncle to whose care he had been entrusted in the south.

These are terrible facts of his childhood that anyone reading Perec is better off for knowing, since not knowing them will make some at least of his writings seem much less affecting than they actually are. For example, there is the 'short story' here called 'The Scene of a Flight', which has an eleven-year-old boy playing truant from home and school. The story is simply, concretely, yet quite artfully told, or told not quite straight, since Perec has shuffled the chronology of the day's events around. In the end we can't be altogether sure whether it is *his* story or not, even though the 'he' of the earlier pages is withdrawn finally in favour of a nakedly authorial 'I'.

This is Perec all over, present in detail on the page while at the same time displaying his author's licence to deceive. At the age of eleven, in 1947, he was indeed living in the quarter of western Paris where his story starts and ends – a much more prosperous quarter than the Rue Vilin, since his uncle dealt in pearls and lived well – and his life with his surrogate parents wasn't a smooth one, so an episode of truancy is highly plausible. We have no reason to doubt that there *was* such a day in the boy Georges's life, some reason to doubt that it happened *exactly* as it is told here. What the story leaves behind is the bleak sense in a young boy of alienation, of belonging neither at home nor anywhere else, of his deep need to experience hospitality. That bleak sense is something that Georges Perec seems to have lived with all his life.

'I was born in France, I am French, I bear a French first name, Georges, and a French surname, or almost, Perec.' In that throwaway 'almost' there lay a painful and incurable awareness of difference for Perec. His surname didn't have quite the written form it should have done; had it been a truly French name it would have been written Pérec, with an acute accent, or possibly Perrec, with a double *r* to ensure that the first *e* was given the right value. The faintly foreign form that it in fact took was for him the tell-tale mark of his difference. His was the uncertainty of the assimilated but still identifiable Jew. To the French he was different for being by birth Jewish; to other, unassimilated Jews, including members of his own family, he was different because he was French, steeped in a Gentile culture (this is a theme of 'Ellis Island').

The terrible fate suffered by his mother, and by others of his Polish relatives, is to be borne in mind when reading what is inevitably the most sombre of the pieces I have included here, which is a review that Perec wrote in his mid-twenties of a book by Robert Antelme describing his wartime imprisonment in a Nazi camp (p. 249). The review is quite impersonal: it nowhere so much as hints that the life of the man writing it had itself been profoundly affected by the evil institution Antelme is concerned with. It's as if Perec were relieved to be able to remain in the role of reporter, rather than having to declare himself emotively as another victim of the concentration camp system.

This is very much a *willed* objectivity on his part, poignant to us because we know it was hard-won. It might be used also to explain his commitment to the 'infra-ordinary', or the belief he had that we none of us give enough attention to what is truly daily in our daily lives, to the banal habits, settings and events of which these lives almost entirely consist. The infra-ordinary is what goes, literally, without saying. Perec, however, the modest, watchful student of the everyday, will take on the job of saying it, as he does in *Species of Spaces* and in other pieces translated here.

At one stage of Perec's life, this unusually concrete mode of literary sociology had a political point to it. It's not hard indeed to see it as deriving from Marxian notions of the use- and labour-value attaching to even the most nondescript products of human making.

But Perec's left-wing political allegiance was shallow and it didn't last; it is detectable here only when he draws hopeful lessons from the camp experience of Robert Antelme and tries to superimpose them on the class structure of postwar France. But if politics are otherwise out of sight in this volume, that only serves to make Perec's unregenerate materialism the more effective, since it is no longer at the distracting service of an ideology.

It was a materialism that extended also to writing and to language. Materialists of language are distinctive for taking full advantage of the fact that language's constituents, words, are so many objects existing materially, in the form either of a graphic inscription or acoustically, as a sound made in the mouth and received by the ear. All materialists do is to exploit the possibilities inherent in words as things, or signifiers, rather than doing what most of us do most of the time, which is to overlook the materiality or thingness of words and pass directly on to their meaning, or the signified. Perec was a writer waiting, you might say, for Structuralism to happen and to bring to the fore this suggestive division of language into its material and its semantic aspects. It is a division rich in possibilities for anyone who has decided, as he already had, that language is a raw material to be enjoyed and worked on.

He wasn't alone in this, because there were other writers in France who felt the same way. A key moment in Perec's life came with his co-opting in 1967 by the OuLiPo, a literary association of the like-minded that has by this time acquired a certain celebrity but which was then more or less unknown. There is a nice pedantry to the acronym, with its upper- and lower-case letters, apt because it is the acronym of a body as fond of pedantry as it is of word-play. The Ouvroir de Littérature Potentielle or 'Workshop for Potential Literature' was formed in 1960 by a subset of writers and mathematicians who were all interested in the possible connections between the practice of mathematics and the various formal constraints that have to be satisfied in the writing of poetry. Perec was no sort of mathematician, but the interests, and above all the advanced experiments in constraint that the members of the OuLiPo went in for, were right up his street. He became a key and resourceful member of the group, proving himself capable of OuLiPian feats of transcendent skill.

The most celebrated was the novel he wrote in the form of a lipogram, a lipogram being a text from which a certain letter (or letters) of the alphabet has been banned. Most lipograms are short; this one of Perec's was not. *La Disparition*, which was published in 1969, ran to more than 300 pages, and is riotous, a wonderfully inventive virtuoso display of how much can be done without once using the letter *e*, the hardest letter to do without in French as it is in English (Gilbert Adair's English version of this *e*-less extravaganza, published as *A Void* in 1994, is a brilliant verbal exercise in its own right). Almost as astonishing as his lipogram is Perec's Great Palindrome, a less than meaningful but still stunningly ingenious reversible construction containing more than 5,000 characters. (When I was a schoolboy, the paltry nineteen characters of the Napoleonic 'Able was I ere I saw Elba' were held to be quite something.) These and other, lesser games were at once a test for Perec and a solace; they were demonstrations of verbal expertise freed from the need to be expressive.

Perec's life was not a long one – he died four days before his forty-sixth birthday, of lung cancer, brought on by a disastrous liking for nicotine. He had decided he wanted to be a writer while he was still at school, and a writer he there and then became, unpublishable to begin with but determined. His formal education did not go well, either at school or during the two years he spent failing to finish a history degree at the Sorbonne. But though he was set on becoming a writer, and even after he began to get published, he seems not to have had sufficient confidence in his success to become a writer pure and simple: he remained nearly all his life in what was – nominally – a full-time job as archivist in a science laboratory, giving it up only four years before his death. He was by every account an unusually thoughtful bibliographer, alert to ways of improving on old methods of classification. So the job was never the chore it may sound, or would have been for someone less temperamentally attuned to it. Perec positively enjoyed classification, in practice and in theory – for the evidence of that you have only to read what he has to say about its charms and oddities in 'Think/Classify'.

At the time of his death, Georges Perec had a small but select following in his own country and none at all to speak of outside it. The first book that he succeeded in getting published (in 1965), *Things*, won the Prix Renaudot, which is one of the literary prizes that actually count for something in France; and *Life a User's Manual* won the equally worthwhile Prix Médecis when it appeared in 1978, having been shortlisted for the Prix Goncourt. This wasn't great fame, but fame enough for a discreet writer like Perec, whose *oeuvre* was so various and so undemanding, and who away from his writings was too mild and shy a man ever to go in for self-promotion. Outside France, he was hardly known when he died and it was some years before any publisher was brave enough to bring out *Life a User's Manual* in English. Since then, we have had not only all the translations I listed earlier, but a large, not to say exhaustive biography of Perec by his most dedicated English-language translator, David Bellos (a book I was grateful to be able to draw on in the writing of this Introduction). With the addition of this *Species of Spaces and Other Pieces* Perec is now with us in full, and I know of no more pleasurable literary company.

I have added footnotes to my translations where they seem likely to be of help in explaining Perec's allusions; these are marked by asterisks and daggers. All the numbered footnotes are Perec's own. I needed help myself, needless to say, in pursuing some of the more arcane details and allusions, and I here record my thanks to Harry Mathews, Georges Perec's old friend and fellow-OuLiPian, and to Marie-José Minassian. In making a number of small changes to both the Introduction and the text of the new edition of *Species of Spaces*, I am most grateful for the suggestions of Mme Ela Bienenfeld, Georges Perec's cousin and literary executor.

John Sturrock, 1999

Species of Spaces / Espèces d'espaces (1974)

For Pierre Getzler

Figure 1: Map of the Ocean
(taken from Lewis Carroll's *Hunting of the Snark*)

SPACE
OPEN SPACE
ENCLOSED SPACE
OUTER SPACE
SPACE SUIT
SPACE AGE
LIVING SPACE
PROJECTIVE SPACE
SPACE CAPSULE
LACK OF SPACE
SPACE BAND
SPACE HEATER
DEEP SPACE
SPACE ODYSSEY
SPACE SALESMAN
EUCLIDEAN SPACE
SPACE CADET
SPACE STATION
BLANK SPACE
SPACE OUT
PARKING SPACE
SPACE INVADERS
SPACE WALK
SPACE TIME CONTINUUM
SPACE BAR
LOST IN SPACE
STARING INTO SPACE
WATCH THIS SPACE
SPACE CURVE
SPACE LATTICE
SPACE OPERA
CATCHER SPACE
SPACE SICKNESS
BUNCHER SPACE
THREE-DIMENSIONAL SPACE
HAIR SPACE
SPACE RACE
NULL SPACE

LEAVE A SPACE
SPACE OF A MOMENT
INTERCOSTAL SPACE
AVAILABLE SPACE
SPACE NEEDLE
POSITION IN SPACE
EDGES OF SPACE
SPACE WRITER
WIDE OPEN SPACES
LACK OF SPACE
SPACE SAVING
ENCLOSED SPACE
SPACE FILLER
WASTED SPACE

Foreword

The subject of this book is not the void exactly, but rather what there is round about or inside it (cf Fig. 1). To start with, then, there isn't very much: nothingness, the impalpable, the virtually immaterial; extension, the external, what is external to us, what we move about in the midst of, our ambient milieu, the space around us.

Space. Not so much those infinite spaces, whose mutism is so prolonged that it ends by triggering off something akin to fear, nor the already almost domesticated interplanetary, intersidereal or intergalactic spaces, but spaces that are much closer to hand, in principle anyway: towns, for example, or the countryside, or the corridors of the Paris Métro, or a public park.

We live in space, in these spaces, these towns, this countryside, these corridors, these parks. That seems obvious to us. Perhaps indeed it should be obvious. But it isn't obvious, not just a matter of course. It's real, obviously, and as a consequence most likely rational. We can touch. We can even allow ourselves to dream. There's nothing, for example, to stop us from imagining things that are neither towns nor countryside (nor suburbs), or Métro corridors that are at the same time public parks. Nor anything to forbid us imagining a Métro in the heart of the countryside [*campagne*] (I've even before now seen an advertisement to that effect, but it was – how shall I put it? – a publicity campaign [*campagne*]).

What's certain, in any case, is that at a time too remote no doubt for any of us to have retained anything like a precise memory of it, there was none of all this: neither corridors, nor parks, nor towns, nor countryside. The problem isn't so much to find out how we have reached this point, but simply to recognize that we have reached it, that we are here. There isn't one space, a beautiful space, a beautiful space round about, a beautiful space all around us, there's a whole lot of small bits of space, and one of these bits is a Métro corridor, and another of them is a public park. Another – and here we suddenly enter into much more particularized spaces – originally quite modest in size, has attained fairly colossal dimensions and has become Paris, whereas a space near by, not necessarily any less well endowed to begin with, has been content to remain Pontoise. Still another space, much larger and vaguely hexagonal, has been surrounded by a broad dotted line (innumerable events, some of them particularly weighty, had as their sole purpose the tracing out of this dotted line) and it has been decided that everything found *inside* this dotted line should be coloured violet and be called France, while everything found *outside* this dotted line should be in a different colour (although, outside the aforesaid hexagon, they weren't in the least anxious to be of a uniform colour: one bit of space wanted its colour and another bit its, whence the famous problem in topology of the four colours, unresolved to this day) and have a different name (in point of fact and for quite a few years, there was a strong insistence on colouring violet – and thereby calling France – bits of space that didn't belong to the aforesaid hexagon, but were often far distant from it, but, generally speaking, that didn't last half so well).

In short, spaces have multiplied, been broken up and have diversified. There are spaces today of every kind and every size, for every use and every function. To live is to pass from one space to another, while doing your very best not to bump yourself.

or, if you prefer:

ACT ONE

A voice (off):
To the North, nothing.
To the South, nothing.
To the East, nothing.
To the West, nothing.
In the centre, nothing.
The curtain falls. End of Act One.

ACT TWO

A voice (off):
To the North, nothing.
To the South, nothing.
To the East, nothing.
To the West, nothing.
In the centre, a tent.
The curtain falls. End of Act Two.

ACT THREE AND LAST

A voice (off):
To the North, nothing.
To the South, nothing.
To the East, nothing.
To the West, nothing.
In the centre, a tent,
and,
in front of the tent,
an orderly busy polishing a pair
of boots
with 'LION NOIR' boot polish!
The curtain falls. End of Act Three and Last.

(Author unknown. Learnt around 1947, recalled in 1973.)

Or again:

In Paris, there is a street;
in that street, there is a house;
in that house, there is a staircase;
on that staircase, there is a room;
in that room, there is a table;
on that table, there is a cloth;
on that cloth, there is a cage;
in that cage, there is a nest;
in that nest, there is an egg;
in that egg, there is a bird.

The bird knocked the egg over;
the egg knocked the nest over;
the nest knocked the cage over;
the cage knocked the cloth over;
the cloth knocked the table over;
the table knocked the room over;
the room knocked the staircase over;
the staircase knocked the house over;
the house knocked the street over;
the street knocked the town of Paris over.

Children's song from Les Deux-Sèvres
(Paul Eluard, *Poésie involontaire*
et poésie intentionelle)

The Page

'I write in order to peruse myself'

Henri Michaux

1

I write . . .

I write: I write . . .
I write: 'I write . . .'
I write that I write . . .
etc.

I write: I trace words on a page.
Letter by letter, a text forms, affirms itself, is confirmed, is frozen, is fixed:
a fairly strictly h
o
r
i
z
o
n
t
a
l
line is set down on the blank sheet of paper, blackens the virgin space, gives it a direction, vectorizes it:
from left   to right
f
r
o
m

t
o
p
t
o
b
o
t
t
o
m

Before, there was nothing, or almost nothing; afterwards, there isn't much, a few signs, but which are enough for there to be a top and a bottom, a beginning and an end, a right and a left, a recto and a verso.

2

The space of a sheet of paper (regulation international size, as used in Government departments, on sale at all stationers) measures 623.7 sq. cm. You have to write a little over sixteen pages to take up one square metre. Assuming the average format of a book to be 21 by 29.7 cm, you could, if you were to pull apart all the printed books kept in the Bibliothèque Nationale and spread the pages carefully out one beside the other, cover the whole, either of the island of St Helena or of Lake Trasimeno.

You could also work out the number of hectares of forest that have had to be felled in order to produce the paper needed to print the works of Alexandre Dumas (*père*), who, it will be remembered, had a tower built each stone of which had the title of one of his books engraved on it.

3

I write: I inhabit my sheet of paper, I invest it, I travel across it.

I incite *blanks*, *spaces* (jumps in the meaning: discontinuities, transitions, changes of key).

I write in the margin

I start a new

paragraph. I refer to a footnote[1]

I go to a new sheet of paper.

1. I am very fond of footnotes at the bottom of the page, even if I don't have anything in particular to clarify there.

4

There are few events which don't leave a written trace at least. At one time or another, almost everything passes through a sheet of paper, the page of a notebook, or of a diary, or some other chance support (a Métro ticket, the margin of a newspaper, a cigarette packet, the back of an envelope etc.) on which, at varying speeds and by a different technique depending on the place, time or mood, one or another of the miscellaneous elements that comprise the everydayness of life comes to be inscribed. Where I'm concerned (but I'm no doubt too choice an example, writing being in fact one of my principal activities), this goes from an address caught in passing, an appointment noted down in haste, or the writing-out of a cheque, an envelope or a package, to the laborious drafting of an official letter, the tedious filling-in of a form (tax return, sickness note, direct debit for gas and electricity bills, subscription form, contract, lease, endorsement, receipt etc.), to a list of urgently needed supplies (coffee, sugar, cat litter, Baudrillard book, 75-watt bulb, batteries, underwear etc.), from the sometimes rather tricky solution to a Robert Scipion crossword to the fair copy of a finally completed text, from notes taken at some lecture or other to the instant scribbling-down of some device that may come in useful (verbal play, verbal ploy, play on letters, or what's commonly known as an 'idea'), from a piece of literary 'work' (writing, yes, sitting down at the table and writing, sitting at the typewriter and writing, writing right through the day, or right through the night, roughing out a plan, putting down capital *I*s and small *a*s, drawing sketches, putting one word next to another, looking in a dictionary, recopying, rereading, crossing-out, throwing away, rewriting, sorting, rediscovering, waiting for it to come, trying to extract something that might resemble a text from something that continues to look like an insubstantial scrawl, getting there, not getting there, smiling (sometimes), etc.) to work full stop (elementary, alimentary): i.e. to ticking, in a journal containing a summary of almost all the others in the field of the life sciences, the titles that may be of interest to the research-workers whose bibliographical documentation I am supposed to provide, filling in index-cards, assembling references, correcting proofs, etc.

Et cetera.

5

This is how space begins, with words only, signs traced on the blank page. To describe space: to name it, to trace it, like those portolano-makers who saturated the coastlines with the names of harbours, the names of capes, the names of inlets, until in the end the land was only separated from the sea by a continuous ribbon of text. Is the aleph, that place in Borges from which the entire world is visible simultaneously, anything other than an alphabet?

Space as inventory, space as invention. Space begins with that model map in the old editions of the *Petit Larousse Illustré*, which used to represent something like 65 geographical terms in 60 sq. cm., miraculously brought together, deliberately abstract. Here is the desert, with its oasis, its wadi and its salt lake, here are the spring and the stream, the mountain torrent, the canal, the confluence, the river, the estuary, the river-mouth and the delta, here is the sea with its islands, its archipelago, its islets, its reefs, its shoals, its rocks, its offshore bar, and here are the strait, the isthmus and the peninsula, the bight and the narrows, and the gulf and the bay, and the cape and the inlet, and the head, and the promontory, here are the lagoon and the cliff, here are the dunes, here are the beach, and the saltwater lakes, and the marshes, here is the lake, and here are the mountains, the peak, the glacier, the volcano, the spur, the slope, the col, the gorge, here are the plain and the plateau, and the hillside and the hill, here is the town and its anchorage, and its harbour and its lighthouse . . .

Virtual space, a simple pretext for a nomenclature. But you don't even need to close your eyes for the space evoked by these words, a dictionary space only, a paper space, to become alive, to be populated, to be filled: a long goods train drawn by a steam locomotive passes over a viaduct; barges laden with gravel ply the canals; small sailing boats manoeuvre on the lake; a big liner escorted by tugs enters the anchorage; children play ball on the beach; an Arab wearing a big straw hat trots down the shady paths of the oasis on his donkey . . .

The streets of the town are full of cars. A turbaned housewife is beating a carpet at her window. In small suburban plots, dozens of nurserymen are pruning fruit trees. A detachment of soldiers presents arms as an official wearing a tricolour sash unveils the statue of a general.

There are cows in the pasture, winegrowers in the vineyards, lumberjacks in the forests, climbers roped together in the mountains. A postman on his bicycle pedals laboriously up the hairpin bends of a lane. There are washerwomen beside the river, roadmenders beside the roads, and farmers' wives feeding the hens. Rows of children are coming out in twos into the school yard. A *fin-de-siècle* villa stands all on its own surrounded by tall glass buildings. There are little gingham curtains in the windows, drinkers on the terraces of the cafés, a cat warming itself in the sun, a lady weighed down by parcels hailing a taxi, a sentry mounting guard in front of a public building. There are garbage-collectors filling refuse trucks, decorators putting up scaffolding. There are nannies in the squares, second-hand booksellers along the quays; there's a queue in front of the bakery, one gentleman walking his dog, another reading his newspaper sitting on a bench, another watching workmen demolishing a block of houses. There's a policeman controlling the traffic. There are birds in the trees, sailors on the river, fishermen on the embankment. There's a woman raising the iron shutter of her haberdashery. There are chestnut-vendors, sewermen, newspaper-sellers. There are people doing their shopping.

Studious readers are reading in the libraries. Teachers are giving their lessons. Students are taking notes. Accountants are lining up columns of figures. Apprentice pastry cooks are stuffing cream into rows of cream puffs. Pianists are playing their scales. Sitting deep in thought at their tables, writers are forming lines of words.

An idealized scene. Space as reassurance.

The Bed

'For a long time I went to bed in writing'
Parcel Mroust*

1

We generally utilize the page in the larger of its two dimensions. The same goes for the bed. The bed (or, if you prefer, the page) is a rectangular space, longer than it is wide, in which, or on which, we normally lie longways. 'Italian' beds are only to be found in fairy tales (Tom Thumb and his brothers, or the seven daughters of the Ogre, for example) or in altogether abnormal and usually serious circumstances (mass exodus, aftermath of a bombing raid, etc.). Even when we utilize the bed the more usual way round, it's almost always a sign of a catastrophe if several people have to sleep in it. The bed is an instrument conceived for the nocturnal repose of one or two persons, but no more.

The bed is thus the individual space *par excellence*, the elementary space of the body (the bed-monad), the one which even the man completely crippled by debts has the right to keep: the bailiffs don't have the power to seize *your* bed. This also means – this is easily verified in practice – that we have only one bed, which is *our* bed. When there are other beds in a house or an apartment, they are said to be guest beds or spare beds. It seems we only sleep well in our own bed.

*A play on the first sentence of Proust's great novel, *A la recherche du temps perdu*, which reads: 'For a long time I went to bed early.'

2

*'Lit = île'**
Michel Leiris

It was lying face-down on my bed that I read *Twenty Years After*, *The Mysterious Island* and *Jerry on the Island*. The bed became a trapper's cabin, or a lifeboat on the raging ocean, or a baobab tree threatened by fire, a tent erected in the desert, or a propitious crevice that my enemies passed within inches of, unavailingly.

I travelled a great deal at the bottom of my bed. For survival, I carried sugar lumps I went and stole from the kitchen and hid under my bolster (they scratched . . .). Fear – terror even – was always present, despite the protection of the blankets and pillow.

Bed: where unformulated dangers threatened, the place of contraries, the space of the solitary body encumbered by its ephemeral harems, the foreclosed space of desire, the improbable place where I had my roots, the space of dreams and of an Oedipal nostalgia:

> Happy he who can sleep without fear and without remorse
> In the paternal bed, massive, venerable,
> Where all his kinsfolk were born and where they died.
>
> José-Maria de Heredia, *Trophées*

3

I like my bed. I've had it for a little over two years. Before that, it belonged to a woman friend of mine who had just moved into an apartment so tiny that her bed, though of perfectly orthodox dimensions, would barely fit in the room intended to receive it,

*Literally 'bed = island', Leiris's point being that the closeness in sound between the two French words has somehow determined the closeness (for him) in their meaning.

so she swapped it for the one I then had, which was slightly narrower.

(One day I shall write – see the next chapter – the history of, among others things, my beds.)

I like my bed. I like to stretch out on my bed and to gaze at the ceiling with a tranquil eye. I would gladly devote the major part of my time to this (the mornings mainly) were I not so often prevented by supposedly more urgent occupations (to list them would be tedious). I like ceilings, I like mouldings and ceiling roses. They often serve me instead of a Muse and the intricate embellishments in the plasterwork put me readily in mind of those other labyrinths, woven from phantasms, ideas and words. But people no longer pay any attention to ceilings. They are made dispiritingly rectilinear or, worse still, done up with so-called exposed beams.

A huge plank has long served me as a bedhead. With the exception of solid foodstuffs (I'm not usually hungry when I stay in bed), everything I couldn't do without was to be found assembled there, in the areas of both the necessary and the pointless: a bottle of mineral water, a glass, a pair of nail-scissors (chipped unfortunately), a collection of crosswords by Robert Scipion (I take the opportunity to address a tiny reproach to him: in the 43rd grid of the said collection, excellent otherwise, he has – implicitly – got *néanmoins* with two *m*s, which, obviously, means that the corresponding word across is wrong [it couldn't decently be written as *assomnoïr*] and that the solution to the puzzle has been palpably compromised), a packet of paper handkerchiefs, a hard brush that enabled me to give my (female as it happens) cat's fur a sheen that was the admiration of all, a telephone, thanks to which I was able, not only to give my friends reports on my state of health, but to inform numerous callers that I was not the Michelin Company, a fully transistorized radio playing all day long, should the mood take me, various kinds of music interspersed with whispered news items about traffic jams, a few dozen books (some that I had intended to read and didn't read, others that I re-read constantly), albums of strip cartoons, piles of newspapers, a complete smoker's kit, various diaries, notebooks, exercise-books and loose sheets of paper, an alarm-clock, naturally, a tube of Alka-Seltzer (empty), another of aspirins (half full or, if you prefer, half empty), yet another of cequinyl (an anti-flu treatment, more or less untouched), a torch, of course, numerous handouts I had neglected to throw away, letters, felt-pens, ballpoints (both these last often dry), pencils, a pencil-sharpener, an eraser (these three last articles intended for the solving of the aforesaid crosswords), a pebble picked up on the beach at Dieppe, a few other small mementoes and a post office calendar.

4
A few other banalities:

We spend more than a third of our lives in a bed.

The bed is one of the rare places where we adopt roughly speaking a horizontal posture. The others are much more specialized: operating table, bench in a sauna, chaise-longue, beach, psychoanalyst's couch . . .

Techniques of sleeping: the idea that lying down is something natural is quite inaccurate (see Marcel Mauss, 'Techniques of the Body', in *Sociologie et Anthropologie*, p. 378; the whole paragraph – too succinct, alas! – would be worth quoting).

And what about hammocks? And paliasses? And bedsteads? And box-beds? And divans deep as the grave? And straw pallets? And railway couchettes? And camp beds? And sleeping-bags resting on air-beds themselves resting on a carpet of earth?

The Bedroom

1
Fragments from a Work in Progress

I have an exceptional, I believe fairly prodigious even, memory of all the places I have slept in, with the exception of those from my earliest childhood – up until the end of the war – which have all merged in the undifferentiated greyness of a school dormitory. For the others, all I need to do, once I'm in bed, is to close my eyes and to think with a minimum of application of a given place for the bedroom to come instantly back into my memory in every detail – the position of the doors and windows, the arrangement of the furniture – for me to feel, more precisely still, the almost physical sensation of being once again in bed in that room.

Thus:

ROCK (Cornwall) Summer 1954

When you open the door, the bed is almost immediately on the left. It's a very narrow bed, and the room, too, is very narrow (give or take a few centimetres, the width of the bed plus the width of the door, i.e. hardly more than one metre fifty), and not much longer than it is wide. In extension of the bed, there is a small hanging cupboard. At the far end, a sash window. To the right, a washstand with a marble top, with a basin and a water jug, which I don't think I used much.

I'm almost certain there was a framed print on the left-hand wall, facing the bed; not just any old coloured print, but a Renoir perhaps or a Sisley.

There was lino on the floor. There was no table, or any armchair, but a chair without arms perhaps, against the left-hand wall: I used to throw my clothes on to it before getting into bed. I don't think I sat on it; I only came into this room to sleep. It was on the third and last floor of the house, I had to be careful going upstairs when I came in late not to wake up my landlady and her family.

I was on holiday, I had just passed my *bac*. In theory, I should have been living at a boarding-house that took in French schoolchildren whose parents wanted them to improve their use of English. But the boarding-house was full and I had been billeted on a family.

Each morning, my landlady would open my door and put down a steaming cup of 'morning tea' at the foot of my bed, which I invariably drank cold. I always got up too late, and only once or twice did I manage to arrive in time to eat the copious breakfast that was served in the boarding-house.

It will no doubt be remembered that during that summer, following the Geneva Agreements and the negotiations with Tunisia and Morocco, the entire planet experienced peace for the first time in several decades: a situation that lasted for only a few days and which I don't think has recurred since.

My memories are attached to the narrowness of that bed, to the narrowness of that room, to the lingering bitterness of the tea that was too strong and too cold. That summer, I drank 'pink gins', or glasses of gin improved by a drop of angostura, I flirted, somewhat fruitlessly, with the daughter of a cotton-mill-owner who had recently returned from Alexandria, I decided to become a writer, I slaved away at playing, on country harmoniums, the one tune I've ever succeeded in learning: the 54 opening notes – for the right hand, the left hand most often failing to follow – of a Bach prelude.

The resurrected space of the bedroom is enough to bring back to life, to recall, to revive memories, the most fleeting and anodyne along with the most essential. The coenesthetic certainty of my body in the bed, the topographical certainty of the bed in the room, these alone reactivate my memory, and give it an acuity and a precision it hardly ever has otherwise. Just as a word brought back from a dream can, almost before it is written down, restore a whole memory of that dream, here, the mere fact of knowing (almost without having needed to search for it, simply by having stretched out for a few moments and having closed my eyes) that the wall was on my right, the door beside me on the left (by raising my arm I could touch the handle), the window facing me, instantly evokes in me a chaotic flood of details so vivid as to leave me speechless: the young girl with the doll-like manner, the immensely long Englishman whose nose was slightly crooked (I saw him again in London, when I went to spend three days there at the end of this pseudo-linguistic holiday; he took me into a pub smothered in greenery that, sadly, I've never managed to find again since, and to a promenade concert at the Albert Hall, where I was very proud to hear, conducted it may well be by Sir John Barbirolli, a concerto for mouth organ and orchestra written especially for Larry Adler), marshmallows, Rock rock (decorated barley sugar, a speciality of seaside resorts; the best known is Brighton rock, which is – apart from being a play on words: there are rocks in Brighton just as there are cliffs in Etretat – the title of a novel by Graham Greene; even at Rock it was hard to escape it), the grey beach, the cold sea, and the wooded countryside, with its old stone bridges, where you might have expected sprites and will o' the wisps to appear at any moment.

It's no doubt because the space of the bedroom works for me like a Proustian madeleine (the whole project is of course invoked by this; all it is is nothing more than a rigorous extension of paragraphs 6 and 7 of the first chapter of the first part [*Combray*] of the first volume [*Du côté de chez Swann*] of *A la recherche du temps perdu*) that I undertook, several years ago now, to make an inventory, as exhaustive and as accurate as possible, of all the 'Places Where I Have Slept'. As yet, I've scarcely begun to describe them; on the other hand, I believe I've just about listed them all. There are about two hundred of them (barely half a dozen get added every year; I have become something of a home body). I haven't yet finally settled on the manner in which I shall classify them. Certainly not in chronological order. Doubtless not in alphabetical order (although it's the only order whose pertinence requires no justification). Maybe according to their geographical arrangement, which would emphasize the 'guidebook' aspect of the work. Or else, according rather to a thematic perspective which might result in a sort of typology of bedrooms:

1. *My* bedrooms
2. Dormitories and barrack-rooms
3. Friends' bedrooms
4. Guest rooms
5. Makeshift beds (settee, moquette plus cushions, carpet, chaise-longue, etc.)
6. Houses in the country
7. Rented villas
8. Hotel rooms
   a. scruffy hotels, boarding houses
   b. luxury hotels
9. Unusual conditions: nights on a train, on a plane, in a car; nights on a boat; nights on guard duty; nights in a police station; nights under canvas; nights in hospital; sleepless nights, etc.

I spent several months or years in a small number of these rooms; in most, I spent only a few days or a few hours. It's foolhardy perhaps on my part to claim I shall be able to remember every one of them: what was the pattern of the wallpaper in that room in the Hôtel du Lion d'Or in Saint-Chély-d'Apcher (the name – much more surprising when spoken than when written – of that cantonal capital in the Lozère has been anchored for some unknown reason in my memory since I was in the third form and had been very insistent we should stop there)? But it's from the resurrected memories of these ephemeral bedrooms that I expect the greatest revelations obviously.

2
Minor problem

When, in a given bedroom, you change the position of the bed, can you say you are changing rooms, or else what?

(cf. topological analysis.)

3

What does it mean, to live in a room? Is to live in a place to take possession of it? What does taking possession of a place mean? As from when does somewhere become truly yours? Is it when you've put your three pairs of socks to soak in a pink plastic bowl? Is it when you've heated up your spaghetti over a camping-gaz? Is it when you've used up all the non-matching hangers in the cupboard? Is it when you've drawing-pinned to the wall an old postcard showing Carpaccio's 'Dream of St Ursula'? Is it when you've experienced there the throes of anticipation, or the exaltations of passion, or the torments of a toothache? Is it when you've hung suitable curtains up on the windows, and put up the wallpaper, and sanded the parquet flooring?

4
Placid small thought no 1

Any cat-owner will rightly tell you that cats inhabit houses much better than people do. Even in the most dreadfully square spaces, they know how to find favourable corners.

Placid small thought no 2

The passage of time (my History) leaves behind a residue that accumulates: photographs, drawings, the corpses of long since dried-up felt-pens, shirts, non-returnable glasses and returnable glasses, cigar wrappers, tins, erasers, postcards, books, dust and knickknacks: this is what I call my fortune.

The Apartment

1

For two years, I had a very old neighbour. She had lived in the building for seventy years, had been a widow for sixty. In the last years of her life, after she had broken the neck of her femur, she never went further than the landing on her own floor. The concierge, or a young boy from the building, ran her errands. Several times she stopped me on the stairs to ask me what day it was. One day I went to get her a slice of ham. She offered me an apple and invited me in. She lived surrounded by exceedingly gloomy furniture that she spent her time rubbing.

2

A few years ago, one of my friends had the idea of living for a whole month in an international airport, without ever leaving it (unless, all international airports being by definition identical, to catch a plane that would have taken him to another international airport). To my knowledge, he has never realized this project, but it's hard to see what, objectively, there might be to prevent him. The activities essential to life, and most social activities, can be carried out without difficulty within the confines of an international airport: there are deep armchairs and bench seats that aren't too uncomfortable, and often restrooms even, in which passengers in transit can take a nap. You've got toilets, baths and showers, and often saunas and Turkish baths. You've got hairdressers, pedicurists, nurses, masseurs and physiotherapists, bootblacks, dry cleaners who are equally happy to mend heels and make duplicate keys, watchmakers and opticians. You've got restaurants, bars and cafeterias, leather shops and perfumeries, florists, bookshops, record shops, tobacconists and sweet shops, shops selling pens and photographers. You've got food shops, cinemas, a post office, flying secretarial services and, naturally, a whole host of banks (since it's practically impossible, in this day and age, to live without having dealings with a bank).

The interest of such an undertaking would lie above all in its exoticism: a displacement, more apparent than real, of our habits and rhythms, and minor problems of adaptation. It would quite soon become tedious no doubt. All told, it would be too easy and, as a consequence, not very testing. Seen in this light, an airport is no more than a sort of shopping mall, a simulated urban neighbourhood. Give or take a few things, it offers the same benefits as a hotel. So we could hardly draw any practical conclusion from such an undertaking, by way of either subversion or acclimatization. At most, we might use it as the subject-matter for a piece of reportage, or as the point of departure for an umpteenth comic screenplay.

3

A bedroom is a room in which there is a bed; a dining-room is a room in which there are a table and chairs, and often a sideboard; a sitting-room is a room in which there are armchairs and a couch; a kitchen is a room in which there is a cooker and a water inlet; a bathroom is a room in which there is a water inlet above a bathtub; when there is only a shower, it is known as a shower-room; when there is only a wash-basin it is known as a cloakroom; an entrance-hall is a room in which at least one of the doors leads outside the apartment; in addition, you may find a coat-rack in there; a child's bedroom is a room into which you put a child; a broom closet is a room into which you put brooms and the vacuum cleaner; a maid's bedroom is a room that you let to a student.

From this list, which might easily be extended, two elementary conclusions may be drawn that I offer by way of definitions:

1. Every apartment consists of a variable, but finite, number of rooms.
2. Each room has a particular function.

It would seem difficult, or rather it would seem derisory, to question these self-evident facts. Apartments are built by architects who have very precise ideas of what an entrance-hall, a sitting-room (living-room, reception room), a parents' bedroom, a child's room, a maid's room, a box-room, a kitchen, and a bathroom ought to be like. To start with, however, all rooms are alike, more or less, and it is no good their trying to impress us with stuff about modules and other nonsense: they're never anything more than a sort of cube, or let's say rectangular parallelepiped. They always have at least one door and also, quite often, a window. They're heated, let's say by a radiator, and fitted with one or two power points (very rarely more, but if I start in on the niggardliness of building contractors, I shall never stop). In sum, a room is a fairly malleable space.

I don't know, and don't want to know, where functionality begins or ends. It seems to me, in any case, that in the ideal dividing-up of today's apartments functionality functions in accordance with a procedure that is unequivocal, sequential and nycthemeral.[1] The activities of the day correspond to slices of time, and to each slice of time there corresponds one room of the apartment. The following model is hardly a caricature:

07.00	The mother gets up and goes to get breakfast in the	KITCHEN
07.15	The child gets up and goes into the	BATHROOM
07.30	The father gets up and goes into the	BATHROOM
07.45	The father and the child have their breakfast in the	KITCHEN
08.00	The child takes his coat from the	ENTRANCE-HALL

1. This is the best phrase in the whole book!

	and goes off to school	
08.15	The father takes his coat	
	from the	ENTRANCE-HALL
	and goes off to his office	
08.30	The mother performs her	
	toilet in the	BATHROOM
08.45	The mother takes the	
	vacuum cleaner from the	BROOM CLOSET
	and does the housework	
	(she then goes through all	
	the rooms of the apartment	
	but I forbear from listing	
	them)	
09.30	The mother fetches her	
	shopping basket from the	KITCHEN
	and her coat from the	ENTRANCE-HALL
	and goes to do the shopping	
10.30	The mother returns from	
	shopping and puts her coat	
	back in the	ENTRANCE-HALL
10.45	The mother prepares lunch	
	in the	KITCHEN
12.15	The father returns from	
	the office and hangs his	
	coat up in the	ENTRANCE-HALL
12.30	The father and the mother	
	have lunch in the	DINING-ROOM
	(the child is a day boarder)	
13.15	The father takes his coat	
	from the	ENTRANCE-HALL
	and leaves again for his	
	office	
13.30	The mother does the dishes	
	in the	KITCHEN
14.00	The mother takes her coat	
	from the	ENTRANCE-HALL
	and goes out for a walk or	

	to run some errands before going to fetch the child from school	
16.15	The mother and the child return and put their coats back in the	ENTRANCE-HALL
16.30	The child has his tea in the	KITCHEN
16.45	The child goes to do his homework in the	CHILD'S ROOM
18.30	The mother gets supper ready in the	KITCHEN
18.45	The father returns from his office and puts his coat back in the	ENTRANCE-HALL
18.50	The father goes to wash his hands in the	BATHROOM
19.00	The whole small family has supper in the	DINING-ROOM
20.00	The child goes to brush his teeth in the	BATHROOM
20.15	The child goes to bed in the	CHILD'S ROOM
20.30	The father and the mother go into the they watch television, or else they listen to the radio, or else they play cards, or else the father reads the newspaper while the mother does some sewing, in short they while away the time	SITTING-ROOM
21.45	The father and the mother go and brush their teeth in the	BATHROOM
22.00	The father and the mother go to bed in their	BEDROOM

You will notice that in this model, which, I would stress, is both fictional and problematic, though I'm convinced of its elementary rightness (no one lives exactly like that, of course, but it is nevertheless like that, and not otherwise, that architects and town planners see us as living or want us to live), you will notice then, that, on the one hand, the sitting-room and bedroom are of hardly any more importance than the broom closet (the vacuum cleaner goes into the broom closet; exhausted bodies into the bedroom: the two functions are the same, of recuperation and maintenance) and, on the other hand, that my model would not be modified in any practical way if, instead of having, as here, spaces separated by partitions delimiting a bedroom, a sitting-room, a dining-room, a kitchen, etc., we envisaged, as is often done these days, a purportedly single, pseudo-modular space (living-room, sitting-room, etc.). We would then have, not a kitchen but a cooking-area, not a bedroom but a sleeping-area, not a dining-room but an eating-area.

It's not hard to imagine an apartment whose layout would depend, no longer on the activities of the day, but on functional relationships is between the rooms. That after all was how the so-called reception rooms were divided up ideally in the large town houses of the eighteenth century or the great bourgeois apartments of the *fin de siècle*: a sequence of drawing-rooms en suite, leading off a large vestibule, whose specification rested on minimal variations all revolving around the notion of reception: large drawing-room, small drawing-room, Monsieur's study, Madame's boudoir, smoking-room, library, billiard-room, etc.

It takes a little more imagination no doubt to picture an apartment whose layout was based on the functioning of the senses. We can imagine well enough what a gustatorium might be, or an auditory, but one might wonder what a seeery might look like, or an smellery or a feelery.

It is hardly any more transgressive to conceive of a division based, no longer on circadian, but on heptadian rhythms.[1] This would give us apartments of seven rooms, known respectively as the Mondayery, Tuesdayery, Wednesdayery, Thursdayery, Fridayery, Saturdayery, and Sundayery. These two last rooms, it should be observed, already exist in abundance, commercialized under the name of 'second' or 'weekend homes'. It's no more foolish to conceive of a room exclusively devoted to Mondays than to build villas that are only *used* for sixty days in the year. The Mondayery could ideally be a laundry-room (our country forebears did their washing on Mondays) and the Tuesdayery a drawing-room (our urban forebears were happy to receive visitors on Tuesdays). This, obviously, would hardly be a departure from the functional. It would be better, while we're at it, to imagine a thematic arrangement, roughly analogous to that which used to exist in brothels (after they were shut down, and until the fifties, they were turned into student hostels; several of my friends thus lived in a former '*maison*' in the Rue de l'Arcade, one in the 'torture chamber', another in the 'aeroplane' [bed shaped like a cockpit, fake portholes, etc.], a third in the 'trapper's cabin' [walls papered with fake logs, etc.]). The Mondayery, for example, would imitate a boat: you would sleep in hammocks, swab down the floor and eat fish. The Tuesdayery, why not, would commemorate one of Man's great victories over Nature, the discovery of the Pole (North or South, to choice), or the ascent of Everest: the room wouldn't be heated, you would sleep under thick furs, the diet would be based on pemmican (corned beef at the end of the month, dried beef when you're flush). The Wednesdayery would glorify children, obviously, being the day on which, for a long time now, they haven't had to go to school; it could be a sort of Dame Tartine's

1. A habitat based on a circa-annual rhythm exists among a few of the 'happy few' who are sufficiently well endowed with residences to be able to attempt to reconcile their sense of values, their liking for travel, climatic conditions and cultural imperatives. They are to be found, for example, in Mexico in January, in Switzerland in February, in Venice in March, in Marrakesh in April, in Paris in May, in Cyprus in June, in Bayreuth in July, in the Dordogne in August, in Scotland in September, in Rome in October, on the Côte d'Azur in November, and in London in December.

Palace,* gingerbread walls, furniture made from plasticine, etc.

4
A space without a use

I have several times tried to think of an apartment in which there would be a useless room, absolutely and intentionally useless. It wouldn't be a junkroom, it wouldn't be an extra bedroom, or a corridor, or a cubby-hole, or a corner. It would be a functionless space. It would serve for nothing, relate to nothing.

For all my efforts, I found it impossible to follow this idea through to the end. Language itself, seemingly, proved unsuited to describing this nothing, this void, as if we could only speak of what is full, useful and functional.

A space without a function. Not 'without any precise function' but precisely without any function; not pluri-functional (everyone knows how to do that), but a-functional. It wouldn't obviously be a space intended solely to 'release' the others (lumber-room, cupboard, hanging space, storage space, etc.) but a space, I repeat, that would serve no purpose at all.

I sometimes manage to think of nothing, not even, like Raymond Queneau's Ami Pierrot,† of the death of Louis XVI. All of a sudden I realize I am here, that the Métro train has just stopped and that, having left Dugommier some ninety seconds before, I am now well and truly at Daumesnil. But, in the event, I haven't succeeded in thinking of nothing. How does one think of nothing? How to think of nothing without automatically putting something round that nothing, so turning it into a hole, into which one will hasten to put something, an activity, a function, a destiny, a gaze, a need, a lack, a surplus . . . ?

I have tried to follow wherever this limp idea led me. I have

*The reference is to a well-known French *comptine*, or nursery rhyme.

†In a novel called *Pierrot mon ami*.

encountered many unusable spaces and many unused spaces. But I wanted neither the unusable nor the unused, but the useless. How to expel functions, rhythms, habits, how to expel necessity? I imagined myself living in a vast apartment, so vast that I could never remember how many rooms it had (I had known, in the old days, but had forgotten, and knew I was too old now to start again on such a complicated enumeration). All the rooms, except one, were used for something. The whole point was to find this last room. It was no harder, when all's said and done, than for the readers in Borges's story of the 'Library of Babel' to find the book that held the key to all the others. Indeed, there is something almost vertiginously Borgesian in trying to imagine a room reserved for listening to Haydn's Symphony Number 48 in C, the so-called Maria Theresa, another devoted to reading the barometer or to cleaning my right big toe.

I thought of old Prince Bolkonsky who, in his anxiety as to the fate of his son, vainly searches all night long, from room to room, torch in hand, followed by his servant Tikhon carrying fur blankets, for the bed where he will be able finally to get to sleep. I thought of a science-fiction novel in which the very notion of habitat has vanished. I thought of another Borges story ('The Immortals'), in which men no longer inhabited by the need to live and to die have built ruined palaces and unusable staircases. I thought of engravings by Escher and paintings by Magritte. I thought of a gigantic Skinner's Box: a bedroom entirely hung in black, a solitary switch on the wall, by pressing which you can make something like a grey Maltese cross appear for a brief flash against a white background; I thought of the Great Pyramids and the church interiors of Saenredam;* I thought of something Japanese. I thought of the vague memory I had of a text by Heissenbüttel in which the narrator discovers a room without either doors or windows. I thought of the dreams I had had on this very subject, discovering a room I didn't know about in my own apartment.

I never managed anything that was really satisfactory. But I

*A Dutch painter (1597–1665).

don't think I was altogether wasting my time in trying to go beyond this improbable limit. The effort itself seemed to produce something that might be a statute of the inhabitable.

5

Moving out

Leaving an apartment. Vacating the scene. Decamping. Clearing up. Clearing out.

Making an inventory tidying up sorting out going through

Eliminating throwing away palming off on

Breaking

Burning

Taking down unfastening unnailing unsticking unscrewing unhooking

Unplugging detaching cutting pulling dismantling folding up cutting off

Rolling up

Wrapping up packing away strapping up tying piling up assembling heaping up fastening wrapping protecting covering surrounding locking

Removing carrying lifting

Sweeping

Closing

Leaving

Moving in

cleaning checking trying out changing fitting signing waiting imagining inventing investing deciding bending folding stooping sheathing fitting out stripping bare splitting turning returning beating muttering rushing at kneading lining up protecting covering over mixing ripping out slicing connecting hiding setting going activating installing botching up sizing breaking threading filtering tamping cramming sharpening polishing making firm driving in pinning together hanging up arranging sawing fixing pinning up marking noting working out climbing measuring mastering seeing surveying pressing hard down on priming rubbing down painting rubbing scrap-ingconnecting climbing stumbling straddling mislaying finding again rummaging around getting nowhere brushing puttying stripping camouflaging puttying adjusting coming and going putting a gloss on allowing to dry admiring being surprised getting worked up growing impatient suspending judgment assessing adding up inserting sealing nailing screwing bolting sewing crouching perching moping centring reaching washing laundering evaluating reckoning smiling main taining sub-tracting multiplying kicking your heels roughing out buying acquiring receiving bringing back unpacking undoing edging framing rivetting observing considering musing fixing scoop-ing out wiping down the plaster camping out going thoroughly into raising procuring sitting down leaning against bracing yourself rinsing out unblocking completing sorting sweeping sighing whistling while you work moistening becoming very keen on pulling off sticking up glueing swearing insisting tracing rubbing down brushing painting drilling plugging in switching on starting up soldering bending unfixing sharpening aiming dillydallying shortening supporting shaking before using grinding going into raptures touching up botching scraping dusting manoeuvring pulverising balancing checking moistening stopping up emptying crushing roughing out explaining shrugging fitting the handle on dividing up walking up and down tightening timing juxtaposing bringing together matching whitewashing varnishing replacing the top insulating assessing pinning up arranging distempering hanging up starting again inserting spreading out washing looking for entering breathing hard

settling in

living in

living

Doors

We protect ourselves, we barricade ourselves in. Doors stop and separate.

The door breaks space in two, splits it, prevents osmosis, imposes a partition. On one side, me and *my place*, the private, the domestic (a space overfilled with my possessions: my bed, my carpet, my table, my typewriter, my books, my odd copies of the *Nouvelle Revue Française*); on the other side, other people, the world, the public, politics. You can't simply let yourself slide from one into the other, can't pass from one to the other, neither in one direction nor in the other. You have to have the password, have to cross the threshold, have to show your credentials, have to communicate, just as the prisoner communicates with the world outside.

From the triangular shape and phenomenal size of the doors in the film of *Forbidden Planet*, you can deduce some of the morphological characteristics of their very ancient builders. The idea is as spectacular as it is gratuitous (why triangular?), but if there hadn't been any doors at all, we would have been able to draw far more startling conclusions.

How to be specific? It's not a matter of opening or not opening the door, not a matter of 'leaving the key in the door'. The problem isn't whether or not there are keys: if there wasn't a door, there wouldn't be a key.

It's hard obviously to imagine a house which doesn't have a door. I saw one one day, several years ago, in Lansing, Michigan. It had been built by Frank Lloyd Wright. You began by following a gently winding path to the left of which there rose up, very gradually, with an extreme nonchalance even, a slight declivity that was oblique to start with but which slowly approached the vertical. Bit by bit, as if by chance, without thinking, without your having any right at any given moment to declare that you had remarked anything like a transition, an interruption, a passage, a break in continuity, the path became stony, that's to say that at first there was only grass, then there began to be stones in the middle of the grass, then there were a few more stones and it became like a paved, grassy walkway, while on your left, the slope of the ground began to resemble, very vaguely, a low wall, then a wall made of crazy paving. Then there appeared something like an open-work roof that was practically indissociable from the vegetation that had invaded it. In actual fact, it was already too late to know whether you were indoors or out. At the end of the path, the paving stones were set edge to edge and you found yourself in what is customarily called an entrance-hall, which opened directly on to a fairly enormous room that ended in one direction on a terrace graced by a large swimming-pool. The rest of the house was no less remarkable, not only for its comfort, its luxury even, but because you had the impression that it had slid on to its hillside like a cat curling itself up in a cushion.

The punch line of this anecdote is as moral as it is predictable. A dozen more or less similar houses were scattered through the surrounds of a private golf club. The course was entirely closed off. Guards who it was all too easy to imagine as being armed with sawn-off shotguns (I saw lots of American movies in my youth) were on duty at the one entrance gate.

Staircases

We don't think enough about staircases.

Nothing was more beautiful in old houses than the staircases. Nothing is uglier, colder, more hostile, meaner, in today's apartment buildings.

We should learn to live more on staircases. But how?

Walls

'Granted there is a wall, what's going on behind it?'
Jean Tardieu

I put a picture up on a wall. Then I forget there is a wall. I no longer know what there is behind this wall, I no longer know there is a wall, I no longer know this wall is a wall, I no longer know what a wall is. I no longer know that in my apartment there are walls, and that if there weren't any walls, there would be no apartment. The wall is no longer what delimits and defines the place where I live, that which separates it from the other places where other people live, it is nothing more than a support for the picture. But I also forget the picture, I no longer look at it, I no longer know how to look at it. I have put the picture on the wall so as to forget there was a wall, but in forgetting the wall, I forget the picture, too. There are pictures because there are walls. We have to be able to forget there are walls, and have found no better way to do that than pictures. Pictures efface walls. But walls kill pictures. So we need continually to be changing, either the wall or the picture, to be forever putting other pictures up on the walls, or else constantly moving the picture from one wall to another.

We could write on our walls (as we sometimes write on the fronts of houses, on fences round building sites and on the walls of prisons), but we do it only very rarely.

The Apartment Building

1
Project for a novel

I imagine a Parisian apartment building whose façade has been removed – a sort of equivalent to the roof that is lifted off in *Le Diable boiteux*, or to the scene with the game of go in *The Tale of Genji* – so that all the rooms in the front, from the ground floor up to the attics, are instantly and simultaneously visible.

The novel – whose title is *Life a User's Manual* – restricts itself (if I dare use that verb for a project that will finally extend to something like four hundred pages) to describing the rooms thus unveiled and the activities unfolding in them, the whole in accordance with formal procedures which it doesn't seem necessary to go into here in detail, but the mere stating of which seems to me rather alluring: a polygraph of the moves made by a chess knight (adapted, what's more, to a board of 10 squares by 10), a pseudo-quenine of order 10, an orthogonal Latin bi-square of order 10 (the one that Euler conjectured didn't exist, but which was demonstrated in 1960 by Bose, Parker and Shrikhande).*

This project has more than one source. One is a drawing by Saul Steinberg that appeared in *The Art of Living* (1952) and

*This obscure formula describes the complex structure underlying the multiple (to say the least) narratives of Perec's wonderful novel, *Life a User's Manual*. A 'bi-square' is an elaboration on the familiar 'magic square' in which no number recurs and in which all the rows and columns add up to the same total. In a 'bi-square' each space or location is occupied by two elements instead of just one: e.g. by a letter of the alphabet as well as a number or by two numbers drawn from independent series. Perec's 'bi-square' has ten locations in each direction and thus is 'of order 10'. A 'quenine' is a mathematical formula invented as a formal constraint in the writing of poetry by Raymond Queneau – hence its name. A fuller description of these devices can be found in David Bellos's *Georges Perec: A Life in Words*.

shows a rooming-house (you can tell it's a rooming-house because next to the door there is a notice bearing the words *No Vacancy*) part of the façade of which has been removed, allowing you to see the interior of some twenty-three rooms (I say 'some' because you can also see through into some of the back rooms). The mere inventory – and it could never be exhaustive – of the items of furniture and the actions represented has something truly vertiginous about it:

3 bathrooms. The one on the third floor is empty, in the one on the second, a woman is taking a bath; in the one on the ground floor, a man is having a shower.
3 fireplaces, varying greatly in size, but all on the one axis. None of them is working (no one has lit a fire in them, if you prefer). The ones on the first and second floors are equipped with fire-dogs; the one on the first floor is split into two by a partition which also divides the mouldings and the ceiling rose.
6 candelabra and one Calder-style mobile
5 telephones
1 upright piano with stool
10 adult individuals of the male sex, of whom
    1 is having a drink
    1 is typing
    2 are reading the newspaper, one sitting in an armchair, the other stretched out on a divan
    3 are asleep
    1 is having a shower
    1 is eating toast
    1 is coming through the doorway into a room where there is a dog
10 adult individuals of the female sex, of whom
    1 is doing her chores
    1 is sitting down
    1 is holding a baby in her arms
    2 are reading, one, sitting down, the newspaper, the other, lying down, a novel
    1 is doing the washing-up

1 is having a bath
1 is knitting
1 is eating toast
1 is sleeping

6 young children, 2 of whom are certainly little girls and 2 certainly little boys
2 dogs
2 cats
1 bear on wheels
1 small horse on wheels
1 toy train
1 doll in a pram
6 rats or mice
a fair number of termites (it's not certain they are termites; the sorts of animals in any case that live in floorboards and walls)
at least 38 pictures or framed engravings
1 negro mask
29 lights (over and above the candelabra)
10 beds
1 child's cot
3 divans, one of which serves uncomfortably as a bed
4 kitchens or rather kitchenettes
7 rooms with parquet flooring
1 carpet
2 bedside rugs or mats
9 rooms where the floor is no doubt covered with moquette
3 rooms with tiled floors
1 interior staircase
8 pedestal tables
5 coffee tables
5 small bookcases
1 shelf full of books
2 clocks
5 chests of drawers
2 tables
1 desk with drawers with blotting-pad and inkwell
2 pairs of shoes

1 bathroom stool
11 upright chairs
2 armchairs
1 leather briefcase
1 dressing gown
1 hanging cupboard
1 alarm clock
1 pair of bathroom scales
1 pedal bin
1 hat hanging on a peg
1 suit hanging on a hanger
1 jacket hanging on the back of a chair
washing drying
3 small bathroom cabinets
several bottles and flasks
numerous objects hard to identify (carriage clocks, ashtrays, spectacles, glasses, saucers full of peanuts, for example)

Which is to describe only the 'defaçaded' part of the building. The remaining quarter of the drawing enables us to register a section of pavement strewn with rubbish (old newspaper, tin can, three envelopes), an overflowing dustbin, a porch, once luxurious now tatty, and five figures at the windows: on the second floor, amidst potplants, an old man smoking his pipe with his dog, on the third floor, a bird in its cage, a woman and a young girl.

I fancy it is summertime. It must be something like eight o' clock in the evening (it's odd that the children aren't in bed). Television hasn't been invented yet. There's not a single radio set to be seen either. The owner of the building is no doubt the woman who is knitting (she isn't on the first floor, as I first of all thought, but, in view of the position of the porch, on the ground floor, and what I've been calling the ground floor is in fact a basement – the house has only two storeys). She has fallen on hard times and has been forced, not only to turn her house into a rooming-house, but to divide her best rooms into two.

Examine the drawing a bit more closely and the details of a

voluminous novel could easily be extracted from it. It's obvious, for example, that we are at a time when the fashion is for curly hair (three women have curlers in). The gentleman asleep on his uncomfortable divan is no doubt a teacher; the leather briefcase belongs to him and on his desk he has something that looks very much like a pile of school exercises. The woman doing her chores is the mother of the girl who is sitting down and it's extremely likely that the gentleman leaning on the mantelpiece, a glass in his hand and looking somewhat perplexedly at the Calder-style mobile, is her future son-in-law. As for her neighbour, who has four children and a cat, he seems to be slaving away at his typewriter like someone whose manuscript the publisher has been waiting for the past three weeks.

2
Things we ought to do systematically, from time to time

In the building you live in:

> go and call on your neighbours; look at what there is on the party wall, for example; confirm, or belie, the homotopology of the accommodation. See what use they have made of it;
>
> notice how unfamiliar things may come to seem as a result of taking staircase B instead of staircase A, or of going up to the fifth floor when you live on the second;
>
> try to imagine on what a collective existence might be based, within the confines of this same building. (In an old house in the 18th arrondissement I saw a WC that was shared by four tenants. The landlord refused to pay for the lighting of the said WC, and none of the four tenants was willing to pay for the three others, or had accepted the idea of a single meter and a bill divisible into four. So the WC was lit by four separate bulbs, each controlled by one of the four tenants. A single bulb

burning night and day for ten years would have obviously been less expensive than installing a single one of these exclusive circuits.)

In apartment buildings in general:

look closely at them;

look upwards;

look for the name of the architect, the name of the contractor, the date when it was built;

ask yourself why it often says 'gas on every floor';

in the case of a new building, try to remember what was there before;

etc.

The Street

1

The buildings stand one beside the other. They form a straight line. They are expected to form a line, and it's a serious defect in them when they don't do so. They are then said to be 'subject to alignment', meaning that they can by rights be demolished, so as to be rebuilt in a straight line with the others.

The parallel alignment of two series of buildings defines what is known as a street. The street is a space bordered, generally on its two longest sides, by houses; the street is what separates houses from each other, and also what enables us to get from one house to another, by going either along or across the street. In addition, the street is what enables us to identify the houses. Various systems of identification exist. The most widespread, in our own day and our part of the world, consists in giving a name to the street and numbers to the houses. The naming of streets is an extremely complex, often even thorny, topic, about which several books might be written. And numbering isn't that much simpler. It was decided, first, that even numbers would be put on one side and odd numbers on the other (but, as a character in Raymond Queneau's *The Flight of Icarus* very rightly asks himself, 'Is 13A an even or an odd number?'); secondly, that the even numbers would be on the right (and odd numbers on the left) relative to the direction of the street; and thirdly, that the said direction of the street would be determined generally (but we know of many exceptions) by the position of the said street in relation to a fixed axis, in the event the River Seine. Streets parallel with the Seine are numbered starting upstream, perpendicular streets starting from the Seine and going away from it (these explanations apply to Paris obviously; one might reasonably suppose that analogous solutions have been thought up for other towns).

Contrary to the buildings, which almost always belong to someone, the streets in principle belong to no one. They are divided up, fairly equitably, into a zone reserved for motor vehicles, known as the roadway, and two zones, narrower obviously, reserved for pedestrians, which are called pavements. A certain number of streets are reserved exclusively for pedestrians, either permanently, or else on particular occasions. The zones of contact between the roadway and the pavements enable motorists who don't wish to go on driving to park. The number of motor vehicles not wishing to go on driving being much greater than the number of spaces available, the possibilities of parking have been restricted, either, within certain perimeters known as 'blue zones', by limiting the amount of parking time, or else, more generally, by installing paid parking.

Only infrequently are there trees in the streets. When there are, they have railings round them. On the other hand, most streets are equipped with specific amenities corresponding to various services. Thus there are street lights which go on automatically as soon as the daylight begins to decline to any significant degree; stopping places at which passengers can wait for buses or taxis; telephone kiosks, public benches; boxes into which citizens may put letters which the postal services will come to collect at set times; clockwork mechanisms intended to receive the money necessary for a limited amount of parking time; baskets reserved for waste paper and other detritus, into which numbers of people compulsively cast a furtive glance as they pass; traffic lights. There are likewise traffic signs indicating, for example, that it is appropriate to park on this side of the street or that according to whether we are in the first or second fortnight of the month (what is known as 'alternate side parking'), or that silence is to be observed in the vicinity of a hospital, or, finally and especially, that the street is one-way. Such is the density of motor traffic indeed that movement would be almost impossible if it had not become customary, in the last few years, in a majority of built-up areas, to force motorists to circulate in one direction only, which, obviously, sometimes obliges them to make long detours.

At certain road junctions deemed especially dangerous, communication between the pavements and the roadway, normally free, has been prevented by means of metal posts linked by chains. Identical posts, set into the pavements themselves, serve sometimes to stop motor vehicles from coming and parking on the pavements, which they would frequently tend to do if they weren't prevented. In certain circumstances, finally – military parades, Heads of State driving past, etc. – entire sections of the roadway may be put out of bounds by means of light metal barriers that fit one inside the other.

At certain points in the pavement, curved indentations, familiarly known as '*bateaux*',* indicate that there may be motor vehicles parked inside the buildings themselves which should always be able to get out. At other points, small earthenware tiles set into the edge of the pavement indicate that this section of the pavement is reserved for the parking of hire vehicles.

The junction of the roadway and the pavements is known as the gutter. This area has a very slight incline, thanks to which rainwater can flow off into the drainage system underneath the street, instead of spreading right across the roadway, which would be a considerable impediment to the traffic. For several centuries, there was only one gutter, to be found in the middle of the roadway, but the current system is thought to be better suited. Should there be a shortage of rainwater, the upkeep of the roadway and pavements can be effected thanks to hydrants installed at almost every intersection; these can be opened with the help of the T-shaped keys with which the council employees responsible for cleaning the streets are provided.

In principle, it is always possible to pass from one side of the street to the other by using the pedestrian crossings that motor vehicles

*Called 'boats' because of their shape.

must only drive over with extreme caution. These crossings are signalled, either by two parallel rows of metal studs, perpendicular to the axis of the street, whose heads have a diameter of about twelve centimetres, or else by broad bands of white paint running at an angle across the whole width of the street. This system of studded or painted crossings no longer seems as effective as it no doubt was in the old days, and it is often necessary to duplicate it by a system of traffic lights of three colours (red, amber and green) which, as they have multiplied, have ended up causing extraordinarily complex problems of synchronization that certain of the world's largest computers and certain of what are held to be the age's most brilliant mathematical brains are working tirelessly to resolve.

At various points, remote-controlled cameras keep an eye on what is going on. There is one on top of the Chambre des Députés, just underneath the big tricolour; another in the Place Edmond-Rostand, in continuation of the Boulevard Saint-Michel; others still at Alésia, the Place Clichy, the Châtelet, the Place de la Bastille, etc.

2

I saw two blind people in the Rue Linné. They were walking holding one another by the arm. They both had long, exceedingly flexible sticks. One of the two was a woman of about fifty, the other quite a young man. The woman was feeling all the vertical obstacles that stood along the pavement with the tip of her stick, and guiding the young man's stick so that he, too, touched them, indicating to him, very quickly and without ever being mistaken, what the obstacles consisted of: a street light, a bus stop, a telephone kiosk, a waste-paper bin, a post box, a road sign (she wasn't able to specify what the sign said obviously), a red light . . .

3
Practical exercises

Observe the street, from time to time, with some concern for system perhaps.
Apply yourself. Take your time.
Note down the place: the terrace of a café near the junction of the Rue de Bac and the Boulevard Saint-Germain
the time: seven o' clock in the evening
the date: 15 May 1973
the weather: set fair
Note down what you can see. Anything worthy of note going on. Do you know how to see what's worthy of note? Is there anything that strikes you?
Nothing strikes you. You don't know how to see.

You must set about it more slowly, almost stupidly. Force yourself to write down what is of no interest, what is most obvious, most common, most colourless.

The street: try to describe the street, what it's made of, what it's used for. The people in the street. The cars. What sort of cars? The buildings: note that they're on the comfortable, well-heeled side. Distinguish residential from official buildings.
The shops. What do they sell in the shops? There are no food shops. Oh yes, there's a baker's. Ask yourself where the locals do their shopping.
The cafés. How many cafés are there? One, two, three, four. Why did you choose this one? Because you know it, because it's in the sun, because it sells cigarettes. The other shops: antique shops, clothes, hi-fi, etc. Don't say, don't write 'etc.'. Make an effort to exhaust the subject, even if that seems grotesque, or pointless, or stupid. You still haven't looked at anything, you've merely picked out what you've long ago picked out.

Force yourself to see more flatly.

Detect a rhythm: the passing of cars. The cars arrive in clumps because they've been stopped by a red light further up or down the street.
Count the cars.
Look at the number plates. Distinguish between the cars registered in Paris and the rest.
Note the absence of taxis precisely when there seem to be a lot of people waiting for them.

Read what's written in the street: Morris columns,* newspaper kiosks, posters, traffic signs, graffiti, discarded handouts, shop signs.

Beauty of the women.
The fashion is for heels that are too high.

Decipher a bit of the town, deduce the obvious facts: the obsession with ownership, for example. Describe the number of operations the driver of a vehicle is subjected to when he parks merely in order to go and buy a hundred grams of fruit jelly:

- parks by means of a certain amount of toing and froing
- switches off the engine
- withdraws the key, setting off a first anti-theft device
- extricates himself from the vehicle
- winds up the left-hand front window
- locks it
- checks that the left-hand rear door is locked;
  if not:
    opens it
    raises the handle inside
    slams the door
    checks it's locked securely

*The sturdy columns that carry posters advertising theatrical and other entertainments.

– circles the car; if need be, checks that the boot is locked properly
– checks that the right-hand rear door is locked; if not, recommences the sequence of operations already carried out on the left-hand rear door
– winds up the right-hand front window
– shuts the right-hand front door
– locks it
– before walking away, looks all around him as if to make sure the car is still there and that no one will come and take it away.

Decipher a bit of the town. Its circuits: why do the buses go from this place to that? Who chooses the routes, and by what criteria? Remember that the trajectory of a Paris bus *intra muros* is defined by a two-figure number the first figure of which describes the central and the second the peripheral terminus. Find examples, find exceptions: all the buses whose number begins with a 2 start from the Gare St-Lazare, with a 3 from the Gare de l'Est. All the buses whose number ends in a 2 terminate roughly speaking in the 16th arrondissement or in Boulogne.
(Before, they used letters: the S, which was Queneau's favourite, has become the 84. Wax sentimental over the memory of buses that had a platform at the back, the shape of the tickets, the ticket collector with his little machine hooked on to his belt.)

The people in the streets: where are they coming from? Where are they going to? Who are they?

People in a hurry. People going slowly. Parcels. Prudent people who've taken their macs. Dogs: they're the only animals to be seen. You can't see any birds – yet you know there are birds – and can't hear them either. You might see a cat slip underneath a car, but it doesn't happen.

Nothing is happening, in fact.

Try to classify the people: those who live locally and those who don't live locally. There don't seem to be any tourists. The season doesn't lend itself to it, and anyway the area isn't especially touristy. What are the local attractions? Salomon Bernard's house? The church of St Thomas Aquinas? No 5, Rue Sébastien-Bottin?*

Time passes. Drink your beer. Wait.
Note that the trees are a long way off (on the Boulevard Saint-Germain and the Boulevard Raspail), that there are no cinemas or theatres, that there are no building sites to be seen, that most of the houses seem to have obeyed the regulations so far as renovation is concerned.

A dog, of an uncommon breed (Afghan hound? saluki?).

A Land Rover that seems to be equipped for crossing the Sahara (in spite of yourself, you're only noting the untoward, the peculiar, the wretched exceptions; the opposite is what you should be doing).

Carry on
Until the scene becomes improbable
until you have the impression, for the briefest of moments, that you are in a strange town or, better still, until you can no longer understand what is happening or is not happening, until the whole place becomes strange, and you no longer even know that this is what is called a town, a street, buildings, pavements . . .

Make torrential rain fall, smash everything, make grass grow, replace the people by cows and, where the Rue de Bac meets the Boulevard Saint-Germain, make King Kong appear, or Tex Avery's herculean mouse, towering a hundred metres above the roofs of the buildings!

Or again: strive to picture to yourself, with the greatest possible

*The address of the largest and most glamorous of French publishing houses, Editions Gallimard, by whom Perec would like to have been published, though he never was.

precision, beneath the network of streets, the tangle of sewers, the lines of the Métro, the invisible underground proliferation of conduits (electricity, gas, telephone lines, water mains, express letter tubes), without which no life would be possible on the surface.

Underneath, just underneath, resuscitate the eocene: the limestone, the marl and the soft chalk, the gypsum, the lacustrian Saint-Ouen limestone, the Beauchamp sands, the rough limestone, the Soissons sands and lignites, the plastic clay, the hard chalk.

4
Or else:
Rough draft of a letter

I think of you, often
sometimes I go back into a café, I sit near the door, I order a coffee
I arrange my packet of cigarettes, a box of matches, a writing pad, my felt-pen on the fake marble table
I spend a long time stirring my cup of coffee with the teaspoon (yet I don't put any sugar in my coffee, I drink it allowing the sugar to melt in my mouth, like the people of the North, like the Russians and Poles when they drink tea)
I pretend to be preoccupied, to be reflecting, as if I had a decision to make
At the top and to the right of the sheet of paper, I inscribe the date, sometimes the place, sometimes the time, I pretend to be writing a letter

I write slowly, very slowly, as slowly as I can, I trace, I draw each letter, each accent, I check the punctuation marks

I stare attentively at a small notice, the price-list for ice-creams, at a piece of ironwork, a blind, the hexagonal yellow ashtray (in actual fact, it's an equilateral triangle, in the cutoff corners of which semi-circular dents have been made where cigarettes can be rested)

(. . .)

Outside there's a bit of sunlight
the café is nearly empty
two renovators' men are having a rum at the bar, the owner is dozing behind his till, the waitress is cleaning the coffee machine

I am thinking of you
you are walking in your street, it's wintertime, you've turned up your foxfur collar, you're smiling, and remote

(. . .)

5
Places
(Notes on a work in progress)

In 1969, I chose, in Paris, twelve places (streets, squares, circuses, an arcade), where I had either lived or else was attached to by particular memories.

I have undertaken to write a description of two of these places each month. One of these descriptions is written on the spot and is meant to be as neutral as possible. Sitting in a café or walking in the street, notebook and pen in hand, I do my best to describe the houses, the shops and the people that I come across, the posters, and in a general way, all the details that attract my eye. The other description is written somewhere other than the place itself. I then do my best to describe it from memory, to evoke all the memories that come to me concerning it, whether events that have taken place there, or people I have met there. Once these descriptions are finished, I slip them into an envelope that I seal with wax. On several occasions, I have got a man or woman photographer friend to go with me to the places I was describing who, either freely, or as indicated by me, took photographs that I then slipped, without looking at them (with a single exception), into the corresponding envelopes. I have also had occasion to slip into these envelopes various items capable later on of serving as evidence: Métro tickets, for example, or bar slips, or cinema tickets, or handouts, etc.

I begin these descriptions over again each year, taking care, thanks to an algorithm I have already referred to (orthogonal Latin bi-square, this time of order 12*), first, to describe each of these places in a different month of the year, second, never to describe the same pair of places in the same month.

This undertaking, not so dissimilar in principle from a 'time capsule', will thus last for twelve years, until all the places have been described twice twelve times. I was too taken up last year by the filming of 'Un Homme qui dort' (in which, as it happens, most of these places appear), so I in fact skipped 1973, and only in 1981 shall I be in possession (if, that is, I don't fall behind again) of the 288 texts issuing from this experiment. I shall then know whether it was worth the effort. What I hope for from it, in effect, is nothing other than the record of a threefold experience of ageing: of the places themselves, of my memories, and of my writing.

*The same schema as Perec used for *Life: A User's Manual* – see the note on p.40; 'of order 12' means simply a 12 × 12 square as opposed to one 10 × 10.

The Neighbourhood

1

The neighbourhood. What is a neighbourhood? D'you live in the neighbourhood? You from the neighbourhood? Moved neighbourhoods, have you? You're in which neighbourhood now?
There's something amorphous about the neighbourhood really: a sort of parish or, strictly speaking, a *quartier* or fourth part of an arrondissement, the small portion of a town dependent on a police station.

More generally: that portion of the town you can get around easily in on foot or, to say the same thing in the form of a truism, that part of the town you don't need to go to, precisely because you're already there. That seems to go without saying. It still needs to be made clear, however, that for most of a town's inhabitants, this has the corollary that the neighbourhood is also that portion of the town in which you don't work. The neighbourhood is what we call the area where we reside, not the area where we work: places of residence and places of work hardly ever coincide. This too is self-evident, but it has countless consequences.

Neighbourhood life

This is a very big word.

Agreed, there are the neighbours, the locals, the tradespeople, the dairy, the everything for the home, the tobacconist who stays open on Sundays, the chemist, the post office, the café where you are, if not an habitué then at least a regular (you shake hands with the *patron* or the waitress).

Obviously, you could cultivate these habits, always go to the same butcher's, leave your parcels at the *épicerie*, open an account at the ironmonger's, call the pharmacist by her first name, entrust your cat to the woman who sells newspapers, but it wouldn't work, it still wouldn't make a life, couldn't even give the illusion of being a life. It would create a familiar space, would give rise to an itinerary (leave home, go and buy the evening paper, a packet of cigarettes, a packet of soap powder, a kilo of cherries, etc.), a pretext for a few limp handshakes (morning Madame Chamissac, morning Monsieur Fernand, morning Mademoiselle Jeanne), but that would only ever be putting a mawkish face on necessity, a way of dressing up commercialism.

Obviously, you could start an orchestra, or put on street theatre. Bring the neighbourhood alive, as they say. Weld the people of a street or a group of streets together by something more than a mere connivance: by making demands on them, making them fight.

Death of the neighbourhood

This too is a very big word

(many other things are dying after all: towns, the countryside, etc.).

What I miss above all is the neighbourhood cinema, with its ghastly advertisements for the dry cleaner's on the corner.

2

From all of the foregoing I can draw the, truth to tell, less than satisfying conclusion that I have only a very approximate idea of what a neighbourhood is. It's true that in recent years I've changed neighbourhoods quite a few times; I haven't had time to get properly used to one.

I make little use of my neighbourhood. It's only by chance that some of my friends live in the same neighbourhood as I do. Relative to my dwelling-place, my main centres of interest are somewhat eccentric. I have nothing against the act of moving, quite the reverse.

Why not set a higher value on dispersal? Instead of living in just one place, and trying in vain to gather yourself together there, why not have five or six rooms dotted about Paris? I'd go and sleep in Denfert, I'd write in the Place Voltaire, I'd listen to music in the Place Clichy, I'd make love at the Poterne des Peupliers,* I'd eat in the Rue de la Tombe-Issoire, I'd read by the Parc Monceau, etc. Is that any more foolish, when all's said and done, than putting all the furniture shops in the Faubourg Saint-Antoine, all the glassware shops in the Rue de Paradis, all the tailors in the Rue du Sentier, all the Jews in the Rue des Rosiers, all the students in the Latin Quarter, all the publishers in Saint-Sulpice, all the doctors in Harley Street, all the blacks in Harlem?

*A leafy spot in the 13th arrondissement.

The Town

1

'The roofs of Paris, lying on their backs, with their little paws in the air.'

Raymond Queneau

Don't be too hasty in trying to find a definition of the town; it's far too big and there's every chance of getting it wrong.

First, make an inventory of what you can see. List what you're sure of. Draw up elementary distinctions: for example, between what is the town and what isn't the town.

Concern yourself with what divides the town from what isn't the town. Look at what happens when the town stops. For example (I've already touched on this subject in connection with streets), one absolutely foolproof method for telling whether you're in Paris or outside Paris consists of looking at the numbers of the buses. If they have two digits, you're in Paris, if they have three digits, you're outside Paris (it isn't, alas, as foolproof as all that, but in principle it ought to be).

Recognize that suburbs have a strong tendency not to remain as suburbs.

Take good note that the town hasn't always been what it was. Remember, for example, that for a long time Auteuil was in the country. Up until the middle of the 19th century, when doctors saw that a child had a bit too much pallor, they recommended the parents to go and spend a few days in Auteuil to breathe the good country air (there's still a dairy in Auteuil, as it happens, which persists in calling itself 'Auteuil Farm').

Remember, too, that the Arc de Triomphe was built in the country (it wasn't really the country, more the equivalent of the Bois de Boulogne, but it wasn't really the town all the same).

Remember, too, that Saint-Denis, Bagnolet and Aubervilliers are far more sizeable towns than Poitiers, Annecy or Saint-Nazaire.

Remember that everything calling itself a 'faubourg' used to be outside the town (Faubourg Saint-Antoine, Faubourg Saint-Denis, Faubourg Saint-Germain, Faubourg Saint-Honoré).

Remember that if they said Saint-Germain-des-Prés, it's because there were *prés*, or fields, there.

Remember that a 'boulevard' was originally a walk planted with trees which circled the town and usually occupied the space where the old ramparts had been.

Remember, indeed, that it was fortified.

2

The wind comes off the sea: nauseous town smells are driven towards the East in Europe, towards the West in America. That's the reason why the smart districts are in the West in Paris (the 16th arrondissement, Neuilly, Saint-Cloud, etc.) and London (the West End), and in the East in New York (the East Side).

3

A town: stone, concrete, asphalt. Strangers, monuments, institutions.

Megalopolises. Urban sprawl. Traffic arteries. Crowds.

Ant-hills?

What is the heart of a town? The soul of a town? Why is a town said to be beautiful, or said to be ugly? What's beautiful and what's ugly in a town? How do you get to know a town? How do you get to know your town?

Method: you must either give up talking of the town, about the town, or else force yourself to talk about it as simply as possible, obviously, familiarly. Get rid of all preconceived ideas. Stop thinking in ready-made terms, forget what the town planners and sociologists have said.

There's something frightening in the very idea of the town; you get the impression you can fasten only on to tragic or despairing images of it – Metropolis, the mineral universe, the world turned to stone – that you can only go on endlessly piling up unanswerable questions.

We shall never be able to explain or justify the town. The town is there. It's our space, and we have no other. We were born in towns. We grew up in towns. It's in towns that we breathe. When we catch the train, it's to go from one town to another town. There's nothing inhuman in a town, unless it's our own humanity.

4
My town

I live in Paris. It's the capital of France. At the time when France was called Gaul, Paris was called Lutetia.

Like a lot of other towns, Paris was built in the immediate proximity of seven hills. They are: the Mont Valérien, Montmartre, Montparnasse, Montsouris, the Colline de Chaillot, the Buttes-Chaumont and the Butte-aux-Cailles, the Montagne Sainte-Geneviève, etc.

Obviously, I don't know all the streets of Paris. But I always have some idea of where they're to be found. Even if I wanted to, I'd find it hard to be lost in Paris. I have numerous landmarks to help me. I nearly always know in which direction I need to go on the Métro. I know the itineraries of the buses pretty well. I can explain the route I want to take to a taxi-driver. The names of the streets are hardly ever alien to me, the characteristics of each district are familiar. I can identify the churches and other monuments without too much difficulty. I know where the railway stations are. Numerous locations have precise memories attached to them: houses where friends once lived that I've lost touch with, or else a café in which I played pinball for six hours at a stretch (for an original outlay of a single 20-centimes coin), or else the square in which I read Balzac's *La Peau de Chagrin* while keeping an eye on my little niece as she played.

I like walking in Paris. Sometimes for a whole afternoon, without any precise goal, not really haphazardly, or at random, but trying to let myself be carried along. Sometimes by taking the first bus that stops (you can no longer get on buses when they're moving). Or else by preparing a careful, systematic itinerary. If I had the time, I'd like to think up and solve problems analogous to the one about the bridges of Königsberg* or, for example, find a route that would cross Paris from one side to the other taking only streets beginning with the letter C.

I like my town, but I can't say exactly what I like about it. I don't think it's the smell. I'm too accustomed to the monuments to want to look at them. I like certain lights, a few bridges, café terraces. I love passing through a place I haven't seen for a long time.

5
Foreign towns

You know how to get from the station, or the air terminal, to your hotel. You hope that it isn't too far. You'd like to be central. You study the map of the town with care. You locate the museums, the parks, the places you've been strongly recommended to go and see.

You go and see the paintings and the churches. You'd love to stroll about, to loaf, but you don't dare; you don't know how to drift aimlessly, you're afraid of getting lost. You don't even walk really, you stride. You don't really know what to look at. You're moved almost if you come across the Air France office, on the verge of tears almost if you see *Le Monde* on a news stand. There's nowhere that lets itself be attached to a memory, an emotion, a

*This refers to a celebrated old puzzle, as to whether it was possible to walk round the city of Königsberg, which had seven bridges, crossing each bridge once and no bridge twice. The solution was found in 1736 by the great Swiss mathematician, Leonhard Euler.

face. You locate tearooms, cafeterias, milk-bars, taverns, restaurants. You go past a statue. It's that of Ludwig Spankerfel di Nominatore, the celebrated brewer. You look with interest at a complete set of monkey wrenches (you've got two hours to waste and you walk for two hours; why should you be drawn more particularly by this rather than that? A neutral space, not yet invested, practically without landmarks: you don't know how long it takes to get from one place to another; as a result you're always horribly ahead of time).

Two days may be enough to start to get acclimatized. The day you find out that the statue of Ludwig Spankerfel di Nominatore (the celebrated brewer) is only three minutes from your hotel (at the end of Prince Adalbert Street) whereas you've been taking a good half-hour to get there, you start to take possession of the town. That doesn't mean you start to inhabit it.

We often preserve the memory of an indefinable charm from these towns we've merely brushed against. The memory indeed of our own indecision, our hesitant footsteps, our gaze which didn't know what to turn towards and that found almost anything affecting: an almost empty street lined with large plane trees (were they planes?) in Belgrade, the ceramic tiles on a façade in Saarbrücken, the sloping streets in Edinburgh, the width of the Rhine at Basle, and the rope – the exact term for it would be the suspension cable – guiding the ferry that crosses it . . .

6
On tourism

> 'As for seeing the town, that never entered his head, he being of the English race that makes its servants visit the countries they pass through.'
>
> Jules Verne, *Around the World in Eighty Days*

Rather than visit London, stay at home, in the chimney corner, and read the irreplaceable information supplied by Baedeker (1907 edition):

The season, that is the months of May, June and July, is the most favourable time of year for visiting London. It is now that Parliament is sitting, the aristocracy are at their town-residences, the greatest artistes in the world are performing at the Opera and the picture exhibitions are open. The remainder of the country may be visited all year round, with the exception of the mountains.

. . . If no policeman is to be found in the vicinity, ask for information in a shop. Address a stranger only in cases of absolute necessity, and do not reply to any question from a passer-by, especially in French, for the question is probably the prelude to a theft or confidence trick. The foreigner should remain constantly on his guard and above all keep careful watch on his purse and his timepiece. This recommendation must be borne in mind when boarding a train or omnibus, as well as when alighting, everywhere in short where there is a crowd. It will be noted that it is customary for pedestrians to keep to the right in crowded streets. Avoid also, in the evenings, the poor areas of the town and out-of-the-way streets.

The Metropolitan Railways . . . are an important means of effecting long journeys in London. They pass for the most part a short distance below the surface of the ground, in tunnels or cuttings bordered by high walls . . . The trains run on the inner belt from 5.30 a.m. until around midnight . . . One buys a ticket at the booking-office and descends to the railway. At the bottom of the first flight of stairs, the official who checks the tickets indicates the correct platform, while the tickets themselves are marked with a large red 'O' or 'I' (for 'outer' or 'inner' line of rails). A telegraph-board indicates the destination of the 'next train', and the terminus towards which the train is travelling is also generally placarded on the front of the locomotive. The names of the stations are called out by the porters, and are always painted at different parts of the platform and on the lamps and benches, though frequently difficult to distinguish from the surrounding advertisements. As the stoppages are extremely brief, no time should be lost either in taking seats or in alighting.

Doctors. Recommended are doctors: L. Vintras, doctor to the French Embassy and the French Hospital; H. de Méric (surgeon); H. Dardenne; P. J. Baranoff, doctor at the French Hospital; Naumann, doctor at the Italian Hospital. Dentists: A. A. Goldsmith (American); K. A. Davenport (American); H. L. Coffin (American); Pierrepoint (American), etc. Pharmacies (no French pharmacy).

Time-table: two weeks are barely sufficient, even for an indefatigable traveller content merely with a superficial visit, to have a reasonably clear idea of London and its environs. A methodical distribution of the time will greatly facilitate the task . . . in the mornings and afternoons one can go to visit the churches, many of which remain open all day, and walk in the parks or the botanical and zoological gardens. In the afternoon, from 5 to 7 p.m. before dinner, a turn may be taken in Regent Street or Hyde Park, always animated, with a dense crowd of brilliant horsemen and a large number of equipages. If one is in the vicinity of London Bridge, one should take advantage of every available moment to visit the port and its environs, the ships arriving or departing and the enormous traffic in the docks. For those wishing to enjoy a grand spectacle, unique in the world, the excursion to Gravesend is especially recommended.

7
Exercises

Describe the operations you effect when you catch the Métro with the same meticulousness as Baedeker for the London Underground in 1907.

Reconsider some of the proposals made by the Surrealists for embellishing the town:

The obelisk in the Concorde: round it off and put a steel feather of the right size on the summit

The Tour Saint-Jacques: bend it slightly

The lion of Belfort: have it gnawing a bone and turned to the West

The Panthéon: slice it vertically and separate the two halves by 50 centimetres

By using maps and the appropriate diagrams, try and work out an itinerary that would enable you to take every bus in the capital one after the other.

Try and imagine what Paris will become:

Paris will become a winter garden; espaliered fruit trees on the boulevard. The Seine filtered and warm – an abundance of fake gemstones – a profusion of gilding – the houses lit up – the light will be stored, for there are bodies that have this property, such as sugar, the flesh of certain molluscs and Bologna phosphorus. The fronts of the houses will be made to be daubed with this phosphorescent substance, and their radiance will light the streets.

Gustave Flaubert,
Drafts for the final plan of *Bouvard and Pécuchet*

The Countryside

1

I don't have a lot to say concerning the country: the country doesn't exist, it's an illusion.

For most people of my kind, the country is a decorative space surrounding their second home, bordering a part of the motorways they take on Friday evenings when they go there, and a few metres of which they will pass through, if they have the courage, on Sunday afternoons, before regaining the town, where, throughout the whole of the rest of the week, they will be hymning the return to nature.

Like everyone else, however, I've been to the country on several occasions (the last time, if I remember rightly, was in February 1973; it was very cold). What's more, I like the country (I like the town too, as I've already said, I'm not hard to please). I like being in the country: you eat country bread, you breathe more easily, you sometimes see animals you're hardly in the habit of seeing in the towns, you light a fire in the hearth, you play Scrabble or other party games. It has to be admitted that you often have more room there than in the town, and almost as much comfort, and sometimes as much peace and quiet. But none of this seems to me to be enough to base any pertinent difference on.

The country is a foreign land. It shouldn't be, yet it is. It might not have been so, but it has been so and will be so from now on. It's far too late to change anything.

I am a man of the towns; I was born, I grew up and I have lived in towns. My habits, my rhythms and my vocabulary are the habits, rhythms and vocabulary of a townsman. The town belongs to me. I'm at home there: asphalt, concrete, railings, the network of streets, the dull grey of the façades stretching out of sight, these are things that may surprise or shock me, but in the same way that I might be surprised or shocked by, for example, the extreme difficulty we have when we want to look at the back of our own neck or the unjustifiable existence of the sinuses (frontal or maxillary). In the country, nothing shocks me; I might be conventional and say that everything surprises me; in actual fact, everything leaves me more or less indifferent. I learnt lots of things at school and I still know that Metz, Toul and Verdun constituted the Three Sees, that $\Delta = b^2 - 4ac$,* that acid plus base gives salt plus water, but I didn't learn anything about the country, or else I've forgotten everything I was taught. I've sometimes chanced to read in books that the country was populated by peasants, that peasants got up and went to bed with the sun, and that their work consisted, among other things, in liming, marling, rotating crops, manuring, harrowing, spudding, dressing, hoeing or treading out. For me, the operations concealed beneath these verbs are more exotic than those that preside, for example, over the servicing of a central heating boiler, an area in which I'm not all that well informed.

There are, of course, the great yellow fields furrowed by gleaming machines, the copses, the meadows planted with clover and vines as far as the eye can see. But I know nothing of these spaces, for me they are impracticable. The only things I can know are the little packets from Vilmorin or Truffaut,† the renovated farmhouses where the yokes of the oxen have become wall-hangings and grain measures have become waste-paper baskets (I have one, to which I'm very attached), compassionate articles about the raising of young calves and a nostalgia for cherries eaten sitting in the tree.

*The formula by which quadratic equations were taught in French schools.

†Vilmorin and Truffaut are well-known seed merchants in Paris.

2
Village utopia

For a start, you'd have been at school with the postman.

You'd know that the schoolmaster's honey is better than the station-master's (no, there wouldn't be a station-master any longer, only a level-crossing keeper; the trains haven't been stopping for several years now and a bus service has replaced them, but there would still be a level-crossing that hasn't yet been automated).

You'd know whether it was going to rain by looking at the shape of the clouds above the hill, you'd know the places where there are still crayfish, you'd remember the time when the garage-man shod horses (pile it on a bit, until you almost want to believe it, not too much though).

Of course, you'd know everyone and everyone's stories. Every Wednesday, the *charcutier* from Dampierre would toot in front of your house bringing you your andouillettes. Every Monday, Madame Blaise would come and wash.

You'd go with the children to pick blackberries along the sunken lanes; you'd go with them to the mushrooms; you'd send them off to hunt for snails.

You'd watch out for the 7 o'clock bus to come past. You'd like to go and sit on the village bench, underneath the hundred-year-old elm tree, opposite the church.

You'd go through the fields in ankle boots carrying a stick with a ferrule which you'd use to decapitate the long grasses.

You'd play cards with the gamekeeper.

You'd go and fetch your wood from the communal woodlands.

You'd be able to recognize birds by their song.

You'd know each one of the trees in your orchard.

You'd wait for the seasons to come round.

3
Nostalgic (and false) alternative:

To put down roots, to rediscover or fashion your roots, to carve the place that will be yours out of space, and build, plant, appropriate, millimetre by millimetre, your 'home': to belong completely in your village, knowing you're a true inhabitant of the Cévennes, or of Poitou.

Or else to own only the clothes you stand up in, to keep nothing, to live in hotels and change them frequently, and change towns, and change countries; to speak and read any one of four or five languages; to feel at home nowhere, but at ease almost everywhere.

Of Movement

We live somewhere: in a country, in a town in that country, in a neighbourhood in that town, in a street in that neighbourhood, in a building in that street, in an apartment in that building.

We should long ago have got into the habit of moving about, of moving about freely, without it being too much trouble. But we haven't done so, we've stayed where we were; things have stayed as they were. We haven't asked ourselves why it was there and not somewhere else, why it was like this and not otherwise. Then, obviously, it was too late, our habits were formed. We began to think we were well off where we were. After all, we were as well off there as over the road.

We have difficulty changing, even if it's only the position of our furniture. Moving house is quite a business. We stay in the same neighbourhood, we miss it if we change.

Something extremely serious needs to happen for us to agree to move: wars, famines, epidemics.

We find it hard to get acclimatized. Those who arrived a few days before you did look down on you. You stay in your own small corner, with the people from your corner. You remember with nostalgia your little village, your little river, the big field of mustard you could see when leaving the main road.

The Country

1
Frontiers

Countries are divided from one another by frontiers. Crossing a frontier is quite an emotive thing to do: an imaginary limit, made material by a wooden barrier which as it happens is never really on the line it purports to represent, but a few dozen or hundreds of metres this side or that of it, is enough to change everything, even the landscape. It's the same air, the same earth, but the road is no longer quite the same, the writing on the road signs changes, the baker's shops no longer look altogether like the thing we were calling a baker's shop just a short while earlier, the loaves are no longer the same shape, there are no longer the same cigarette packets lying around on the ground.

(Note what remains identical: the shape of the houses? the shape of the fields? the faces? the 'Shell' emblems at the filling stations, the 'Coca-Cola' signs that are almost identical, as a recent photographic exhibition showed, from Tierra del Fuego to Scandinavia and from Japan to Greenland, the rules of the road [with a few variations], the gauge on the railways [with the exception of Spain], etc.)

In 1952, in Jerusalem, I tried to set foot in Jordan, by getting underneath the barbed wire. I was stopped by the people I was with: it seems it had been mined. It wasn't Jordan I would have touched in any case, but a piece of nothing, of no man's land.

In October 1970, at Hof in Bavaria, I took in at a single glance, as they say, something that was West Germany, something that was East Germany and something that was Czechoslovakia. In the event, it was a vast grey, sullen expanse with a few clumps of trees. The – West German – inn from which you could take in this panorama was much frequented.

In May 1961, not far from the ruins of Sbeitla, in Tunisia, somewhere over towards Kasserine, I saw the frontier with Algeria: a simple row of barbed wire. A few hundred metres away, you could see a ruined farm that was in Algeria. The Morice Line, which was still in operation, passed just behind it, I was told.

Frontiers are lines. Millions of men are dead because of these lines. Thousands of men are dead because they didn't manage to cross them. Survival then depended simply on crossing a river, a small hill, a peaceful forest: on the far side was Switzerland, a neutral country, the Unoccupied Zone.

(*La Grande Illusion*: they didn't fire at escaped prisoners once they were over the frontier.)*

Tiny morsels of space have been fought over, bits of hillside, a few yards of seaside, needles of rock, the corner of a street. Death has come for millions of men from a slight difference in level between two points less than a hundred metres apart: they fought for weeks to capture or recapture Hill 532.

(One of the commanders-in-chief of the French Army in the 1914–18 war was called General Nivelle†.)

2
My country

The national territory (the Motherland – in German, *Vaterland* –, the Nation, the Country, France, the Hexagon) is a state in Western Europe corresponding in large part to Cisalpine Gaul. It is contained between 42° 20′ and 51° 5′ of latitude north, and between 7° 11′ of longitude west and 5° 10′ of longitude east. Its surface area is 528,576 square kilometres.

*The reference is to the celebrated Jean Renoir film.

†The sardonic point being that *niveler* is a French verb meaning 'to level off', making (*il*) *nivelle* the third person singular of the present tense.

For roughly 2,640 kilometres, this territory is bordered by a maritime space constituting French 'territorial waters'.

The entire surface area of the national territory is surmounted by an 'air space'.

The defence, integrity and security of these three spaces, terrestrial, maritime and aerial, are the object of constant concern on the part of the authorities.

I don't think I have anything special, or spatial, to add where my country is concerned.

Europe

One of the five parts of the world.

Old Continent

Europe, Asia and Africa.

New Continent

Hey guys, we've been discovered! (an Indian, catching sight of Christopher Columbus).

The World

The world is big.
Aeroplanes crisscross it at all times and in all directions.

Travelling.
You could set yourself to follow a given degree of latitude (Jules Verne, *The Children of Captain Grant*), or to pass through all the United States of America either in alphabetical order (Jules Verne, *The Testament of an Eccentric*) or by linking the passage from one state to the next to the existence of two towns of the same name (Michel Butor, *Mobile*).

The surprise and disappointment of travelling. The illusion of having overcome distance, of having erased time.
To be far away.

To see something *in reality* that had long been an image in an old dictionary: a geyser, a waterfall, the Bay of Naples, the spot where Gavrilo Princip was standing when he shot at Archduke Franz-Ferdinand of Austria and Duchess Sophia of Hohenberg, on the corner of Franz-Josef Street and the Appel Quay in Sarajevo, just opposite the Simic Brothers' bar on 28 June 1914, at 11.15 a.m.

Or else, rather, to see, far from its presumed place of origin, a perfectly ugly object, for example a box made out of seashells bearing the words 'Souvenir of Dinard' in a chalet in the Black Forest, or a perfectly commonplace one, such as a coathanger stamped 'Hôtel Saint-Vincent, Commercy' in a bed-and-breakfast in Inverness, or a perfectly improbable one, like the *Répertoire archéologique du Département du Tarn*, compiled by Mr H. Crozes, Paris, 1865, quarto, 123pp., in the sitting-room of a family pension in Regensburg (better known in France under the name of Ratisbonne).

To see what you have always dreamed of seeing. But what have you always dreamed of seeing? The Great Pyramids? The portrait of Melancthon by Cranach? Marx's grave? Freud's grave? Bokhara and Samarkand? The hat worn by Katharine Hepburn in *Sylvia Scarlet*? (One day, on my way from Forbach to Metz, I made a detour to go and see the birthplace of General Eblé in Saint-Jean-Rohrbach.)

Or else, rather, to discover what you've never seen, what you didn't expect, what you didn't imagine. But how to give examples? Not what, over time, has come to be listed among the various wonders and surprises of the world; neither the grandiose nor the impressive; nor even the foreign necessarily. But rather the reverse, the familiar rediscovered, a fraternal space . . .

What can we know of the world? What quantity of space can our eyes hope to take in between our birth and our death? How many square centimetres of Planet Earth will the soles of our shoes have touched?

To cover the world, to cross it in every direction, will only ever be to know a few square metres of it, a few acres, tiny incursions into disembodied vestiges, small, incidental excitements, improbable quests congealed in a mawkish haze a few details of which will remain in our memory: out beyond the railway stations and the roads, and the gleaming runways of airports, and the narrow strips of land illuminated for a brief moment by an overnight express, out beyond the panoramas too long anticipated and discovered too late, and the accumulations of stones and the accumulations of works of art, it will be three children perhaps running along a bright white road, or else a small house on the way out of Avignon, with a wooden lattice door once painted green, the silhouetted outline of trees on top of a hill near Saarbrücken, four uproarious fat men on the terrace of a café in the outskirts of Naples, the main street of Brionne, in the Eure, two days before Christmas, around six in the evening, the coolness of a covered gallery in the souk at Sfax, a tiny dam across a Scottish loch, the hairpin bends of a road near Corvol-l'Orgueilleux. And with these, the sense of the world's concreteness, irreducible, immediate, tangible, of something clear and closer to us: of the world, no longer as a journey having constantly to be remade, not as a race without end, a challenge having constantly to be met, not as the one pretext for a despairing acquisitiveness, nor as the illusion of a conquest, but as the rediscovery of a meaning, the perceiving that the earth is a form of writing, a *geography* of which we had forgotten that we ourselves are the authors.

. . . so that the world and space seemed to be the mirror one of the other both minutely storied in hieroglyphs and ideograms, and each of them could equally well be or not be a sign: a calcareous concretion on basalt, a ridge raised by the wind on the coagulated sand of the desert, the arrangement of the eyes in the feathers of the peacock (living in the midst of signs had very slowly brought us to see as so many signs the innumerable things that had at first been there without indicating anything but their own presence, it had transformed them into signs of themselves, and had added them to the series of signs deliberately made by whoever wanted to make a sign), the streaks of fire against a wall of schist, the four hundred and twenty-seventh groove – slightly askew – in the corniche on the pediment of a mausoleum, a sequence of streaks on a screen during a magnetic storm (the series of signs multiplied itself into the series of signs of signs, of signs repeated an innumerable number of times, always the same and always in some way different, for to the sign made on purpose was added the sign fallen there by chance), the badly inked downstroke of the letter R that in a copy of an evening paper had met with a flaw in the fibres of the newsprint, one scratch out of eight hundred thousand on the creosoted wall between two docks in Melbourne, the curve of a statistical graph, brakes being suddenly applied on tarmac, a chromosome . . .

Italo Calvino, *Cosmicomics*

Space

We use our eyes for seeing. Our field of vision reveals a limited space, something vaguely circular, which ends very quickly to left and right, and doesn't extend very far up or down. If we squint, we can manage to see the end of our nose; if we raise our eyes, we can see there's an up, if we lower them, we can see there's a down. If we turn our head in one direction, then in another, we don't even manage to see completely everything there is around us; we have to twist our bodies round to see properly what was behind us.

Our gaze travels through space and gives us the illusion of relief and distance. That is how we construct space, with an up and a down, a left and a right, an in front and a behind, a near and a far.

When nothing arrests our gaze, it carries a very long way. But if it meets with nothing, it sees nothing, it sees only what it meets. Space is what arrests our gaze, what our sight stumbles over: the obstacle, bricks, an angle, a vanishing point. Space is when it makes an angle, when it stops, when we have to turn for it to start off again. There's nothing ectoplasmic about space; it has edges, it doesn't go off in all directions, it does all that needs to be done for railway lines to meet well short of infinity.

On Straight Lines

If I mend at this rate, it is not impossible . . . but I may arrive hereafter at the excellency of going on even thus:

---

which is a line drawn as straight as I could draw it by a writing-master's ruler . . .

This *right line,* – the path-way for Christians to walk in! say Divines, –
– The emblem of moral rectitude! says Cicero, –
– The *best line!* say cabbage planters, – is the shortest line, says Archimedes, which can be drawn from one given point to another.

Lawrence Sterne, *Tristram Shandy*

Measures

Like everyone else, I presume, I feel an attraction for zero points, for the axes and points of reference from which the positions and distances of any object in the universe can be determined:

– the Equator
– the Greenwich Meridian
– sea-level

or the circle on the parvis in front of Notre-Dame (it disappeared, alas, when they were making the carpark and no one has thought to put it back) from which all French distances by road were calculated.

When going from Tunis to Sfax, I used to like passing the sign (it, too, has since vanished) which showed how far it was to Tripoli, Benghazi, Alexandria and Cairo.

I like knowing that Pierre-François-André Méchain, born in Laon in 1744, and Jean-Baptiste-Joseph Delambre, born in Amiens in 1749, went from Dunkirk to Barcelona with the sole object of verifying how long a metre had to be (it seems that Méchain made a mistake in his calculations).

I like knowing that midway between the hamlets of Frapon and La Presle, in the commune of Vesdun, in the department of the Cher, a plaque is to be found indicating that you are at the exact *centre* of metropolitan France.

Right here, at this moment, it wouldn't be altogether impossible for me to determine my position in degrees, minutes, seconds, tenths and hundredths of a second: somewhere in the region of 49° north latitude, somewhere in the region of 2° 10′ 14.4″ east of Greenwich (or only a few fractions of a second west of the Paris meridian), and a few dozen metres above sea-level.

I read recently that a letter had been posted in England whose only address was a latitude and longitude. The sender, obviously, was, if not a geographer, then at least a surveyor or mapmaker, and it's true that the addressee lived on his own in a house sufficiently isolated to be identifiable. The fact remains that the letter arrived. The Postmaster-General, the British equivalent of our own Minister of Posts and Telegraphs, issued a statement in which he expressed the high esteem in which he held his postmen, but warned that in future such forms of address would not be accepted. The same goes for addresses written in verse; postmen have better things to do than solve riddles. The path a letter follows from its point of departure to its point of arrival is a strictly coded affair; Mallarmé, Latis* or cartography can only produce 'noise'.

Space seems to be either tamer or more inoffensive than time; we're forever meeting people who have watches, very seldom people who have compasses. We always need to know what time it is (who still knows how to deduce it from the position of the sun?) but we never ask ourselves where we are. We think we know: we are at home, at our office, in the Métro, in the street.

That of course is obvious – but then what isn't obvious? Now and again, however, we ought to ask ourselves where exactly we are, to take our bearings, not only concerning our state of mind, our everyday health, our ambitions, our beliefs and our *raisons d'être*, but simply concerning our topographical position, not so much in relation to the axes cited above, but rather in relation to a place or a person we are thinking about, or that we shall thus start thinking about. For example, when you get into the coach at the Invalides air terminal to go to Orly, picture the person you're going to meet passing directly above Grenoble, and try, as the coach makes its way with difficulty through the traffic jams in the Avenue de Maine, to imagine his slow progress across a map of France, crossing the Ain, the Saône-et-Loire, the Nièvre and the Loiret. Or else, more systematically, interrogate yourself at some precise moment of the day about the positions occupied

*The pseudonym of Emmanuel Peillet, a philosophy teacher and active member of OuLiPo.

by some of your friends, in relation both to one another and to yourself. List the differences in levels (the ones who, like you, live on the first floor, the ones who live on the fifth, the sixth, etc.), the direction they are facing, imagine their movements through space.

Long ago, like everyone else I presume, and no doubt on one of those little three-month diaries the Librairie Gibert gave away at the start of the autumn term, you went to swap the Carpentier-Fialap and Roux-Combaluzier textbooks of the year before for the Carpentier-Fialap and Roux-Combaluzier of the year ahead, I used to write my address as follows:

Georges Perec
18, Rue de l'Assomption
Staircase A
Third floor
Right-hand door
Paris 16e
Seine
France
Europe
The World
The Universe

playing with space

Play with large numbers (factorials, Fibonacci series, geometric progressions):

Distance from the Earth to the Moon: a sheet of cigarette paper so fine it would take a thousand of them to make a millimetre, folded in two 49 times in a row;

Distance from the Earth to the Sun: ditto, folded in two 58 times in a row;

Distance from Pluto to the Sun: the same again; by folding it four more times you're just about there, but fold it five more times and you pass Pluto by some 3,000,000,000 kilometres;

Distance from Earth to Alpha Centauri: fifteen more foldings.

Play with distances: prepare a journey that would enable you to visit or pass through all the places that are 314.60 kilometres from your house;

Look up the route you've followed on an atlas or army map.

Play with measurements: reacquaint yourself with feet and leagues (if only to make it easier to read Stendhal, Dumas or Jules Verne); try and get once and for all a clear idea of what a nautical mile is (and by the same token, a knot); remember that a *journal* is a unit of space, it's the surface area a farm labourer can work in a day.

Play with space:

Cause an eclipse of the sun by raising your little finger (as Leopold Bloom does in *Ulysses*).

Have yourself photographed holding up the Leaning Tower of Pisa.

Start to get used to living in a state of weightlessness; forget verticals and horizontals: Escher's engravings, the inside of spaceships in *2001: A Space Odyssey*.

Reflect on these two quite brilliant thoughts (complementary as it happens):

I often think about how much beef it would take to turn the Lake of Geneva into consommé. (Pierre Dac, *L'Os à moelle*)

Elephants are generally drawn smaller than life size, but a flea always larger. (Jonathan Swift, *Thoughts on Various Subjects*)

the conquest of space

1
M. Raymond Roussel's Mobile Home
(Extract from the *Revue du Touring Club de France*)

The author of *Impressions of Africa*, whose genius has been extolled by so many distinguished minds, has had an automobile 9 metres long by 2.30 wide built to his own design.

This vehicle is a veritable small house. Thanks to the ingenuity of its arrangement, it contains: a sitting-room, a bedroom, a studio, a bathroom, and even a small dormitory for a staff consisting of three men (two chauffeurs and a manservant).

The very elegant coachwork is by Lacoste and its interior layout is as original as it is ingenious . . . In the daytime the bedroom turns into a studio or sitting-room; in the evening the front section (behind the driver's seat) becomes a small bedroom in which the three men referred to above can relax and perform their toilet (there is a wash-basin in the casing to the left of the driver's seat and steering wheel).

The interior decoration of M. Raymond Roussel's mobile home bears the signature of Maple's.

It is heated electrically and has a petroleum gas-stove with flue. The water-heater likewise works off petroleum gas.

The fittings have been planned to meet all requirements. They even include a Fichet safe.

An excellent wireless set enables one to pick up all the European stations.

This description, brief though it is, is enough to show that this veritable mobile villa – to which a kitchen-trailer can be added – allows its owner to rediscover all the comforts of the family home within an only slightly reduced setting.

This luxurious installation is mounted on a Saurer chassis. On the flat, its normal speed is some 40 kilometres an hour. The steepest descents can be tackled without fear thanks to the motor braking system.

The steering has an excellent 'lock', something much to be desired when taking the hairpin bends on mountain roads.

. . . As soon as it was built, the caravan left . . . to effect a 3,000-kilometre excursion through Switzerland and Alsace. M. Roussel was able to enjoy a fresh horizon each evening.

He has brought back incomparable impressions from his journey.

2
Saint Jerome in his Study
by Antonello da Messina (National Gallery, London)

The study is a piece of wooden furniture standing on the tiled floor of a cathedral. It rests on a dais which is reached by three steps and consists mainly of six compartments filled with books and various other objects (boxes chiefly and a vase), and a working surface the flat part of which supports two books, an inkwell and a quill, and the sloping part the book that the saint is in the midst of reading. All its elements are fixed, i.e. constitute the piece of furniture as such, but on the dais also are a chair, the one on which the saint is sitting, and a chest.

The saint has taken his shoes off in order to mount the dais. He has put his cardinal's hat down on the chest. He is dressed in a (cardinal) red robe and wears a sort of skullcap, also red, on his head. He sits very upright on his chair, and a long way from the book he is reading. His fingers have slipped inside the pages as if he were either only leafing through the book, or rather as if he had a frequent need to refer back to passages he has read earlier. On top of one of the shelves, facing the saint and high above him, there stands a tiny crucifix.

On one side of the shelves are fixed two austere hooks, one of which bears an item of clothing that may be an amice or a stole, but is more likely a towel.

On a projection of the dais are two potted plants, one of which might be a dwarf orange-tree, and a small tabby cat whose position gives one to suppose it is dozing. Above the orange-tree, on the panel of the worktop, a label is fixed, as nearly always with Antonello da Messina, giving the artist's name and the date when the picture was painted.

On either side and above the study, you can get an idea of the rest of the cathedral. It is empty, with the exception of a lion, on the right, which, with one paw raised, seems to be hesitating whether to come and disturb the saint at his work. Seven birds are framed in the tall, narrow upper windows. Through the lower windows can be seen a countryside of low hills, a cypress tree, olive trees, a castle, a river with two people in a boat and three fishermen.

The whole is seen from a vast ogival opening on the sill of which a peacock and a very young bird of prey are obligingly perched next to a magnificent copper basin.

The whole space is organized around *the piece of furniture* (and the whole of the piece of furniture is organized around the book). The glacial architecture of the church (the bareness of the tiling, the hostility of the piers) has been cancelled out. Its perspectives and its vertical lines have ceased to delimit the site simply of an ineffable faith; they are there solely to lend scale to the piece of furniture, to enable it to be *inscribed*; Surrounded by the uninhabitable, the study defines a domesticated space inhabited with serenity by cats, books and men.

3
The Escaped Prisoner

'Thus you think you can see a bridge galloping'

Jacques Roubaud

I've forgotten where this anecdote came from, I can't guarantee its authenticity and I'm far from being certain as to the accuracy of its terminology. Nevertheless, it seems to me to illustrate my purpose admirably.

A French prisoner of war succeeded in escaping in the middle of the night from the train that was taking him to Germany. The night was pitch black. The prisoner was wholly ignorant of his whereabouts. He walked for a long time at random, i.e. straight ahead. At a certain moment he came to the banks of a river. There was the moan of a siren. A few seconds later, the waves raised by the passing boat came and broke on the bank. From the time separating the moan of the siren from the splashing of the waves, the escapee deduced the width of the river. Knowing how wide it was, he identified it (it was the Rhine) and having identified it, knew where he was.

4
Meetings

It would be quite senseless obviously if it were otherwise. Everything has been studied, been worked out, there's no question of getting it wrong, no known case of an error being detected, even of a few centimetres, even of a few millimetres.

Yet I still feel something like amazement when I think of the French and Italian workmen meeting in the middle of the Mont Cenis tunnel.

The Uninhabitable

The uninhabitable: seas used as a dump, coastlines bristling with barbed wire, earth bare of vegetation, mass graves, piles of carcasses, boggy rivers, towns that smell bad

The uninhabitable: the architecture of contempt or display, the vainglorious mediocrity of tower blocks, thousands of rabbit hutches piled one above the other, the cutprice ostentation of company headquarters

The uninhabitable: the skimped, the airless, the small, the mean, the shrunken, the very precisely calculated

The uninhabitable: the confined, the out-of-bounds, the encaged, the bolted, walls jagged with broken glass, judas windows, reinforced doors

The uninhabitable: shanty towns, townships

The hostile, the grey, the anonymous, the ugly, the corridors of the Métro, public baths, hangars, car parks, marshalling yards, ticket windows, hotel bedrooms

factories, barracks, prisons, asylums, old people's homes, lycées, law courts, school playgrounds

space-saving private properties, converted attics, superb bachelor pads, fashionable studio flats in leafy surroundings, elegant pieds-à-terre, triple reception rooms, vast homes in the sky, unbeatable view, double aspect, trees, beams, character, luxurious designer conversion, balcony, telephone, sunlight, hallway, real fireplace, loggia, double (stainless steel) sink, peace and quiet, exclusive small garden, exceptional value

You are asked to give your name after 10 p.m.

Embellishment:

39533/43/Kam/J 6 November 1943

Objective: to assemble the plants for the purpose of providing a border of greenery for the camp's Nos 1 and 2 crematorium ovens.
Ref: Conversation between SS-Obersturmbannführer Höss, Camp Commandant, and Sturmbannführer Bishoff.
To SS-Sturmbannführer Ceasar, Head of Agricultural Services in the Concentration Camp of Auschwitz (Upper Silesia).
In conformity with an order from SS-Obersturmbannführer Höss, Camp Commandant, Nos 1 and 2 crematorium ovens in the camp will be provided with a green border serving as a natural boundary to the camp.
The following is a list of the plants needing to be drawn from our stocks of trees:
200 trees in leaf from three to five metres high; 100 tree shoots in leaf from a metre and a half to four metres high; lastly, 1,000 bushes for use as lining from one to two and a half metres high, all to come from the stocks in our nurseries.

You are requested to place these supplies of plants at our disposal.
Head of the Central Building Directorate of
the Waffen SS and the Police at Auschwitz.
Signed: SS-Obersturmführer
(quoted by David Rousset, *Le Pitre ne rit pas*, 1948)

Space (Continuation and End)

I would like there to exist places that are stable, unmoving, intangible, untouched and almost untouchable, unchanging, deep-rooted; places that might be points of reference, of departure, of origin:

My birthplace, the cradle of my family, the house where I may have been born, the tree I may have seen grow (that my father may have planted the day I was born), the attic of my childhood filled with intact memories . . .

Such places don't exist, and it's because they don't exist that space becomes a question, ceases to be self-evident, ceases to be incorporated, ceases to be appropriated. Space is a doubt: I have constantly to mark it, to designate it. It's never mine, never given to me, I have to conquer it.

My spaces are fragile: time is going to wear them away, to destroy them. Nothing will any longer resemble what was, my memories will betray me, oblivion will infiltrate my memory, I shall look at a few old yellowing photographs with broken edges without recognizing them. The words '*Phone directory available within*' or '*Snacks served at any hour*' will no longer be written up in a semi-circle in white porcelain letters on the window of the little café in the Rue Coquillière.

Space melts like sand running through one's fingers. Time bears it away and leaves me only shapeless shreds:

To write: to try meticulously to retain something, to cause something to survive; to wrest a few precise scraps from the void as it grows, to leave somewhere a furrow, a trace, a mark or a few signs.

PARIS 1973–1974

Index of some of the words used in this work

Since 1984, small planet No 2817 (1982 UJ) has borne the name of Georges Perec

from *Je suis né* (1990)

*I Was Born**

7. ix. 70 Carros

I was born on 7.3.36. How many dozens, how many hundreds of times have I written that sentence? I've no idea. I know I began quite early on, well before forming any plans for an autobiography. I made it the subject-matter of a bad novel entitled *J'Avance masqué* ['I Advance Wearing a Mask'], and of an equally hopeless story (which was simply the foregoing badly recast) entitled *Gradus ad Parnassum.*

It will be observed first of all that such a sentence is complete, it forms a whole. It's hard to imagine a text beginning: I was born.

One might on the other hand stop once the date has been specified.

I was born on 7 March 1936. Full stop. That's what I've been doing these past several months. It's also what I've been doing for 34 and a half years, today!

Normally, one goes on. It's a good beginning, one that invites further details, a lot of details, a whole history.

I was born on 25 December 0000. My father was a jobbing carpenter, so they say. Shortly after my birth, the gentiles weren't so gentle and we had to take refuge in Egypt. That's how I found out I was a Jew and the origin of my firm decision not to remain one has to be seen as lying in these dramatic circumstances. The rest you know.

The near impossibility of going on, once the 'I was born on 7.3.36' has been uttered, formed the actual substance, now I think back on it, of the books referred to above. In *J'Avance masqué* the

*This extract from one of Perec's autobiographical notebooks was first published in the *Cahiers Georges Perec* in 1988.

narrator recounted his life at least three times over, the three narrations being equally false ('a written confession is always untruthful': I was drinking in Svevo at the time) but perhaps significantly different.

The question isn't 'why go on?', nor 'why didn't I manage to go on?' (questions I shall have to answer in the third of my three sections), but 'how to go on?'.

The fact is I'm back again at my starting point. I was born on 7.3.36. So be it. I light a cigarette, I take a turn round the edge of the pool without any intention of swimming, I leaf through books, looking for an exemplary opening (I was born on . . .). I light upon *Too Strong for Fantasy*, Marcia Davenport's autobiography, concerning which all I know is that it talks about music and about Czechoslovakia; it has photographs and an index. I shall read it more carefully. Leaf also through the diary of Anne Frank (not much I can take from that), Elmer Luchterhand's two articles on social behaviour in the camps (offprints I asked for at the lab). Or else I play patience, thump away on the half-dismantled piano (i.e. directly on the strings), glance at a now ancient *France-Soir*, shave, pour myself some beer, etc. (gnaw at a fingernail, pull off toenails, walk up and down).

Or else, obviously, the most subtle(?) form of self-display: write on (so far) 3 pages of this notebook that I can't go on . . .

Either there is a continuation, or there isn't.

Either there is a continuation that can be recounted, or there isn't.

Let's keep tapping the topic: What? Who? When? Where? How? Why?

What? I was born.

Who? I was.

When? 7 March 1936.

More precisely? I don't know what time; I would (will) need to consult a birth certificate. Let's say nine o' clock in the evening. One day I'll also have to go to the Bibliothèque Nationale to get out some of the newspapers for that day and look and see what happened. For a long time I believed 7 March 1936 was when Hitler entered Poland. Either I had the date wrong or the country. Perhaps it was '39 (I don't think so) or else it was Czechoslovakia (plausible?) or Austria, the Sudetenland, the Anschluss or Danzig or the Saar, I don't know that history at all well even though for me it was crucial. Whatever the case, Hitler was already very much in power and there were already concentration camps.

Where? In Paris. Not in the 20th arrondissement, as I long believed, but in the 19th. No doubt in a maternity home. The name of the street still eludes me (I could find that ditto on a birth certificate).

How? Why?

Why? That's a good question, as Lucy Van Pelt* would say.

The best authors give a few details about their parents almost immediately after the announcement of their entry into the world.

My father's name was Icek Judko, that's to say Isaac Joseph, or Isidore if you want. His sister and his niece remember him under the name of Izzy. For my part, I've always insisted on calling him André.

8 Sept. 70. Carros.

Today I've mainly been playing around with various paints: inks and oils, gouaches and knives.

It's four p.m., perhaps I can attempt to work. My intention is clear (if you like), the difficulty put on: the mechanics of writing, the artifice of rhetoric. I'm not held back by modesty (that wouldn't anyway be the main argument). What then? Perhaps the magnitude of the task is putting me off. To unravel the skein one more

*The girl in the *Peanuts* strip.

time, right to the end, to shut myself up for I don't know how many weeks, months or years (12 years if I respect the rule imposed by the writing of *Lieux**) in the enclosed world of my memories, going over and over them until I'm both satiated and nauseated.

*See the description of this unfinished project on pp. 55–6 of this volume.

*The Scene of a Flight**

The stamp market in the Champs-Elysées gardens opened only on Thursdays and Sundays. He knew that, but he'd told himself he might perhaps meet someone, some old fellow at a loose end who would look at his stamp-book, would pause at the sepia Blériot, at the 'Victory of Samothrace', would weigh up the Marianne series, or the crimson Pétain overprinted with the Cross of Lorraine. But there was no one, not even a stroller. Nothing but metal chairs painted green, lined up between the trees. It wasn't even nine a.m. The air was mild. A council sprinkler lorry was going down the Avenue Gabriel. The Champs-Elysées seemed deserted. On the other side of the gardens, between the little swings and the puppet theatre, some workmen were unloading the wooden horses of a roundabout, the skeleton of which had already been erected, from a big yellow lorry and trailer.

He sat down on a seat and opened his satchel. He took out his small stamp-book, the one he used to keep his swaps in. It was quite some time now since he had slipped the best items from his real collection into the little pocket inside the cover, from his beautiful bound album which his aunt kept locked away, in the wardrobe of her bedroom next to her jewellery, and which she never liked letting him look at.

He looked carefully at the stamps, one by one, set them out, tried to estimate what they might give him for them.

Later, he closed the book again and put it into the inside pocket of his jacket.

*French title *Les Lieux d'une fugue*. This account was written in 1965 and first published in a monthly magazine called *Présence et regards* ten years later. In 1976 Perec made a film version of it that was shown on French television.

He got out his homework book. Today, Wednesday, he had an hour of French and an hour of Latin with Monsieur Bourguignon, an hour of history with Monsieur Poirier, an hour of English with Monsieur Normand; in the afternoon, an hour of drawing with Monsieur Joly, an hour of natural science with Monsieur Léonard.

He hadn't done his English homework, or prepared the written questions.

It was nine o' clock; he was late merely. Everything could still be put right.

Often before, he'd had occasion to miss the first class. At half past eight, the porter closed the pupils' entrance. He'd never had the courage to go in through the main entrance on the Avenue du Parc-des-Princes.

He would walk off, intoxicated by freedom, to the Porte de Saint-Cloud, the Avenue de Versailles. He would go into the Prisunic and stop at every counter, in front of the hammers, the bowls, the soap. Sometimes he was lucky enough to steal a nail, a screw, a shoe cleat, a light switch.

He came back for nine-thirty. His absence had been noted down on the class list and earned him two hours' detention on Thursday morning. But his lateness was an alibi: a fault far easier to endure, when faced by his uncle, than indiscipline.

He opened his books and looked through them. He read his exercise-books and his old homework. He opened the green leather pencil-case that his two girl cousins had used. It contained an old chewed ruler, three crayons without any lead in, a black pencil, a broken fountain-pen stuck together with Elastoplast, a Plexiglas protractor, a worn-away rubber, a pair of compasses.

He drew a few circles on the yellow wood of the seat. Then he put the compasses back into the case, and the case, the books and the exercise-books, back into the satchel.

Then he walked quickly off.

He was sitting on a bench, opposite the *Figaro*. The lights had finally gone out in the glass cases where the paper was displayed. The only illumination came from the big capital F with a goose-quill through it above the entrance. The gardens were deserted. The orange and blue canopy of the roundabout could no longer be made out. The few pedestrians on the Champs-Elysées passed within a few yards of him, without seeing him, hurrying to get home. He could hear a jumble of words.

He got up. He crossed the Champs-Elysées, went as far as the Métro station. He saw it was shut and retraced his steps.

He was cold. He lay down on the seat, curled up as tightly as he could, wrapping his arms around his bare knees. The seat was made from two pieces of wood screwed down on to cast-iron legs, and was too narrow.

He got up, turned around, went and sat down again, lay down again, resting his head on his right arm, pulling his knees into his chest.

He closed his eyes, then opened them again.

A few yards away, people were going past like shadows. An occasional car went past behind his back, slowed down, changed gear, sometimes blew its horn.

Later on, a man approached him. He saw him coming in the distance, a dark mass standing out against the even darker background of the *Figaro* building. He closed his eyes, pretended to be asleep. His heart was racing.

What are you doing there? asked the man.

He didn't answer.

What are you doing there? he repeated. Where do you live?

He said nothing.

Where do you live? he repeated.

He didn't answer. He looked at him.

He was a tall man, well dressed, concerned-looking.

He told himself for a moment that he could tell him, could explain. But he had nothing to tell. He thought he understood he'd been waiting for this moment all through the day, for someone to speak to him, to see him, to come looking for him.

Leave me alone, he said.

Come on now, come with me, said the man.

He took him by the hand and led him to the police station in the Grand-Palais.

I found him on a seat, at the Rond-Point, next to the *Figaro*, he said to the policemen.

He had twenty-three francs on him. They soon went. Around the middle of the morning, he went into a baker's in the Rue du Colisée and bought a small milk-loaf for ten francs. He ate it slowly, in small mouthfuls, as he went along. A little time later, he bought an illustrated magazine at a kiosk in the Champs-Elysées. He went and sat down in order to read it, but got no pleasure from it.

He had three francs left: a forty-sou coin and a twenty-sou coin, both stamped with the battle-axe. He couldn't buy anything with them, except perhaps sweets or a piece of chewing-gum, at some stall or other; but he didn't come across one.

Later on, he found a crumpled-up copy of *France-Soir* in one of the waste-paper bins in the Alma-Marceau Métro station. He looked for the sports page, read the strips, the jokes, the gossip column, then got tired and threw it away again where he'd found it.

Later on, much later on, he mingled with the idlers who, all day long, read the *Figaro*, the *Figaro Littéraire* and the *Figaro Agricole* displayed on the walls of the building in the Avenue des Champs-Elysées.

Later on, he drank some water from a public fountain.

His aunt, in her dressing gown, her hair undone, her first cigarette in her mouth, closed the door on him, a thick, heavy door, with three brass locks and a burglar-proof catch, which never slammed. He began to go down the stairs as usual, then stopped, remained motionless for a few moments, between landings. He looked at the marble stairs, the red carpet, the ironwork and glass of the liftshaft.

He began to go down again, slowly, letting himself drop almost from stair to stair, his knees locked, like an automaton or a monster.

He passed, head lowered, in front of the concierge, who was shining the knobs on the lift with a woollen duster, pipe in mouth, a blue apron around his waist.

The mirrors in the big hallway reflected his image back at him for a moment, to infinity. He went out. The Rue de l'Assomption was quiet, almost provincial, still asleep. The dustbins hadn't been emptied; the concierges were shaking out the doormats. Schoolchildren, boys and girls from the lycée, on their way to Janson-de-Sailly or to Claude-Bernard, to La Fontaine or Molière, were going up the street towards the Ranelagh Métro, or going down it to wait in the Rue de Boulainvilliers for the No 52 bus.

He caught the Métro, as every day. He handed his weekly season to the ticket puncher; it had already been perforated four times and the outward journey for Wednesday was punched. The train came in, he got in at the back, as every day. But, at Michel-Ange-Molitor, instead of getting out, he changed, took the same line in the opposite direction. He went past Ranelagh. He got off at Franklin-Roosevelt.

It was the eleventh of May nineteen hundred and forty-seven. He was eleven years and two months old. He had just run away from home, eighteen Rue de l'Assomption in the sixteenth arrondissement. He was wearing a grey woollen jacket with three buttons, a pair of navy blue shorts, brown shoes, blue woollen socks. He was carrying a satchel of black imitation leather. His whole fortune amounted to twenty-three francs and his one hope was a small stamp collection that he was counting on selling as soon as possible.

He could see the woman in the ticket-office was looking at him and he paused from opening the ticket barrier. He didn't move. He pressed himself against the tiled wall and waited.

A long time afterwards, the cashier came out and approached him.

Can't stay there, sonny, you're in the way, she said to him.

He said nothing. He didn't look at her.

What are you doing here? she asked.

I'm not doing anything, he answered.

She asked: Where do you live?

He said, dropping his voice: At Ranelagh.

She said: You must go home to bed.

He said: I don't have a ticket any more.

She went to find him one, came back, held it out to him.

I haven't any money, he said.

She said: That doesn't matter, I'm giving it to you. Now go away to bed.

He ran down on to the platform.

A train passed, nearly empty; he got in. He sat down. The train started, the carriages shook and swayed. The noise of the Métro was almost a comfort to him.

At Trocadéro, he got off, not even daring to go on to Ranelagh. He changed and set off again towards the Mairie de Montreuil. He got off at Alma-Marceau. He hung around for a long time on the platform. He followed the winding tracks of the water left by the sprinklers. He fumbled in the litter bins amongst the piles of tickets.

Later on, he sat down next to the sweet machine. He watched the trains as they came in. He tried to remember the numbers written on the leading carriage. He watched the people as they came and went.

Finally, he took the Métro again, got off at Franklin-Roosevelt, changed and went out via the Vincennes-Neuilly line, on to the Avenue des Champs-Elysées.

At the beginning of the afternoon, with his Wednesday return section, he took the Métro as far as the Pont de Sèvres, going once again through Ranelagh, Michel-Ange-Auteuil and Michel-Ange-Molitor. At the Pont de Sèvres, he crossed the Seine and entered the woods.

He walked for a long time; now and again he caught sight of a gardener trimming a hedge, or a man walking his dog.

He left the broadwalks, plunged down side paths, pushed his way through the bushes. At the top of a small escarpment strewn with stones and brambles, three trees with their trunks set close together formed a sheltered space, a rudimentary cabin. He cleared it carefully, rooting the brambles and grass out with his heel, piling up the stones and loose chalk. Then he sat down, his back against the thickest of the three tree-trunks.

Later on, with the sharp edge of a stone, he made a broad incision in the bark of one of the three trees and marked his return route by various signs.

He no longer had a valid ticket to get back to Franklin-Roosevelt. His season had been used twice. In a timid voice, he asked the ticket-puncher to take his Thursday section. He said he'd made a mistake and had forgotten to get off. The ticket-puncher looked at him and let him through.

He sat down on a seat of green slats and, once again, gazed at the roundabout. The workmen had finished hooking on the horses and pods and were fixing a large canopy of alternately orange and blue canvas on to the conical framework of the roof. It was attached at the top by a huge metal eyelet, and held in place at the bottom by long white canvas laces. These were being interminably plaited by one of the workmen, standing on a double step-ladder, and then masked by an edging of triangular festoons.

Later on, he walked for a time in the rock garden that borders the Grand-Palais next to the river, amongst the fake stone steps, the fake arches, the fake wooden bridge. He leant over the ornamental pond where three small red fish were swimming.

Later on, he found a piece of metalwork in a gutter, a sort of L-shaped copper tube that had a sprung valve at one end and a threaded rod at the other.

He stood at the top of the steps, near to the exit on the Montreuil line. He swung to and fro once or twice, bent over the ticket barrier. Then he looked at the posters.

He heard a train arrive. People came running up the stairs. He could tell they were going to the theatre because they were wearing bow ties. He pulled the barrier towards him and held it open while the people passed.

Trains arrived. People came up in waves, others went down and everyone was in a hurry. He opened and closed the barrier. No one addressed a word to him, no one thanked him. Some of them looked at him, surprised perhaps – the thought suddenly occurred to him – that he should be so well dressed, and he wondered for a second or two whether he should hold out his hand.

He circled the puppet theatre. On the ground he found a marble, an agate, a lump of worn-away white glass, with bubbles and splinters of colour in it, and a bright spiral of blue and yellow.

He bent over the dumb mouths of the fountains, over the empty flower-beds of the Rond-Point.

For a long time he watched the workmen putting up the roundabout. They attached two blue pods decorated with an orange sun, then some stylized horses, white, brown and black, with crinkly manes, blue or yellow, orange or green, and eyes made from two half-billets of wood embedded one inside the other, alternately blue and red.

Later on, he sat down and looked at what he had in his wallet: a school identity card, a Métro ticket, a photo of his girl cousin at a fancy dress ball, in a dress sewn with seashells, a photo of himself on the balcony in the Rue de l'Assomption.

He walked all the way round the Rond-Point, the Avenue Matignon, the Rue du Colisée, as far as Saint-Philippe-du-Roule. It must have been midday. People were queuing in front of the bakers'. The cafés were full.

Later on, he walked slowly in the midst of a crowd that was hurrying off in every direction. Newsvendors were shouting, selling *Le Monde*, or *France-Soir*. Compact knots of people were waiting at the intersections and the bus stops, or being swallowed up by the entrances to the Métro.

Later on still, in the darkness, he went up the Champs-Elysées and down it again, stopping at the entrances to the cinemas, looking into shop windows, weaving between the tables on the café terraces.

Later on, he stopped for a long time next to the newsvendor at Franklin-Roosevelt, who was selling the final editions of the papers underneath his canvas shelter lit by a paraffin lamp.

He confessed almost right away. He said what his name was. He gave the name of his uncle, his telephone number, his address.

He looked at the policeman leaning over him and he cried.

Are you hungry? asked the policeman.

He didn't answer.

Haven't you had anything to eat?

He shook his head.

They brought him a pâté sandwich, so big that he had to make an effort to tear off each mouthful. The bread was a bit stale, the pâté tasted bitter. He was still crying and snivelled as he ate. He was trembling slightly. Fragments of pâté and breadcrumbs fell on to the stained blotter.

Give him something to drink, said a voice.

A policeman came back, holding a bowl filled with water and held it out to him. He put the sandwich down on the blotter and took the bowl in both hands.

It was an enormous, deep bowl of white china, its rim slightly chipped, its bottom lined with greyish streaks. He wet his lips in the water and drank.

Later on, the man who had brought him in went away. He remained alone with the policemen, in front of the half-gnawed sandwich, the white china bowl, the stained blotter, the inkwell, the die stamps.

They motioned him to get up and go and sit further off. He went to the end of the room, sat down on a wooden bench-seat that ran all the way along the wall. His hands on his knees, head bent, staring at the ground, he waited, full of shame and fear.

Later on, his uncle and his girl cousin arrived, and took him away in a car.

When, twenty years later, he undertook to remember (when, twenty years later, I undertook to remember), everything at first was opaque and uncertain. Then the details returned, one by one:

the marble, the seat, the small loaf of bread;

the walk, the wood, the rock garden;

the roundabout, the puppets;

the ticket barrier;

the Rue de l'Assomption, the journey by Métro, the journeys by Métro;

the illustrated magazine, the man, the policemen;

the sandwich and the bowl, the big white china bowl, with the chipped rim and the bottom covered in greyish streaks, out of which he'd drunk water

(out of which I'd drunk water).

And he remained trembling for a long moment, before the blank page

(and I remained trembling for a long moment, before the blank page).

May nineteen hundred and sixty-five

*The Parachute Jump**

[. . .] It's a very personal experience, I'm telling it because I'm a bit . . . because I've drunk a bit. I'd like to talk about a jump I made. There doesn't seem to be any connection at first between a parachute jump and a discussion among intellectuals. In fact, there is no connection. Only, if I manage to talk to you about the way I feel about it today . . . about the way in which *I* made a parachute jump at a particular point in time, I fancy there are a certain number of mutual connections which I can't even try to define, but which will define themselves in one way or another. Right then, I'll start.

We're on an airfield. There are a certain number of parachutists. Only you mustn't take the word 'parachutist' in the sense it has today, simply bear in mind that among all these parachutists there is one parachutist who is me, Georges Perec (*short embarrassed laugh*), that's to say someone possessing, when all's said and done, a certain goodwill, a certain liking for life, a certain number of difficulties, and who is managing to resolve them, or who thinks he can manage to resolve them exactly in so far as he manages to negotiate all the various stages necessary in order to jump. There's a tremendous noise of planes busy turning round on the runway. A wait, extremely slow. A sort of a let-down, inasmuch as we're in the middle of waiting for something, there's a whole lot of people going ahead of us – i.e. a whole lot of people busy risking

*This is the transcript of remarks made by Perec at an editorial meeting in 1959 of the journal *Arguments*, with which he was then associated. It was first published in an accurate version in 1990, as part of the volume entitled *Je suis né*. It needs to be remembered when reading it that Perec had been a conscript in the French Army and that the parachutists had earned for themselves an especially unpleasant reputation for their brutality in fighting against the Nationalists in Algeria, in a war to which Perec, like almost every other intellectual and writer of the time, was passionately opposed. He was himself excused from being sent there by the fact that his father had died in action in 1940.

something before we do – and as for us, we're not feeling as brave as we should. We're busy waiting simply; you smoke a cigarette, you go and pee, because you always pee before moments like this, and then at a given moment, a given instant . . .

If anyone doesn't feel interested, given that I reckon what I'm recounting is completely bloody stupid, I wish he'd interrupt and say it has no connection (*protests*), but anyway, if no one does, I'll go on. You go and pee, then at a given moment an order comes up, the order is called: 'Fall in!' You all run to fall in, you stand to attention. This has no connection, but it all forms part, in a way, of a ritual, of how the whole thing develops . . . of how the fear develops, which is something extremely important. Because from that moment on, you begin to feel afraid. For as long as we hadn't been told to get our equipment on, we weren't afraid because we weren't yet sure we'd be jumping. From the moment you begin to get your equipment on, you are sure of jumping. Then, you begin to check to see your parachute is all there. You check the fastenings, you check the . . . You get your equipment on, you check the length of the harness, you fasten the harness; at that moment, you have the parachute behind your back and in front of you. The parachute weighs 15 kilos, it's something very heavy and very laborious to carry. You are well and truly . . . condemned, well and truly . . . minimized!

Anyway, it's terrible. You can't carry it, can't walk with it. You're forced to put up with it. Your parachute is inspected. A plane arrives, you get into the plane. The plane takes off. And then it's airborne, everyone began singing the moment the plane started moving, and everyone has all of a sudden stopped. When you look at the eyes of the ones facing you, you realize that everyone has something in common, deep down, beyond their fear, beyond the fact that you know they're fascists, you know that these guys are absolute bastards, that these guys are the dregs . . . You feel there's something in common but you can't manage to define exactly what it is. Perhaps it's simply the fact that they're all in the same situation as you are, that they're all going to have to jump out of the plane door when the moment comes. At a given moment, you're told: 'On your feet, hook on.' 'On your feet, hook on,' means you've got to stand up – you're sitting down – you've got to stand up, you've got to hook on the static line, you've got to hook it on to the wire in the plane and take up a certain position in relation to the man in front of you and the one following you, so as to be able to get out as easily as possible.

This is the moment when it all gets very complicated; you can't manage to stand up. Well, *I* couldn't manage to stand up. I don't know exactly what the matter was, I didn't know what was going on, my legs had gone, I had the impression I was going to give up altogether, that I was going to lose every last drop of courage, that I was going to be absolutely incapable of making the totally insignificant movement of standing up, taking hold of the snaphook of my parachute, hooking it on to the static line, then jumping, that is, of moving forward, of preparing myself . . . Well, I couldn't! That's the moment when doubt appears. It was exactly as if everything had been thrown back into question.

That's the moment when the problem of choice poses itself. Exactly the problem of life as a whole. That was the moment when I knew I was going to have to put my trust in things that were wholly alien to me. That I was going to have to begin assuming my situation fully, definitively: the fact that I was a parachutist, the fact that I had a helmet on my head, that I had a parachute on my back and a parachute on my stomach, that the whole thing weighed 15 kilos, that it was very heavy, that my ears were buzzing because I had just climbed 400 metres in twenty seconds, that the plane was going at speed, that everyone I was looking at, all the men I was looking at, were afraid, because they were all obliged to be afraid, and that I, too, was feeling that fear which was making me tense, was stopping me from standing up!

Yet everyone gets up, suddenly. Everyone gets up, and nothing happens. You're hooked on. The people who are going to make you jump, to cast you off, the instructors, check to see that the static lines and parachutes are in order. Everything is always in order. Then, at a given moment, a siren sounds. The moment the siren sounds, you begin jumping. Generally, generally speaking I mean, you're never the first to jump. I'm telling this story because at that moment I wasn't the first to jump. Nor was it my first jump. Nor was it the start of everything. It was simply a repetition. It was the fifth, or sixth, or seventh time I was performing an action I was familiar with, that I was performing action*s* I was familiar with, that I was beginning again on something I had already been through. That didn't stop the fear being always the same. Indeed, it was all the greater in so far as I knew what was going to follow. The moment the siren begins to sound, the first ones, the ones who are first, jump. I had already been first on one jump, but that's part of another story . . .

At that moment everyone begins to move forward. And as you move forward, you gradually lose your awareness of yourself. The one thing left is your determination, the determination to get all this inertia over with, all this heaviness, all the difficulty there is in having a 15-kilo parachute on your back and on your stomach, all the difficulty in walking, the fact you're packed in like sardines . . . you're all in a hurry, in a huge hurry to get out. And you get out very fast. And the moment comes when you find yourself facing into the void. You find yourself in front of a door and 400 metres below you, is . . . 400 metres below is the ground, i.e. there's nothing. There's nothing in front of you. And you have to throw yourself out. That's the moment I want to speak about, the reason I'm telling you this story. The fact is, a moment comes when you're in the presence of . . . it's not even that you're in the presence of a danger, it's that you have at all costs to put your trust in something. In fact, I don't even know any longer why I'm telling you this story, but that doesn't matter very much. You have at all costs to put your trust in your parachute, have at all costs to tell yourself that, yes, the following thing is going to happen, the static line is going to reel out, then the parachute is going to open, then the rigging lines are going to go slack, to unwind, then the parachute is going to open fully, you'll have that tremendous corolla in front of you, and that'll be tremendous, you'll be supported, you'll come down to earth at really quite a limited speed, you'll land, and then it'll be over, you'll have made six jumps instead of five, or made eight instead of seven . . .

Then, at a particular moment, you have doubts. There's really nothing you can do about it. You ask yourself . . . well no, it's not *you*, it's *I*. I've always asked myself why I jumped. At first, to start with, it wasn't a problem; I'd accepted, I'd been posted to the paras, I went, although I could have had other ways of not going, because of my personal situation let's say . . . I accepted to go because I had the impression I would experience something new. I want to say that I was very surprised the day Clara Malraux* told me that a parachute jump was like having psychoanalysis . . . For me, that showed a rather peculiar sense of humour!

In point of fact, I don't think that's exactly it. I think psychoanalysis had given me something quite different. That it wasn't in the same area at all. In this case it really was trust. It really was optimism beginning, optimism becoming absolutely necessary in fact, it really was trusting in life. I fancy that . . . Anyway, you've known me for long enough to know that what I've been saying this evening for example, what I've been saying to you since I came back to Paris, since November, is quite different from what I thought before I left to do my army service.

It doesn't seem to me a matter of complete indifference; there's a common link after all, a possible connection after all with the fact that you may be obliged to feel trust at all costs and that it isn't possible to refuse something, isn't possible to . . . say no, isn't possible to take refuge for example in nihilism, or even intellectualism, no longer possible even to intellectualize! You're facing into the void and you have suddenly to throw yourself out. Suddenly you have to refuse your fear, suddenly have to refuse to give up. And then . . . then, you have to launch yourself. I jumped thirteen times and thirteen times I launched myself. Thirteen times I felt like giving up, I felt like saying to myself: 'Right, it's not worth it, after all if I refuse, now, right, I've qualified, it's quite unimportant, I can lose my nerve.' It wasn't that exactly . . . I think that if there's been one time when I've had the intuition, when I've had the sensation of being . . . I want to say brave – but not in the banal sense, in the way it's usually understood, of continually surpassing yourself – it was in performing this perfectly

*The wife of the writer André Malraux, and a writer herself.

gratuitous action, of throwing oneself into the void 400 metres up, an action with overtones that were . . . fascist.

That's right: fascist overtones. Because the fact of being a parachutist isn't just any old fact. It means living in an environment that's made up of guys with only one aim, which is to be forever destroying the Republic. I mean, the colonels' Algeria, we know all about that. Well, you had to jump all the same, because if I hadn't done so I don't think I could have been here this evening. I had at all costs to launch myself into the void, at all costs to accept that difficulty, which now I compare to the difficulties of the days ahead, which I compare to the situation . . . perhaps because I'm an intellectual, perhaps because I'm inclined to make comparisons that are always a little peculiar . . . You had absolutely to launch yourself. It wasn't possible to do otherwise. It was necessary to jump, necessary to throw yourself out in order to be convinced that it might perhaps have a meaning, might perhaps have repercussions you didn't even know about yourself. On the absolutely individual level, for me it had absolutely unarguable overtones: the fact that prior to 1958 I couldn't manage to accept myself and that now I am constantly managing it, that I couldn't manage to define myself and that now I'm fully capable of doing so, it no longer poses any sort of problem for me in fact. It was even important from a more general point of view. The reason why we're here is, more or less, that we are all participants in a review, and that that review has been searching for itself, searching for the last two years . . . That's my personal impression and mine alone. I think it has to launch itself, has to accept to jump. That's all.

The Gnocchi of Autumn or *An Answer to a Few Questions Concerning Myself**

Across the street, three pigeons have been sitting for a long time, motionless, on the edge of the roof. Above them, to the right, a chimney is smoking; some unadventurous sparrows are perched on the top of the pipes. There is noise down below, in the street.

Monday. Nine a.m. I've already been writing this too long overdue text for two hours.

The first question is this no doubt: why have I waited until the last moment? The second: why this title, why this opening? The third: why start by asking these questions?

Where's the great difficulty? Why begin with a play on words just sufficiently hermetic to bring a smile from only a small number of my friends? Why continue with a description of a neutrality just sufficiently false to give people to understand that if I got up early, it was because I was very behindhand, and that I'm uncomfortable about being behindhand, whereas it's obvious I'm only behindhand precisely because the actual purpose of the few pages that will follow makes me feel uncomfortable. I feel uncomfortable. Is the right question: why do I feel uncomfortable? Why do I feel uncomfortable about feeling uncomfortable? Am I going to have to justify my feeling uncomfortable? Or is it having to justify myself that makes me feel uncomfortable?

*This short piece was first published under the title '*Autoportrait*' or 'Self-Portrait' in the journal *Cause Commune* in 1972. The 'play on words' that Perec refers to is contained in the French title: *Les Gnocchis de l'automne* is a typical Perecquian play on the well-known Greek saying *gnoti se auton*, or 'know thyself'.

This can go on for a long time. It's the peculiarity of the literary man to hold forth about his own nature, to become mired in a mess of contradictions: clear-sighted and despairing, solitary yet at one with others, making fine phrases out of his bad conscience, etc. It's been going on for quite a few years now and has begun to be profitable. But all things considered, I've never found it very interesting. It's not up to me to examine the case against intellectuals, I'm not going to relapse into all that stuff about art for art's sake or commitment.*

My problem is rather to attain, I don't say to the truth (why should I know that any better than anyone else, and by what right therefore would I open my mouth?), nor do I say validity (that's a problem between words and me), but rather sincerity. This isn't a question of morality but of practice. It's not the only question I put to myself no doubt, but I fancy it's the only one that has proved more or less permanently crucial for me. But how to answer (sincerely) when it's sincerity I am calling into question? How to set about avoiding, yet again, those games with mirrors within which a 'self-portrait' will be nothing more than the umpteenth reflection of a consciousness that has been well pruned, a knowledge that has been well polished, a prose made docile by the pains I have taken? A portrait of the artist as a clever monkey; can I say 'sincerely' that I'm a clown? Can I achieve sincerity in spite of a rhetorical toolkit in which the series of question-marks that punctuate the preceding paragraphs was long ago classified as a figure (of doubt)? Can I really hope to extract myself by means of a few more or less subtly balanced sentences?

'The means form part of the truth as well as the result.' I've been dragging that sentence along behind me for ages. But it's become harder and harder for me to believe that I shall extract myself by dint of mottoes, quotations, slogans or aphorisms. I've used up a

*i.e. *engagement*, or that moral, political and philosophical commitment which the Existentialist writers of the late 1940s and 1950s in France saw as the one authentic source of meaning in a human life.

whole supply of them: '*Larvatus prodeo*', 'I write in order to peruse myself', 'Open the door and see all the people',* etc., etc. Some of them still manage at times to delight me, to move me, they still seem to have a lot to teach me, but you do what you like with them, you abandon them, take them up again, they have all the docility you demand from them.

This doesn't prevent . . . What is the right question, the one that will enable me truly to answer, truly to answer myself? Who am I? What am I? Where am I at?

Can I measure some of the road I have travelled? Have I achieved some of the aims I set myself, if I ever really did one day set myself aims? Can I say today that I am what I wanted to be in the old days? I don't ask myself whether the world in which I live answers to my aspirations, for as soon as I've answered no, I shan't have the impression of having progressed any further. But does the life I lead in it correspond to what I wanted, to what I expected?

To begin with, it all seems simple: I wanted to write, and I've written. By dint of writing, I've become a writer, for myself alone first of all and for a long time, and today for others. In principle, I no longer have any need to justify myself (either in my own eyes or in the eyes of others). I'm a writer, that's an acknowledged fact, a datum, self-evident, a definition. I can write or not write, I can go several weeks or several months without writing, or write 'well' or write 'badly', that alters nothing, it doesn't make my activity as a writer into a parallel or complementary activity. I do nothing else but write (except earn the time to write), I don't know how to do anything else, I haven't wanted to learn anything else . . . I write in order to live and I live in order to write, and

* A reference to an English game played with the hands. It starts: 'Here is the church' (hands upraised with fingers interlocked, representing the nave), continues with 'Here is the steeple' (index fingers pointing up), and ends: 'Open the door, etc.' (fingers unlocked, hands turned palms up, fingers raised and wiggling).

I've come close to imagining that writing and living might merge completely: I would live in the company of dictionaries, deep in some provincial retreat, in the mornings I would go for a walk in the woods, in the afternoons I would blacken a few sheets of paper, in the evenings I would relax perhaps by listening to a bit of music . . .

It goes without saying that when you start having ideas like these (even if they are only a caricature), it becomes urgent to ask yourself some questions.

I know, roughly speaking, how I became a writer. I don't know precisely why. In order to exist, did I really need to line up words and sentences? In order to exist, was it enough for me to be the author of a few books?

In order to exist, I was waiting for others to designate me, to identify me, to recognize me. But why through writing? I long wanted to be a painter, for the same reasons I presume, but I became a writer. Why writing precisely?

Did I then have something so very particular to *say*? But what have I said? What is there to say? To say that one *is*? To say that one writes? To say that one is a writer? A need to communicate what? A need to communicate that one has a need to communicate? That one is in the act of communicating? Writing says that it is there, and nothing more, and here we are back again in that hall of mirrors where the words refer to one another, reflect one another to infinity without ever meeting anything other than their own shadow.

I don't know what, fifteen years ago when I was beginning to write, I expected from writing. But I fancy I'm beginning to understand, at the same time, the fascination that writing exercised – and continues to exercise – over me, and the fissure which that fascination both discloses and conceals.

Writing protects me. I advance beneath the rampart of my words, my sentences, my skilfully linked paragraphs, my astutely programmed chapters. I don't lack ingenuity.

Do I still need protecting? And suppose the shield were to become an iron collar?

One day I shall certainly have to start using words to uncover what is real, to uncover my reality.

Today, no doubt, I can say that that's what my project is like. But I know it will not be fully successful until such time as the Poet has been driven from the city once and for all, such time as we can take up a pickaxe or a spade, a sledge-hammer or a trowel, without laughing, without having the feeling, yet again, that what we are doing is derisory, or a sham, or done to create a stir. It's not so much that we shall have made progress (because it's certainly no longer at that level that things will be measured), it's that our world will at last have begun to be liberated.

*Some of the Things I Really Must Do Before I Die**

First of all there are things very easily done, things I could do as from today, for example

1 Take a trip on a bateau-mouche

Then things a tiny bit more significant, things that involve decisions, things which I tell myself that, were I to do them, would perhaps make my life easier, for example

2 Make up my mind to throw out a certain number of things that I keep without knowing why I keep them

or else

3 Arrange my bookshelves once and for all
4 Acquire various household appliances

or again

5 Stop myself smoking (before being forced to)

Then things linked to a more profound desire for change, for example

6 Dress in a completely different way
7 Live in a hotel (in Paris)

*The written version of a radio broadcast made by Perec on France-Culture in 1981.

8 Live in the country
9 Go and live for quite a long time in a foreign city (London)

Then things that are linked to dreams of time or space. There are quite a few:

10 Pass through where the Equator crosses the International Date-Line
11 Go beyond the Arctic Circle
12 To have an 'out-of-time' experience (like Siffre)*
13 Take a trip in a submarine
14 Take a long trip on a boat
15 Make an ascent or a journey in a balloon or airship
16 Go to the Kerguelen Islands (or to Tristan da Cunha)
17 Ride a camel from Morocco to Timbuktu in 52 days

Then, among all the things I don't yet know, there are certain ones I'd like to have the time to discover properly

18 I'd like to go into the Ardennes
19 I'd like to go to Bayreuth, but also to Prague and to Vienna
20 I'd like to go the Prado
21 I'd like to drink some rum found at the bottom of the sea (like Captain Haddock in *The Treasure of Red Rackham*)
22 I'd like to have the time to read Henry James (among others)
23 I'd like to travel along canals

Next there are lots of things that I'd like to learn, but I know I won't because it would take me too long, or because I know I would succeed only very imperfectly, for example

24 Find the solution to the Rubik cube
25 Learn to play the drums
26 Learn Italian

*Jean-Loup Siffre, a well-known photographer.

27 Learn the trade of printer
28 Paint

Then things connected with my work as a writer. There are a lot of them. For the most part these are vague projects; some are perfectly possible and depend only on me, for example

29 Write for very young children
30 Write a science-fiction novel

others depend on things I might be asked to do

31 Write the script for an adventure film in which, for example, you would see 5,000 Kirghiz tribesmen riding across the steppes
32 Write a real serial novel
33 Work with a strip cartoonist
34 Write songs (for Anna Prucnal for example)

There's one more thing I'd like to do, but I don't know where it belongs, it's to

35 Plant a tree, and watch it get bigger

Finally, there are things it's impossible to envisage from now on but which would have been possible not so long ago, for example

36 Get drunk with Malcolm Lowry
37 Make the acquaintance of Vladimir Nabokov

etc., etc.
There are lots of others for sure.
I gladly stop at 37.

*The Work of Memory**

Interview with Frank Venaille

F.V. How does a memory come?

G.P. With *Je me souviens*, they're memories that have been prompted, things I'd forgotten that I will make reappear, an anamnesis, i.e. the opposite of forgetting. The procedure is a little odd. I'm at my work table, in a café, an airport or a train, and I try to recover some quite unimportant event, commonplace, out-of-date, but which will set something going the moment I recover it. In a way, the initial idea wasn't mine but I've incorporated it totally. It was Joe Barnard's, an American poet who wrote *I Remember*, a disguised autobiography in actual fact but organized around micro-memories. *Je me souviens* rather hinges on the same theme, i.e. it attempts to recover elements that form part of the texture of everyday life and that it may well be you didn't notice. The most clear-cut example is when you used to give your Métro ticket to the ticket puncher so he could make a hole in it. No one paid that any attention! But if you put it into a book, it forms part of memory. You know, I saw somewhere on the Ligne de Sceaux – which isn't called the Ligne de Sceaux any more as it happens – a sort of shed filled with old ticket barriers from the Métro and for me all that is a sort of active memory. I try to remember, I force myself to remember. I say to myself, let's take the subject of food, or sport, or politics, a song, a subject of the 'holiday souvenirs' kind. Do you get it?

F.V. Yes, I can see for the time being you want to do two things. To work with the everyday and then to de-consecrate memory, or at least the event you're going to bring back. Do you agree?

*An interview first published in a magazine called *Monsieur Bloom* in 1979. *Je me souviens* is a book that appeared in 1978 in which Perec lists more than four hundred tiny 'memories' of a generational, rather than a subjective kind, in accordance with the 'unanimist' principles that he explains here to his interviewer.

G.P. Yes, it's both deconsecrating it and replacing it in its collectivity, let's say. When I was working on *Je me souviens*, what came out most clearly for me was that I wasn't the only one to be remembering. It's a book I might call 'sympathetic', I mean it's in sympathy with its readers, that readers are perfectly at home in it. It works like a sort of appeal to memory because it's something that is shared. It's very different from autobiography, from the exploration of your own prominent, occluded memories. It's a book that starts out from a common memory, a collective memory.

F.V. You're touching there on a subject I'd like to press you about. 'Collective' memory and 'individual' memory. The first seems to me like a sort of magma from which we have all come. And that seems to be the sort of memory that interests you, the things that belong to everyone but which you present with the drama removed as it were, and so with a wish to deny the tragic element in autobiography, to bring out your own life-story.

G.P. That's work of another kind. I've also written an autobiography called *W or The Memory of Childhood*, and all that autobiographical writing is organized around a single memory which for me was deeply occluded, deeply buried and in some sense denied. The problem was to get round that approach, let's say, to my own life-story, and in fact I started on *Je me souviens* at more or less the same time. They're paths that aren't altogether parallel, but which meet somewhere and which start out from the same need to explore something fully in order to situate it. It isn't given all at once. Above all it isn't the tragic event like when the violins start up! It has to remain buried the whole time! The autobiography of my childhood was done from descriptions of photos, from photographs that served as a relay, as a means of approaching a reality of which I used to declare I had no memory. In fact it was done by way of a meticulous investigation, obsessive almost, it was so precise and detailed. Because the decomposition was so meticulous, something was revealed. *Je me souviens* is situated in a sort of in-between and could continually be toppling over into my own relationship with the memory in question. When I write

'I remember that my first bicycle had solid tyres' that isn't innocent! I still have the physical sensation of it, yet it seems quite neutral.

F.V. Yes, and where that pseudo-innocence is concerned, that false appearance of neutrality, don't you think you could have worked just as well from a box of photos that someone had brought you, from a family you didn't know, so that they would have been providing you with the ingredients of a fiction?

G.P. I did that! I took part in a television programme called 'The French on Film' that was a montage of amateur films made between 1930 and 1936 and for which I wrote the commentary. So I was working on documents in which I almost rediscovered my own life-story. One of the films took place in the part of town I grew up in and it was as if I'd been in the picture with my mother and my relations! In one of the things I'm starting on now, there's something that might be called a fictive memory, a memory that might have belonged to me. I'm going to start on a film with Robert Bober about Ellis Island, an island in New York, near the Statue of Liberty. It was the centre where immigrants were processed between 1880 and 1940. I don't know how many millions of Europeans, above all Italians, and Polish and Russian Jews, passed through there; it's since been turned into a museum. So it's rather like the crucible of America and we're going to make a film that will be an evocation of that movement that neither Robert nor I experienced (since we remained in France) but which we might have experienced, which was somewhere inscribed among our possibilities, since Robert Bober came from Berlin and my parents came from a small town near Warsaw. So it's a work about memory and a memory that concerns us, although it's not ours, but is, how shall I put it, adjacent to ours and almost as determining for us as our own life-story. So, if you like, there are three aspects to the work on memorization. First of all, the everyday examined from every angle, next the search by traditional means for my own life-story, then finally this fictive memory. There's even a fourth one, that would lie in the realm, how shall I put it, of the 'encrypted', of being inscribed completely in code, and that would be the notation of elements of memories in a fiction like

Life a User's Manual, but practically speaking for internal use only. I mean that only I and a few other people could be aware of them. It's a sort of resonance, a theme running underneath the fiction, which feeds it but doesn't appear as such . . .

F.V. Which means that the degree of reading depends on however much we know about you and your life?

G.P. Yes, the biographical or everyday elements that come in have a function in the fiction. It could be compared with the technique of William Burroughs because it's almost a biographical 'cut-up'.

F.V. But don't you think that the will, the desire to find roots, the determination to work from memories or from the memory, is the will above all to stand out against death, against silence?

G.P. It certainly has to do with the idea of the trace, of the inscription, of the need to inscribe . . .

F.V. Yes, you draw your own heart on trees or park benches, and you try to have it both ways, i.e. you offer both a 'traditional' fiction and, at the same time, in that fiction, we rediscover your personal life-story!

G.P. How is it organized? How is it articulated? I don't really know. But there was a period in my life (corresponding as it happens to a course of psychoanalysis) when I had a veritable phobia about forgetting. I published a text in *Action poétique* called 'Attempt at an inventory of all the liquid and solid foodstuffs ingurgitated by me in the course of a year'! I kept a journal. I noted down my meals and that produced a result that was both monstrous and altogether curious. It was a completely compulsive move! The fear of forgetting! I kept that journal, I noted down every event, not thoughts no, facts of the 'Ate leg of lamb and drank a bottle of Gigondas' kind.

F.V. So, anyway, your work is really the opposite of the 'forgetful memory' . . .

G.P. Yet at the same time there's something about it that comes under the heading of the derisory. I don't really know how it works. Look, I know people for whom *Je me souviens* is a practical joke, a gimmick, something throwaway! Right. I can just about understand what they mean in relation to its insignificance, but at the same time writing it was very odd. There was usually between quarter of an hour and three quarters of an hour of being adrift, of searching completely vaguely, before one of the memories appeared. And at that instant heaps of interesting things occurred which might be the subject of another text, demonstrating this suspending of time, the moment when I went in search of this derisory memory.

F.V. How do you experience this searching, the determination to draw up these moments of your past life out of yourself? I mean, is it tragic?

G.P. Well, as I say, it happens in this sort of state of suspension! I think there's something not unlike meditation, a wanting to create a void . . .

F.V. . . . to bring to light a minuscule but at the same time crucial event!

G.P. Yes, two or three of them in fact very much surprised me. And then at the moment when you bring out the memory you really have the impression you're wrenching it away from a place where it had always been.

F.V. So in fact what you write is originally tied to your own experience, or to the fictional version of it that you organize yourself. Does that imply you are submitting yourself to the facts, to your memories, to reality?

G.P. Except that it's an experience that will never be apprehended by – how shall I put it? – by my consciousness, my feelings, by an idea, by any ideological elaboration! There's never any psychology involved. This is experience at ground level, what you might call background noise. It's experience grasped at the level of the setting in which your body moves, the gestures it makes, all the ordinariness connected with your clothes, with food, with travelling, with your daily routine, with the exploring of your space. The rest goes unsaid, it's outside, even if it gets reintroduced when fashioned into fiction, but then it's by other means: the dictionary, the encyclopedia, the imagination, by the system of constraints. The submission to experience is a work of meticulous description . . .

F.V. From which, then, we can say you're a realist when you write?

G.P. Yes, I would claim that. If you like, right from the moment when I began to pursue this relationship with autobiography, I've been writing pieces of autobiography that were constantly being sidetracked. It wasn't 'I thought this or that', but the desire to write a history of my clothes or my cats! Or accounts of dreams. My mentor in this vein was a Japanese woman, Sei Shonagan, whose *Pillowbook* is a collection of thoughts about nothing in the end, about waterfalls, clothes, the things that give pleasure, the things that have a refined grace, the things without value, and so on. For me that's true realism: to rely on a description of reality divested of all presumptions. It seems so to me anyway!

F.V. So you feel a need, a desire, a necessity to classify, to make lists, in fact not to be taken in by anything.

G.P. Anyway, I know that if I classify, if I make inventories, somewhere there are going to be events that will step in and throw the order out. I know for example that *Je me souviens* is stuffed with mistakes, therefore that my memories are false! That forms part of the opposition between life and the user's manual, between the rules of the game you've set yourself and the paroxysms of real life that submerge, that are continually undoing the work of setting in order – luckily, moreover.

F.V. Listening to you and reading you, one gets the feeling that the child Perec is no more important than the adolescent or the adult, that you don't want to stress the preponderance of that passage of your life over all the rest. You seem determined about that.

G.P. I don't know how to reply to that question. It's certainly the first time I've been asked it. In point of fact, what I'm trying to get at in my work is the manner in which that childhood is given back to me. The work of writing is always done in relation to something that no longer exists, which may be fixed for a moment in writing, like a trace, but which has vanished. I don't know how the present intervenes. One day I was offered a photograph from a film by Marcel l'Herbier and, well, the next day, I used it in one of the chapters of *Life a User's Manual* and its present became the source of a story, of something that happened earlier.

F.V. So each day you live through brings something to the fiction you're laying bare? That's where the realism's to be found perhaps, and in a certain way it's all being done against individualism!

G.P. It's all done for sharing with others, it forms part of something the outcome of which is a material object, a book, that will belong to others, that'll be shared, exchanged. It's all an approach to my own life-story but only to the extent that that is collective, shareable.

F.V. Yes, one could say that in some of your books you aren't keen to bring out your own uniqueness.

G.P. The idea would be that everyone could write a *Je me souviens*, but that no one else could write the 455 'je me souviens' that are in the book, that no one else could write the same ones. It's like in set theory, I share memories with X that I don't share with Y, and everyone could choose for themselves a unique configuration from out of the complete set of our memories. It's the description of a conjunctive tissue of a kind, in which a whole generation might recognize itself.

F.V. So it has an element of sociality!

G.P. Yes, something I'd like to call unanimist, a literary movement that didn't produce much but whose name I very much like. A movement that starts with yourself and goes towards others. It's what I call sympathy, a sort of projection, and at the same time an appeal!

*Ellis Island: Description of a Project**

'The Statue of Liberty, which he had been observing for a long time, appeared to him in a burst of light. It was as if the arm brandishing the sword had been raised at that very instant, and the free air was blowing around that great body.'

Franz Kafka, *Amerika*

Perhaps this was very precisely what being an emigrant meant: to see a sword where the sculptor, in all good faith, had thought he was putting a torch. And not really to be wrong. For at the very moment when Emma Lazarus's celebrated lines were being engraved on the pedestal of the Statue of Liberty:

Give me your tired, your poor,
Your huddled masses yearning to breathe free,
The wretched refuse of your teeming shore,
Send these, the tempest-tossed, to me:
I lift my lamp beside the golden door.

a whole series of laws was being set in place to try to control and a little later on contain the incessant influx of emigrants coming from southern Italy, Central Europe and Russia. Up until around 1875 the entry of foreigners on to the soil of the United States had been virtually free, but had then become progressively subject to restrictive measures, elaborated and applied to start with at the local level (municipal and harbour authorities), and afterwards regrouped within a Secretariat for Immigration answerable to the Federal Government.

The Ellis Island reception centre was opened in 1892 on a small island of a few hectares situated a few hundred metres from Liberty Island. It marks the end of an almost uncontrolled emigration

*First published in *Catalogue pour des Juifs de maintenant* by the journal *Recherches* in 1979.

and the coming of an official, institutionalized and so to speak industrialized emigration. Between 1892 and 1924, close on sixteen million people were to pass through Ellis Island, at a rate of five to ten thousand a day. The majority spent only a few hours there; a mere two to three per cent were turned away.

In sum, Ellis Island was to be nothing other than a factory for making Americans, for turning emigrants into immigrants, an American-style factory, as quick and efficient as a Chicago pork-butcher's. At one end of the assembly line, they would put an Irishman, a Ukrainian Jew or an Italian from Apulia, at the other end – after their eyes and pockets had been inspected, and they had been vaccinated and disinfected – there emerged an American. But at the same time, as the years passed, the conditions for admission became increasingly strict. Gradually the 'golden door' was closed into this fabulous America where turkeys fell ready roasted into your plate, where the streets were paved with gold and where the land belonged to everyone. In fact, after 1914, emigration began to stop, first because of the war, then because of a series of discriminatory qualitative (the Literacy Act) and quantitative measures (quotas) which prevented the 'wretched refuse' and 'huddled masses' from entering the United States.

In 1924, immigration formalities were handed over to American consulates in Europe and Ellis Island became a detention centre simply for emigrants whose papers were not in order. During and immediately after the Second World War, it took its implicit vocation to its logical conclusion and became a prison for individuals suspected of anti-American activities (Italian fascists, pro-Nazi Germans, Communists or supposed Communists). In 1954, Ellis Island was finally shut down. Today it is a national monument, like Mount Rushmore, Old Faithful and the statue of Bartholdi, run by Rangers in Boy Scout hats who show people round four times a day for six months in the year.

My purpose here is not to evoke what the dreams and disillusionment may have been of the millions of emigrants for whom Ellis Island was the first step in what they intended should be a new life, nor to retrace the circumstances which led me to make a film about Ellis Island with Robert Bober, but simply to define more clearly what my own connection with it may be. For me it is the very place of exile, that is, the place of the absence of place, the place of dispersal. In this sense, it concerns me, it fascinates me, it involves me, it questions me, as if the search for my own identity went via the appropriation of this depository where harassed functionaries baptized Americans by the boatload, as if it were inscribed somewhere in a life-story that might have been mine, formed part of a probable autobiography, a potential memory. What is to be found there is certainly not roots or traces, but the opposite: something without shape, at the limits of the sayable, that I might call a closing-off, a scission, or a break, and which for me is very intimately and confusedly linked to the actual fact of being a Jew.

I don't know exactly what being a Jew means, what it does to me. It's an obvious fact, if you like, yet a mediocre one, a mark, yet a mark that links me to nothing either precise or concrete. It's not a sign of belonging, not linked to a belief, a religion, a praxis, a culture, a folklore, a history, a destiny, a language. It is an absence rather, a question, a throwing into question, a floating, an anxiety, an anxious certainty behind which there is the outline of another certainty, abstract, heavy, insupportable: that of having been designated as a Jew, and therefore as a victim, and of owing my life simply to chance and to exile. My grandparents or parents might have been able to emigrate to Argentina, to the United States, to Palestine, to Australia. I might have been born, like my close or distant cousins, in Haifa or Baltimore or Vancouver, but one thing alone in this almost limitless range of possibilities was forbidden to me, that of being born in the land of my ancestors, in Poland, in Lubartów, Puławy or Warsaw, and of growing up there in the continuity of a tradition, a language and an affiliation.

I was born in France, I am French, I bear a French first name, Georges, and a French surname, or almost, Perec. The difference is minuscule: there's no acute accent on the first e of my name because Perec is the way the Poles write Peretz. If I had been born in Poland, I would have been called, let's say, Mordecai Perec, and everyone would have known I was a Jew. But I wasn't born in Poland, luckily for me, and I have an almost Breton name which everyone spells as Pérec or Perrec – my name isn't written exactly as it is pronounced.

To this insignificant contradiction there attaches the tenuous but insistent, insidious, unavoidable feeling of being somewhere alien in relation to some part of myself, of being 'different', different not so much from 'others' as from 'my own kin'. I don't speak the language that my parents spoke, I don't share any of the memories they may have had. Something that was theirs, which made them who they were, their history, their culture, their creed, their hope, was not handed down to me.

The awareness of this dispossession does not go with any nostalgia, any predilection for what would be closer to me because I am a Jew. For several years I have been writing a history of my family, based on the memories passed down to me by my aunt, trying to retrace their adventure, their wandering, that long and improbable journeying that led them everywhere and nowhere, that continual splintering the survivors from which no longer have anything in common except for having all been, somewhere, deprived of their history. But I have no wish to go to see whether the big square house my grandfather had built in Lubartów is still standing. Anyway it isn't, there are no Jews any more in Lubartów, any more than there are any left in Radom, where Robert Bober went in vain in search of memories of his father.

What I went to seek on Ellis Island was the actual image of this point of no return, the consciousness of this radical fracture. What I wanted to interrogate, to throw into question, to test, were my own roots in this non-place, this absence, this fissure, on which any such quest for the trace, the word, the Other is based.

At a time when tens of thousands of Vietnamese and Cambodians are adrift on rotting vessels in search of increasingly hostile refuges, it may seem, if not wholly pointless, then at least singularly smug, to be going back over in sorrow what is by now ancient history. But by coming close to this abandoned island, and by trying to engage in dialogue with some of those – Jews and Italians – who passed through Ellis Island in the old days, I fancy that at moments I have succeeded in giving resonance to some of the words that are for me inexorably attached to the very name of Jew: journey, expectation, hope, uncertainty, difference, memory; and to those two weak, unlocatable, unstable, fugitive concepts whose fitful light reflects from one on to the other: Native Land and Promised Land.

from *Penser/Classer* (1985)

*Notes on What I'm Looking For**

If I try to define what I've been looking to do since I began writing, the first thought that comes to mind is that I've never written two books the same, have never wanted to repeat in one book a formula, a system or a manner developed in an earlier book.

This systematic versatility has more than once flummoxed certain critics anxious to rediscover the writer's 'trademark' from one book to the next; and it may also have disconcerted some of my readers. It has earned me the reputation of being a sort of computer, a machine for producing texts. For my part, I would liken myself rather to a peasant cultivating several fields; in one he grows beetroot, in another lucerne, in a third maize, etc. In the same way, the books I've written are linked to four different fields, four modes of interrogation that may in the last resort pose the same question, but pose it in a particular perspective corresponding in each instance for me to a different kind of literary work.

The first of these modes might be described as 'sociological': how to look at the everyday. This lies behind texts like *Things*,† 'Species of Spaces', 'An Attempt at a Description of Certain Locations in Paris',‡ and the work I did with the *Cause Commune* team around Jean Duvignaud and Paul Virilio.§ The second mode is of an autobiographical order: *W or The Memory of Childhood*, *La*

*First published in the *Figaro* in December 1978.

†i.e. *Les Choses*, a novel published in 1965 which gave Perec a certain fame by winning the Prix Renaudot for that year. It describes the life of a young French couple exclusively in external terms of the objects they own and those they would like to own.

‡Or *Les Lieux*, see note on p. 56.

§*Cause Commune* was a review, started in 1971–2, whose general purpose was to 'undertake an anthropology of everyday life', and to do so without subscribing to any ideology.

Boutique obscure,* *Je me souviens*,† 'Places Where I've Slept', etc. The third is ludic and relates to my liking for constraints, for feats of skill, for 'playing scales', for all the work the idea and means for which I got from the researches of the OuLiPo group: palindromes, lipograms, pangrams, anagrams, isograms, acrostics, crosswords, etc.‡ The fourth mode, finally, involves the fictive, the liking for stories and adventures, the wish to write the sort of books that are devoured lying face down on your bed: *Life a User's Manual* is the typical example.

This division is somewhat arbitrary and could be much more nuanced. Hardly any of my books is altogether free from certain traces of the autobiographical (for example, the insertion into the chapter I'm writing of an allusion to an incident that has occurred that same day). Hardly any of them has been composed either without my having recourse to one or other OuLiPian constraint or structure, albeit only symbolically, without the said structure or constraint having constrained me in any way at all.

Aside from these four poles that define the four horizons of my work – the world around me, my own history, language and fiction – it seems to me in fact that my ambition as a writer would be to traverse the whole literature of my own time without ever having the sense that I was turning back or treading in my own footsteps, and to write all that it's possible for a man of today to write: fat books and short books, novels and poems, plays, opera libretti, detective stories, adventure novels, science-fiction novels, serials, books for children . . .

I've never felt comfortable talking about my work in abstract, theoretical terms. Even if what I produce seems to derive from a programme worked out a long time ago, from a long-standing project, I believe rather that I discover – that I prove – the direction I am moving in by moving. From the succession of my books I

*A book in which Perec recounted more than a hundred of his dreams.

†See note on p. 123.

‡For the OuLiPo see the Introduction to this volume. A lipogram is a text from which a given letter (or letters) of the alphabet has been excluded; a pangram contains all the letters of the alphabet; an isogram contains lines which all have the same number of (the same) letters.

get the sense, sometimes reassuring, sometimes uncomfortable (because forever dependent on the unfinished, on the 'book to come' that points to the unsayable towards which the desire to write despairingly tends), that they are following a path, are marking out a space, are tracing a tentative itinerary, are describing point by point the stages of a search the 'why' of which I can't tell, only the 'how'. I have a confused sense that the books I've written are inscribed in, that they get their meaning from, a global image I have formed of literature, but it seems I shall never be able to grasp that image exactly, that for me it lies beyond writing, it's a 'why do I write' to which I can reply only by writing, by endlessly deferring that moment when I cease from writing and the image becomes visible, like a puzzle that has been inexorably completed.

*Notes Concerning the Objects that are on my Work-table**

There are a lot of objects on my work-table. The oldest no doubt is my pen; the most recent is a small round ashtray that I bought last week. It's of white ceramic and the scene on it shows the war memorial in Beirut (from the 1914 war, I presume, not yet the one that's breaking out now).

I spend several hours a day sitting at my work-table. Sometimes I would like it to be as empty as possible. But most often, I prefer it to be cluttered, almost to excess. The table itself is made from a sheet of glass 1 metre 40 in length and 70 centimetres across, resting on metal trestles. Its stability is far from perfect and it's no bad thing in actual fact that it should be heavily loaded or even overloaded; the weight of the objects it supports helps to keep it steady.

I tidy my work-table quite frequently. This consists of putting all the objects somewhere else and replacing them one by one. I wipe the glass table with a duster (sometimes soaked in a special product) and do the same with each object. The problem is then to decide whether a particular object should or should not be on the table (next a place has to be found for it, but usually that isn't difficult).

This rearrangement of my territory rarely takes place at random. It most often corresponds to the beginning or end of a specific piece of work; it intervenes in the middle of those indecisive days when I don't quite know whether I'm going to get started and when I simply cling on to these activities of withdrawal: tidying, sorting, setting in order. At these moments I dream of a work surface that is virgo intacta: everything in its place, nothing superfluous, nothing sticking out, all the pencils well sharpened (but why have several pencils? I can see six merely at a glance!),

*First published in *Les Nouvelles littéraires* in February 1976.

all the paper in a pile or, better still, no paper at all, only an exercise book open at a blank page. (Myth of the impeccably smooth desk of the Managing Director: I have seen one that was a small steel fortress, crammed with electronic equipment, or what purported to be so, which appeared and disappeared when you pressed the controls on a superior sort of dashboard.)

Later on, once my work is advancing or else stalled, my work-table becomes cluttered with objects that have sometimes accumulated there purely by chance (secateurs, folding rule), or else by some temporary necessity (coffee cup). Some will remain for a few minutes, others for a few days, others, which seem to have got there in a somewhat contingent fashion, will take up permanent residence. We're not dealing exclusively with objects directly connected with the business of writing (paper, stationery, books); others are connected with a daily practice (smoking) or a periodical one (taking snuff, drawing, eating sweets, playing patience, solving puzzles), with some perhaps superstitious foible (setting a little push-button calendar), or linked not to any particular function but to memories perhaps, or to some tactile or visual pleasure, or simply to a liking for the knick-knack in question (boxes, stones, pebbles, bud-vase).

On the whole, I could say that the objects that are on my work-table are there because I want them to be. This isn't connected simply with their function or with my own negligence. For example, there's no tube of glue on my work-table; that's to be found in a small set of drawers at the side. I put it back there a moment ago after using it. I could have left it on my work-table, but I put it away almost automatically (I say 'almost' because, since I've been describing what there is on my work-table, I am paying closer attention to my movements). Thus, there are objects useful for my work which aren't or aren't always on my work-table (glue, scissors, sticky tape, bottles of ink, stapler), others which aren't immediately useful (sealing wax), or useful for some other purpose (nail file), or not useful at all (ammonite), but which are there all the same.

These objects have in a way been chosen, been preferred to others. It's obvious, for example, that there will always be an ashtray on my work-table (unless I give up smoking), but it won't always be the same ashtray. Generally speaking, the same ashtray stays there for quite some time; one day, in accordance with criteria that it mightn't be without interest to investigate further, I shall put it somewhere else (near the table on which I do my typing, for example, or near the plank on which my dictionaries are, or on a shelf, or in another room) and another ashtray will replace it. (An obvious invalidation of what I've just been claiming: at this precise moment, there are three ashtrays on my work-table, that is, two surplus ones which are as it happens empty; one is the war memorial, acquired very recently; the other, which shows a charming view of the roofs of the town of Ingolstadt, has just been stuck together again. The one in use has a black plastic body and a white perforated metal lid. As I look at them, and describe them, I realize in any case that they're not among my current favourites. The war memorial is definitely too small to be anything more than an ashtray for mealtimes, Ingolstadt is very fragile, and as for the black one with the lid, the cigarettes I throw away in it go on smouldering for ever.)

A desk-lamp, a cigarette box, a bud-vase, a matchbox-holder, a cardboard box containing little multi-coloured index-cards, a large carton bouilli inkwell incrusted with tortoiseshell, a glass pencil-box, several stones, three hand-turned wooden boxes, an alarm-clock, a push-button calendar, a lump of lead, a large cigar box (with no cigars in, but full of small objects), a steel spiral into which you can slide letters that are pending, a dagger handle of polished stone, account books, exercise books, loose sheets, multiple writing instruments or accessories, a big hand-blotter, several books, a glass full of pencils, a small gilded wooden box. (Nothing seems easier than to draw up a list, in actual fact it's far more complicated than it appears; you always forget something, you are tempted to write, etc., but an inventory is when you don't write, etc. With rare exceptions (Butor), contemporary writing has lost the art of enumeration: the catalogues of Rabelais, the Linnaean list of fish in *Twenty Thousand Leagues Under the Sea*, the list of the geographers who've explored Australia in *Captain Grant's Children*.)

It's several years now since I contemplated writing the history of some of the objects that are on my work-table. I wrote the beginning of it nearly three years ago; re-reading it, I notice that, of the seven objects I talked about, four are still on my work-table (although I've moved house in between). Two have been changed: a hand-blotter, which I've replaced by another hand-blotter (they're very much alike, but the second one is bigger), and a battery alarm-clock (whose normal position, as I've already noted, is on my bedside table, where it is today), replaced by another, wind-up alarm-clock. The third object has disappeared from my work-table. This was a Plexiglas cube made up of eight cubes attached to each other in such a way as to enable it to take on a great many shapes. It was given to me by François le Lionnais* and is now in another room, on the shelf above a radiator, next to several other brainteasers and puzzles (one of these is on my work-table: a double tangram, i.e. twice seven bits of black and white plastic that can be used to form an almost infinite number of geometrical figures).

Before, I didn't have a work-table, I mean there was no table for that express purpose. It still quite often happens today that I do my work in a café. At home, however, it's very rare for me to work (write) anywhere except at my work-table (for example, I almost never write in bed) and my work-table isn't used for anything except my work. (Once again, even as I write these words, this turns out to be not wholly accurate; two or three times a year, when I give a party, my work-table is entirely cleared and covered in paper tablecloths – like the plank on which my dictionaries are piled – and becomes a sideboard.)

Thus a certain history of my tastes (their permanence, their evolution, their phases) will come to be inscribed in this project. More precisely, it will be, once again, a way of marking out my space, a somewhat oblique approach to my daily practice, a way of talking about my work, about my history and my preoccupations, an attempt to grasp something pertaining to my experience, not at the level of its remote reflections, but at the very point where it emerges.

*A mathematician who was one of the founders of the OuLiPo.

*Brief Notes on the Art and Manner of Arranging One's Books**

Every library[1] answers a twofold need, which is often also a twofold obsession: that of conserving certain objects (books) and that of organizing them in certain ways.

One of my friends had the idea one day of stopping his library at 361 books. The plan was as follows: having attained, by addition or subtraction, and starting from a given number *n* of books, the number K = 361, deemed as corresponding to a library, if not an ideal then at least a sufficient library, he would undertake to acquire on a permanent basis a new book X only after having eliminated (by giving away, throwing out, selling or any other appropriate means) an old book Z, so that the total number K of works should remain constant and equal to 361: $K + X > 361 > K - Z$.

As it evolved this seductive scheme came up against predictable obstacles for which the unavoidable solutions were found. First, a volume was to be seen as counting as one (1) book even if it contained three (3) novels (or collections of poems, essays, etc.); from which it was deduced that three (3) or four (4) or *n* (*n*) novels by the same author counted (implicitly) as one (1) volume by that author, as fragments not yet brought together but ineluctably bringable together in a Collected Works. Whence it was adjudged that this or that recently acquired novel by this or that English-language novelist of the second half of the nineteenth century could not logically count as a new work X but as a work Z belonging

*First published in *L'Humidité* in 1978.

1. A library I call a sum of books constituted by a non-professional reader for his own pleasure and daily use. This excludes the collections of bibliophiles and fine bindings by the yard, but also the majority of specialized libraries (those in universities, for example) whose particular problems match those of public libraries.

to a series under construction: the set T of all the novels written by the aforesaid novelist (and God knows there are some!). This didn't alter the original scheme in any way at all: only instead of talking about 361 books, it was decided that the sufficient library was ideally to be made up of 361 *authors*, whether they had written a slender opuscule or enough to fill a truck.

This modification proved effective over several years. But it soon became apparent that certain works – romances of chivalry, for example – had no author or else had several authors, and that certain authors – the Dadaists, for example – could not be kept separate from one another without automatically losing 80 to 90 per cent of what made them interesting. The idea was thus reached of a library restricted to 361 *subjects* – the term is vague but the groups it covers are vague also at times – and up until now that limitation has been strictly observed.

So then, one of the chief problems encountered by the man who keeps the books he has read or promises himself that he will one day read is that of the increase in his library. Not everyone has the good fortune to be Captain Nemo: '. . . the world ended for me the day my *Nautilus* dived for the first time beneath the waves. On that day I bought my last volumes, my last pamphlets, my last newspapers, and since that time I would like to believe that mankind has neither thought nor written.'

Captain Nemo's 12,000 volumes, uniformly bound, were thus classified once and for all, and all the more simply because the classification, as is made clear to us, was uncertain, at least from the language point of view (a detail which does not at all concern the art of arranging a library but is meant simply to remind us that Captain Nemo speaks all languages indiscriminately). But for us, who continue to have to do with a human race that insists on thinking, writing and above all publishing, the increasing size of our libraries tends to become the one real problem. For it's not too difficult, very obviously, to keep ten or twenty or let's say even a hundred books; but once you start to have 361, or a thousand, or three thousand, and especially when the total starts to increase every day or thereabouts, the problem arises, first of all of arranging all these books somewhere and then of being able to lay your hand on them one day when, for whatever reason, you either want or need to read them at last or even to reread them.

Thus the problem of a library is shown to be twofold: a problem of space first of all, then a problem of order.

1. *Of Space*

1.1. *Generalities*

Books are not dispersed but assembled. Just as we put all the pots of jam into a jam cupboard, so we put all our books into the same place, or into several same places. Even though we want to keep them, we might pile our books away into trunks, put them in the cellar or the attic, or in the bottoms of wardrobes, but we generally prefer them to be visible.

In practice, books are most often arranged one beside the other, along a wall or division, on rectilinear supports, parallel with one another, neither too deep nor too far apart. Books are arranged – usually – standing on end and in such a way that the title printed on the spine of the work can be seen (sometimes, as in bookshop windows, the cover of the book is displayed, but it is unusual, proscribed and nearly always considered shocking to have only the edge of the book on show).

In current room layouts, the library is known as a 'corner' for books. This, most often, is a module belonging as a whole to the 'living-room', which likewise contains a

drop-leaf drinks cabinet
drop-leaf writing desk
two-door dresser
hi-fi unit
television console
slide projector
display cabinet
etc.

and is offered in catalogues adorned with a few false bindings.

In practice books can be assembled just about anywhere.

1.2. *Rooms where books may be put*

in the entrance hall
in the sitting room
in the bedroom(s)
in the bog

Generally speaking, only one kind of book is put in the room you cook in, the ones known as 'cookery books'.

It is extremely rare to find books in a bathroom, even though for many people this is a favourite place to read in. The surrounding humidity is unanimously considered a prime enemy of the conservation of printed texts. At the most, you may find in a bathroom a medicine cupboard and in the medicine cupboard a small work entitled *What to do before the doctor gets there.*

1.3. *Places in a room where books can be arranged*

On the shelves of fireplaces or over radiators (it may be thought, even so, that heat may, in the long run, prove somewhat harmful),
between two windows,
in the embrasure of an unused door,
on the steps of a library ladder, making this unusable (very chic),
underneath a window,
on a piece of furniture set at an angle and dividing the room into two (very chic, creates an even better effect with a few pot-plants).

1.4. *Things which aren't books but are often met with in libraries*

Photographs in gilded brass frames, small engravings, pen and ink drawings, dried flowers in stemmed glasses, matchbox-holders containing, or not, chemical matches (dangerous), lead soldiers, a photograph of Ernest Renan in his study at the Collège de France,* postcards, dolls' eyes, tins, packets of salt, pepper and mustard from Lufthansa, letter-scales, picture hooks, marbles, pipe-cleaners, scale models of vintage cars, multicoloured pebbles and gravel, ex-votos, springs.

2. *Of Order*

A library that is not arranged becomes disarranged: this is the example I was given to try and get me to understand what entropy was and which I have several times verified experimentally.

Disorder in a library is not serious in itself; it ranks with 'Which drawer did I put my socks in?'. We always think we shall know instinctively where we have put such and such a book. And even if we don't know, it will never be difficult to go rapidly along all the shelves.

Opposed to this apologia for a sympathetic disorder is the small-minded temptation towards an individual bureaucracy: one thing for each place and each place for its one thing, and vice versa. Between these two tensions, one which sets a premium on letting things be, on a good-natured anarchy, the other that exalts the virtues of the *tabula rasa*, the cold efficiency of the great arranging, one always ends by trying to set one's books in order. This is a trying, depressing operation, but one liable to produce pleasant surprises, such as coming upon a book you had forgotten because you could no longer see it and which, putting off until tomorrow what you won't do today, you finally re-devour lying face down on your bed.

2.1. *Ways of arranging books*

ordered alphabetically
ordered by continent or country

*A famously pompous, highminded nineteenth-century scholar and writer, unlikely to have appealed to GP.

ordered by colour
ordered by date of acquisition
ordered by date of publication
ordered by format
ordered by genre
ordered by major periods of literary history
ordered by language
ordered by priority for future reading
ordered by binding
ordered by series

None of these classifications is satisfactory by itself. In practice, every library is ordered starting from a combination of these modes of classification, whose relative weighting, resistance to change, obsolescence and persistence give every library a unique personality.

We should first of all distinguish stable classifications from provisional ones. Stable classifications are those which, in principle, you continue to respect; provisional classifications are those supposed to last only a few days, the time it takes for a book to discover, or rediscover, its definitive place. This may be a book recently acquired and not yet read, or else a book recently read that you don't quite know where to place and which you have promised yourself you will put away on the occasion of a forthcoming 'great arranging', or else a book whose reading has been interrupted and that you don't want to classify before taking it up again and finishing it, or else a book you have used constantly over a given period, or else a book you have taken down to look up a piece of information or a reference and which you haven't yet put back in its place, or else a book that you can't put back in its rightful place because it doesn't belong to you and you've several times promised to give it back, etc.

In my own case, nearly three-quarters of my books have never really been classified. Those that are not arranged in a definitively provisional way are arranged in a provisionally definitive way, as at the OuLiPo. Meanwhile, I move them from one room to another, one shelf to another, one pile to another, and may spend three hours looking for a book without finding it but sometimes having the satisfaction of coming upon six or seven others which serve my purpose just as well.

2.2. *Books very easy to arrange*

The big Jules Vernes in the red binding, very large books, very small ones, Baedekers, rare books or ones presumed to be so, hardbacks, volumes in the Pléiade collection, the Présence du Futur series, novels published by the Editions de Minuit, collections, journals of which you possess at least three issues, etc.

2.3. *Books not too difficult to arrange*

Books on the cinema, whether essays on directors, albums of movie stars or shooting scripts, South American novels, ethnology, psychoanalysis, cookery books (see above), directories (next to the phone), German Romantics, books in the Que Sais-je? series (the problem being whether to arrange them all together or with the discipline they deal with), etc.

2.4. *Books just about impossible to arrange*

The rest: for example, journals of which you possess only a single issue, or else *La Campagne de 1812 en Russie* by Clausewitz, translated from the German by M. Bégouën, Captain-Commandant in the 31st Dragoons, Passed Staff College, with one map, Paris, Librairie Militaire R. Chapelot et Cie, 1900; or else fascicule 6 of Volume 91 (November 1976) of the *Proceedings of the Modern Language Association of America* (*PMLA*) giving the programme for the 666 working sessions of the annual congress of the said Association.

2.5.

Like the librarians of Babel in Borges's story, who are looking for the book that will provide them with the key to all the others, we oscillate between the illusion of perfection and the vertigo of the unattainable. In the name of completeness, we would like to believe that a unique order exists that would enable us to accede to knowledge all in one go; in the name of the unattainable, we would like to think that order and disorder are in fact the same word, denoting pure chance.

It's possible also that both are decoys, *a trompe l'oeil* intended to disguise the erosion of both books and systems. It is no bad thing in any case that between the two our bookshelves should serve from time to time as joggers of the memory, as cat-rests and as lumber-rooms.

*Twelve Sidelong Glances**

1. *The ready-to-wear manufacturer*

Jacket, rounded neck, jacquard design (215fr) over flannel dress in pure wool (420 fr); skirt in Liberty wool, sunray pleats (295fr), jacket, openwork design backed with tweed (360 fr) over woollen sweater, jacquard design neck (185fr).

Plus fours in pure wool material (250 fr), jacquard jacket, shawl neck (225 fr), over matching tanktop (165fr); tartan skirt, pure wool (230 fr), woollen jacket, pattern forming sailor collar (250 fr).

Tartan skirt cut on the cross, flap pockets, in pure wool (235fr); V-necked waistcoat, buttoned front (195fr); check flannel skirt, sunray pleats (280 fr), jacket, Peter Pan collar in pure wool (265 fr).

Dress in printed muslin, round collar, plain silk cuffs, sunray pleated skirt (400 fr).

V-necked jumper, viscose, graduated horizontal stripes (175fr), matching scarf (65fr), over acetate mix culottes (300 fr); flowing rayon dress (370 fr) under long viscose cardigan with geometric pattern (235fr).

Suit in printed viscose crepe, straight jacket with pleated collar, pleated skirt (450 fr); suit in viscose muslin, small floral print, sunray pleated skirt, high square collar over V-neck, godet sleeves (500fr).

Pure wool jersey dress, shawl collar, silk cuffs, ribbed bodice, pleated skirt (450 fr); pure wool jersey suit, jacket with silk sailor collar, ribbed sleeves and pockets, pleated skirt, buttoning down the side (525fr).

Pure wool flannel suit, jacket with tailored collar, short buttoned waistcoat, fully pleated skirt (790 fr), silk blouse, round collar with bow (250 fr).

*First published in *Traverses* in 1976.

Pleated jersey cape, with matching skirt, box pleats in front (420 fr).

Children's collection. Printed sateen smock, 4-year-olds, 90fr.

Jacquard sweaters and blouson jackets, 115 to 155fr (6- to 8-year-olds), according to model. Scarves (65fr), matching bérets (55 and 75fr).

For one or two weeks, around last October, on an imposing number of poster-sites on the still recent bus shelters, three toddlers looking dreadfully *child-like* were showing off to good advantage the sweaters, scarves and bérets described above. Their poses, their expressions, their clothes, their relationship, both on the mythological plane of the advert and on that of what one might suppose to be reality (their existence qua models, the role they were being made to play, the role they were playing to themselves, the successive investments, psychic as well as economic, in which they were both the stake and the means) struck me as a peculiarly sordid manifestation of the world we are living in.

2. *The craftsman in leather*

Fashion might be as much what distinguishes as what brings together: the sharing in some superior quality, 'happy few'-ism, and so on. That is at least conceivable. But at the risk of being taxed with élitism, I shall continue to ask myself why so very many people take pride in showing off handbags bearing the monogram of their manufacturer. I can understand people attaching some importance to having their initials on the things they are fond of (shirts, suitcases, napkin rings, etc.), but the initials of a supplier? That really is beyond me.

3. *'Musts'*

In fashion the crucial words aren't 'Do you like it?', but 'You must'. As in the English phrase 'It's a must'. Which is the name a jeweller in the Rue de la Paix has given to his watches and cigarette lighters. What strikes me isn't so much the name itself but the fact that it is followed by a small letter R with a circle round it, which means that the manufacturer is keeping an exclusive right to this label.

It hardly matters in the event what the fashionable object may be. What counts is the name, the label, the signature. You might even say that if the object weren't named and signed, it wouldn't exist. It is nothing more than its sign. But signs quickly wear out, quicker than lighters and watches do. That is why fashions change. A benign tyranny, so it's said; but I'm not so sure.

4. *Anecdotal parenthesis*

A few years ago I had occasion, within the space of three months, to eat four meals in four Chinese restaurants situated respectively in Paris (France), Saarbrücken (Germany), Coventry (Great Britain) and New York (United States of America). The décor of the restaurants was roughly speaking the same, their Chineseness depending in each case on almost identical signifiers (dragons, Chinese characters, lanterns, lacquer, red hangings, etc.). Where the food was concerned it was less obvious, however. For want of any referent, I had naïvely thought up until then that (French) Chinese cuisine was Chinese cuisine; but that (German) Chinese cuisine resembled German cuisine, (English) Chinese cuisine resembled English cuisine (green peas), and (American) Chinese cuisine resembled something that was definitely not Chinese, if not something truly American.

This anecdote seems to me significant, but I'm not sure of what exactly.

5. *Quotations*

Fashion: the fickle and capricious element in human behaviour, exercising its sway over personal adornment, dress, furnishings, equipages, etc. The term properly signifies *a way*, that is, the *right* way par excellence, brooking no further argument. Fashion, however, is an ephemeral usage originating in the fancies of an often corrupt taste that seeks to satisfy the vanity and lend variety to the enjoyments of the great, the rich and the indolent. Almost unknown among the lower orders, it yet provides the livelihood of a great many hardworking artisans. The Asians have passions rather than tastes, strength of purpose and few caprices. Among them, institutions, ideas and customs are of an almost unfailingly stable kind. Fashion, of which they have no experience, is on the contrary all-powerful in civilized Europe, particularly in France, where superficial impressions follow one another in rapid succession. (Bachelet and Dezobry, *Dictionnaire Général des Lettres, des Beaux-Arts et des Sciences Morales et Politiques*, Paris, 1882.)

Paris fashions, admired above all for their good taste and elegance, are adopted almost universally by foreign nations, and fashion articles are a principal source of exports. The duty raised by the French Customs on such articles alone amounts to more than five million francs annually. (Bouillet, *Dictionnaire Universel des Sciences, des Lettres et des Arts*, Paris, 1854.)

6. *Questions 1*

Why talk about fashion? Is it really an interesting subject? A fashionable subject?

One might ask a more general question. It would concern such contemporary institutions as fashion, sport, the holiday trade, community life, pedagogy, the 'protection of nature', the cultural environment, etc., which, it seems to me, are turning activities that at the outset were only, or only intended to be, a pleasure or enjoyment into an ordeal, if not into a form of suffering or even a torment.

We say of things that are in fashion that they are all the craze. But isn't there something crazy, truly crazy, about fashion? And not only crazy, moreover, but also noisy, very noisy, thunderous. Fashion has no time for silence; it bursts your eardrums.

7. *And yet . . .*

What it ought to be about is pleasure: pleasure of the body, of play, of dressing, of dressing alike or else differently, the pleasure sometimes of disguising yourself, of discovering, of imagining, the pleasure of rediscovering something, of changing.

That would be called fashion: a way of enjoyment, the sense of a small celebration, of waste. Something futile, useless, gratuitous, agreeable. We might invent a dish, a gesture, an expression, a game, a costume, a place to go walking, a dance, and then share our invention and share the inventions of others. This might last for several hours or several months. We would grow tired of it or pretend to grow tired of it. It would return, or not. It would be like at school, during break. There it was prisoner's base, then ball tag, then marbles, then an orchestra with combs and bog paper, then collections of cigarette packets.

Yet it's not that obviously, not that at all. Even before we start to talk about fashion, before its facts have been illuminated by the more or less brilliant light of the various contemporary ideologies, we already know it won't be that.

Yet fashion speaks of caprice, of spontaneity, fantasy, invention, frivolity. But these are falsehoods. Fashion is entirely on the side of violence, the violence of conformity, of adhering to models, the violence of the social consensus and the contempt it conceals within it.

8. *Questions 2*

There's nothing much to be gained from putting fashion in the dock. Fashion exists, that we know. It is made and unmade, manufactured and distributed, it is consumed. It enters into the majority of our daily activities.

All the phenomena of fashion converge on one elementary recognition: that fashion produces neither objects nor facts, but only signs, points of reference to which a collectivity can attach itself. The one question then is this: why do we need these signs? Or, if you prefer: can we not look elsewhere for them?

What can you do when the very fact of fashion strikes you as an uncouth institution (something like a carrot on the end of a stick) relating only to the weary convulsions of our commercial civilization? Can we circumvent fashion? Turn fashion aside? Or else what?

9. *Alternatives*

Without contesting its existence or casting doubt on the validity of its principles, one might put forward various modifications to the phenomena of fashion.

a) Vary their periodicity. Fashion is generally seasonal. It could be monthly, weekly, or better still, daily. For example, there would be Monday clothes, Tuesday clothes, Wednesday clothes, Thursday clothes, Friday clothes, Saturday clothes and Sunday clothes. And the same would go, obviously, for all the other facts of fashion. The expression 'today's fashion' would then at last mean exactly what it says.

b) Multiply their areas of application. Lots of objects, places and people are in fashion. One could start even more fashions, in areas where up until now it has scarcely ventured. For example, start a fashion for even-numbered dates. Or else for banks. Cafés, restaurants and shops collect oil lamps and old shop tills; where is the bold banker who will dare to open a branch decorated like a saloon (success guaranteed)? Or again, who will start a fashion for the Corentin-Celton Métro station? 'Get off at Corentin-Celton, the station of the élite!'

c) Exacerbate their laxity. It has been observed often enough that fashion is eclectic, it proposes at one and the same time models, men and works that one might have supposed were incompatible (this isn't true only of fashion in clothes, where skirts of all lengths can now cohabit, but of most aesthetic fashions). One wouldn't have to force this tendency unduly to end up with a world in which *everything* was fashionable.

d) Exasperate their biases. This would be the contrary tendency. At any given moment and in any given domain only *one* thing would be in fashion: basketball boots, for example, or chili con carne, or Bruckner's symphonies. Then it would change: sewerman's boots, tarte Tatin, Corelli's church sonatas. To lend the whole thing greater weight (and enable the leaders of our country to stand up more effectively to the economic crises they have to confront), one might assume that these imperatives had the force of law. The population would be warned in good time via the press of the conditions under which they would henceforth be required to be shod, to eat and to listen to music.

e) Finally, one might conceive of a fashion whose point of application would no longer be temporal but spatial, so that the facts of fashion would be distributed not in time but in space. Their existence would no longer be subject to fluctuating rhythms or imponderable contingencies. They would not be ineluctably condemned to a more or less rapid erosion. They would no longer vanish within a single day or have to endure the mediocrity of an episodic and disillusioned renewal.

All fashions would exist simultaneously and be distributed across the entire surface of the globe; experiencing them would no longer be a question of the season but of distance. One would never meet elsewhere with what one had already found here. Travelling then would perhaps recover its meaning: we should feel like genuine strangers. Inside each one of us there would be a small sleeping Marco Polo, dreaming of going to visit the land of furs, the land of eaters of sauerkraut, the land of knitted wool balaclavas.

10. *Or rather . . .*

Fashion emphasizes the unstable, the elusive, oblivion. It mocks real life by reducing it to signs that are themselves a mockery, to the artifices of veneer and leatherette, to the crudeness of its imitations. It is the mockery of a truth that is itself a mockery, reduced to its fraudulently authenticated skeleton: to the shiny new antique look, to the pseudo-imitation of fake paste. It is a factitious connivance, an absence of dialogue; we share in the indigence of a code without substance: the code of *the very latest thing*.

The opposite of the fashionable obviously isn't the unfashionable. It can only be what is present, what is there, anchored, permanent, resistant, inhabited. The object and its memory, being and its history.

It's not much use going or seeking to go against the fashion. All that we can seek to do perhaps is to be to one side of it, in a place where the exclusions imposed by the very fact of fashion (in fashion/out of fashion) cease to pertain. This could happen simply by the attention we give to a garment, to a colour, to a gesture, by the pleasure merely of a shared taste, in the secret serenity of a custom, a history, an existence. Thus:

11. *The Pillow-Book*

Undergarments
In winter the colour I prefer is 'azalea'.
I like also clothing of brilliant silk and garments that are white on one side and a sombre red on the back.
In summer, I like violet, and white.

Frames for fans
With a green-yellow paper I like a red frame.
With a violet-purple paper I like a green frame.

Women's cloaks
I like bright colours. The colour of a vine, a soft green, a 'cherry' tint, a 'plumtree red' shade, all bright colours are pretty.

Chinese cloaks
I like red, 'wistaria' colour. In summer, I prefer violet; in autumn, a 'dry moorland' tint.

Ceremonial skirts
I like skirts bearing a design of sea coral. Over-skirts.

Jackets
In spring, I like an 'azalea' shade, and a 'cherry' tint. In summer, I like 'green and dead leaf' or 'dead leaf' jackets.

Fabrics
I like violet-purple, and white materials, ones where jagged oak leaves have been woven on a soft green background. Plumtree red fabrics are pretty also, but one sees so many of them that I am tired of them, more than of anything else.

The Pillow-Book of Sei Shonagon

12. *Or else, finally:*

Rather than attempting to define this improbable object, I would rather have begun to recount, under the gentle tutelage of this lady-in-waiting who died around the year 1000, the history of a few of the objects to be found on my work-table: a hand blotter, a carved stone dagger handle, a bud-vase of Britannia metal, three turned wooden boxes, a small matchbox-holder with an orange base in the shape of a truncated cone, a thin slab of sandstone, a carton bouilli penholder incrusted with tortoiseshell, a teapot shaped like a cat, a box of 144 Baignol and Farjon steel-nibbed pens, etc.

Stories like these would no doubt have been traversed by fashion, but there would be more to them than simply fashion.

*The Scene of a Stratagem**

During four years, from May 1971 to June 1975, I was in analysis. Hardly was it ended before I was assailed by the desire to say, or more precisely to write about, what had taken place. Shortly afterwards, Jean Duvignaud suggested to the editors of *Cause Commune* that an issue of the review be organized around the theme of the Stratagem, and it was within this framework, whose contours were ill-defined but characterized by being unstable, blurred and oblique, that I decided, spontaneously, my text would most obviously be at home.

Fifteen months have since gone by, during which time I have written the opening sentences of this text (roughly speaking, the ones I've just written) perhaps fifty times and have each time without fail become thoroughly snared in rhetorical devices. I wanted to write, I had to write, had to rediscover in writing, through writing, the trace of what had been said (all those pages recommenced, those unfinished drafts, those lines left hanging, are like souvenirs of the amorphous sessions in which I had the unspeakable sensation of being a machine for grinding out words without weight), but the words hardened into carefully chosen phrases and what one might assume to be preliminary questions: why do I need to write this text? Who is it really intended for? Why choose to write, and to publish, to make public, what was perhaps named only in the secrecy of the analysis? Why choose to attach this uncertain search to the ambiguous theme of the Stratagem? All questions that I posed with a suspect determination – lower-case one, lower-case two, lower-case three, lower-case four – as if there absolutely had to be questions, as if, were there no questions, there couldn't be any answers. But what I want to say

*First published in the journal *Cause Commune* in 1977. Perec was analysed by one of France's best known psychoanalytical authors, J.-B. Pontalis.

is not an answer, it's an affirmation, a hard fact, something that occurred, that gushed out. Not something that might have been lying curled up inside a problem, but something that was there, close beside me, something of mine needing to be said.

The stratagem is something that circumvents, but how to circumvent the stratagem? The question is a trap, a pre-text, preceding the text, in order each time to defer the ineluctable moment of writing. Each word I put down was not a marker but a detour, something to set me daydreaming. During those fifteen months, I daydreamed over these verbal meanderings just as, for four years, on the couch, I had daydreamed as I gazed at the mouldings and the cracks in the ceiling.

There as here, it was almost reassuring to tell yourself that one day the words would come. One day you would get to talking, would get to writing. For a long time you believe that talking will mean finding, discovering, understanding, finally understanding, being illuminated by the truth. But no: when that happens, you know only that it's happening; it's there, you're talking, you're writing. Talking is talking only, merely talking, writing is only writing, tracing characters on a blank sheet of paper.

Did I know that this was what I had gone looking for? This fact so long unsaid but always to be said, this expectation merely, this tension, rediscovered in an almost intangible mumbling?

It happened one day and I knew it. I'd like to be able to say I knew it at once, but that wouldn't be true. The tense doesn't exist in which to say when it was. It happened, it had happened, it is happening, it will happen. You knew it already, you know it. Something has simply opened and is opening: the mouth in order to speak, the pen in order to write; something has moved, something is moving and is being traced out, the sinuous line of the ink on the paper, all upstrokes and downstrokes.

I posit as self-evident from the start this equivalence between speaking and writing, just as I assimilate the blank sheet of paper to that other scene of hesitations, illusions and erasures that was the ceiling of the analyst's consulting-room. That doesn't automatically follow, I know, but it will do for me from now on: this is precisely what was at stake in the analysis. It was this that happened, that was fashioned, session by session, in the course of those four years.

Psychoanalysis isn't really like those advertisements for hair restorers: there wasn't any 'before' and 'after'. There was a present of the analysis, a 'here and now', that began, lasted and ended. I could just as well write 'which took four years to start' or 'which ended during four years'. There was no beginning or end. The analysis had already begun long before the first session, if only in the slow making-up of my mind to undergo one and in the choice of analyst. The analysis continues, long after the final session, if only in this solitary duplication of it, which mimics both its obstinacy and its failures to move forward. In an analysis you are either stuck fast in time or else time is inflated. For four years, the analysis had its everyday, its ordinary side: small marks in diaries, the work spaced out through the successive sessions, the regularity with which they came round, their rhythm.

The analysis was first of all this: a certain dividing-up of the days – into days with and days without – and on days with something resembling a fold, a pleat, a pocket: in the stratification of the hours a moment that was suspended, was other; a sort of halt or interval in the continuity of the day.

There was something abstract about this arbitrary time, something at once both reassuring and frightening, an immutable, intemporal time, an immobile time in an improbable space. Yes of course, I was in Paris, in a neighbourhood I knew well, in a street where I'd even lived at one time, a few yards from my favourite bar and several familiar restaurants, and I could have amused myself by working out my longitude, latitude, altitude and which way I was facing (my head west-north-west, my feet east-south-east). But the ritual protocol of the sessions extruded space and time from these landmarks. I arrived, I rang the bell, a girl came and opened the door. I waited for a few minutes in a room intended for that purpose; I could hear the analyst showing his previous patient to the door. A few moments later, the analyst would open the door of the waiting-room. He never crossed the threshold. I went ahead of him and entered his consulting-room. He followed me in, closed the doors – there were two of them, forming a tiny entrance-lobby, something like an airlock that accentuated the sense of enclosure – and went and sat in his armchair as I stretched out on the couch.

I am stressing these banal details because they were repeated, two or three times a week, throughout those four years, just as the rites at the end of the session were repeated: the ring on the bell of the next patient, the analyst muttering something that sounded like 'good', without it ever implying the least evaluation of the matters mulled over in the course of the session, then standing up, my standing up and, if need be, settling his fee (I didn't pay him at every session, but every other week), his opening the doors of his consulting-room for me, showing me as far as the front door and closing it behind me after a formal leave-taking which consisted, most often, in confirming the day of my next session ('till Monday' or 'till Tuesday', for example).

At the session following, the same identical movements, the same gestures, were repeated exactly. On the rare occasions when they chanced not to be, and however trivial the modification might then have been to some element of the protocol, it meant something, even if I don't know what, it denoted something, quite simply perhaps that I was in analysis, and that the analysis was this and not some other thing. It hardly matters, in the event, whether these modifications came from the analyst, or from me, or were accidental. Whether these minuscule departures caused the analysis to flow over into the conventions in which it was swathed (as, for example, when, very rarely, I took the initiative going out by opening the doors myself), or whether on the contrary they subtracted from the analysis a small morsel of the time set aside for it (the analyst's secretary being away, for example, and his having to answer the telephone himself, or go and open the door to the next patient or to someone collecting for the Salvation Army), either way they all indicated the function that these rites had for me: the temporal and spatial framework of the unending discourse which, session by session, month by month, year by year, I was going to try and make my own, going to attempt to assume responsibility for, in which I was going to seek to recognize myself and to give myself a name.

The regularity of these rites of entry and departure thus constituted for me a first rule (I'm not talking about psychoanalysis in general, but of the one experience of it I have been affected by and the memories of it that remain to me). Their quiet repetition, their conventional immutability, indicated, with a serene courtesy, the limits of that enclosed space in which, far from the din of the town, outside of time, outside of the world, something was going to be said that perhaps would come from me, would be mine, would be for me. They as it were stood surely for the benign neutrality of the motionless ear into which I was going to attempt to say something, like the limits – polished, civilized, a little austere, a little cold, a shade stilted – within which there would explode the muffled, sealed-in violence of the analytical dialogue.

And so, stretched out on the couch, my head on a white handkerchief that before the next patient came into the consulting-room the analyst would toss carelessly on top of a small Empire filing cabinet already strewn with crumpled handkerchiefs from earlier sessions, my hands joined behind my neck or on my stomach, my right leg out straight, my left slightly bent, for four years I sank deeply into that history-less time, into that non-existent place that was to become the place of my history, of my as yet absent words. I was able to see three walls, three or four items of furniture, two or three engravings, a few books. There was a moquette carpet on the floor, mouldings on the ceiling, fabric on the walls: a severe, always very tidy décor, seemingly neutral, changing little from session to session or year to year. A dead, a tranquil place.

There was little sound. A piano or a radio, at times, some way off, someone somewhere using a vacuum cleaner or, when the weather was fine and the analyst had left the window open (he often aired the room between sessions), birds singing in a small garden near by. As I've said, the telephone hardly ever rang. The analyst himself made very little sound. I could sometimes hear his breathing, a sigh, a cough, his stomach rumbling, or the crackle of a match.

I had to talk, then. That was what I was there for. That was the rule of the game. I was shut in with this other person in this other space. The other person was sitting in an armchair, behind me, he could see me, he could speak or not speak, and chose generally not to speak; I was stretched out on the couch, in front of him, I couldn't see him, I had to speak, my words had to fill that empty space.

Speaking wasn't hard in any case. I had a need to speak, and I had a whole arsenal of stories, problems, questions, associations, phantasms, plays on words, memories, hypotheses, explanations, theories, points of reference [*repères*], hiding-places [*repaires*].

I travelled cheerfully down the too clearly marked-out paths of my labyrinths. Everything meant something, everything was linked together, everything was clear, everything allowed itself to be dissected at leisure, a great waltz of signifiers unrolling their pleasing anxieties. Beneath the ephemeral glitter of these verbal collisions, the measured titillations of this little illustrated Oedipus, my voice met only its own emptiness: neither the feeble echo of my life-story, nor the uncertain tumult of the enemies I should be facing up to, but the threadbare Daddy/Mummy, prick/pussy routine; not my emotion, nor my fear, nor my desire, nor my body, but responses that were ready-made, an anonymous ironmongery, and all the exaltation of a ride on a scenic railway.

The verbal intoxication of these brief moments of pansemic delirium was not long in fading, it took only a few seconds, a few seconds of silence during which I was watching for an acknowledgement from the analyst which never came, and I would then go back to feeling bitter and morose, further off than ever from my own words, my own voice.

Behind me, the other said nothing. At each session I waited for him to speak. I was convinced he was hiding something from me, that he knew much more than he was willing to say, that he was thinking it none the less, that he had his own idea there in the back of his brain. A little as if the words that were passing through my head were going to lodge in the back of his head, to bury themselves there for ever, giving rise, as the sessions came and went, to a ball of silence that was as heavy as my words were hollow, as full as my words were empty.

From then on, everything became mistrust, my words and his silence alike, a tedious game with mirrors in which the Möbius strips of images reflected one another endlessly, dreams too beautiful to be dreams. Where was the true, where the false? Whenever I tried to be silent, to no longer let myself be ensnared by this derisory harking back, by these illusory outcrops of words, the silence all of a sudden became unbearable. Whenever I tried to speak, to say something of my own, to confront the clown within who was juggling so cleverly with my life-story, the conjuror who was so good at deceiving himself, I suddenly had the impression that I was starting on the same puzzle all over again, as if, by using up one by one all the possible combinations, I could one day arrive at the image I was searching for.

At the same time it was as if my memory were bankrupt. I began to be afraid of forgetting, as if, unless I noted everything down, I wasn't going to be able to retain anything of the life that was escaping from me. Scrupulously, every evening, with a maniacal conscientiousness, I began to keep a sort of journal. It was the exact opposite of a *journal intime*: all I put into it were the 'objective' things that had happened to me: the time I woke up, how I spent the day, my movements, what I had bought, the progress – measured in lines or pages – of my work, the people I had met or simply caught sight of, the details of the meal I had had in the evening in one or other restaurant, my reading, the records I had listened to, the films I had seen, etc.

With this panic about losing track of myself there went a fury for preserving and for classifying. I kept everything: letters with their envelopes, cinema checkouts, airline tickets, bills, cheque stubs, handouts, receipts, catalogues, notices of meetings, weekly papers, dried-up felt pens, empty cigarette lighters, even gas and electricity receipts for a flat I hadn't lived in for more than six years; and sometimes I spent a whole day sorting and sorting, imagining a classification that would fill every year, month and day of my life.

I'd long been doing the same thing with my dreams. Well before the start of my analysis, I'd begun waking up during the night in order to note them down in black exercise-books that never left me. I'd very soon become so practised at it that my dreams came to me already written out, their titles included. Whatever liking I may still feel today for these terse, secret forms of words, in which the reflections of my life-story seem to reach me through innumerable prisms, I have finally come to admit that these dreams weren't lived in order to be dreamt, but dreamt in order to become texts, that they weren't the royal road I thought they would be, but tortuous paths that led me ever further away from self-recognition.

Made cautious perhaps by my oneiric stratagems, I transcribed nothing, or almost nothing, of the analysis itself. A symbol in my diary – the analyst's initial – marked the day and time of the session. In my journal, I wrote simply 'session' sometimes followed by a – generally pessimistic – adjective: 'sad', 'drab', 'long-winded', 'not much fun', 'a pain in the arse', 'crap', 'pretty dim', 'pretty shitty', 'depressing', 'laughable', 'anodyne', 'nostalgisome', 'feeble and forgettable', etc.

Very occasionally, I characterized it by something the analyst had said to me that day, by an image, or a sensation ('cramp' for example), but most of these notations, whether positive or negative, are today devoid of meaning, and all the sessions – bar the few exceptions when the words that were to make the analysis a success came to the surface – have merged for me with the memory of that ceilinged-in expectancy, of my troubled gaze as I searched unremittingly among the mouldings for the outline of an animal, or a man's head: for signs.

Of the actual movement that enabled me to emerge from these repetitive and exhausting gymnastics, and gave me access to my own story and my voice, I shall only say that it was infinitely slow: it was the movement of the analysis itelf, but I only found that out later on. First, the carapace of writing behind which I had concealed my desire to write had to crumble, the great wall of ready-made memories to erode, the rationalizations I had taken refuge in to fall into dust. I had to retrace my steps, to remake the journey I had already made all of whose threads I had broken.

Of this subterranean place I have nothing to say. I know that it happened and that, from that time on, its trace was inscribed in me and in the texts that I write. It lasted for the time it took for my story to come together. It was given to me one day, violently, to my surprise and amazement, like a memory restored to its space, like a gesture, like a warmth I had rediscovered. On that day, the analyst heard what I had to say to him, what for four years he had listened to without hearing, for the simple reason that I wasn't telling it to him, because I wasn't telling it to myself.

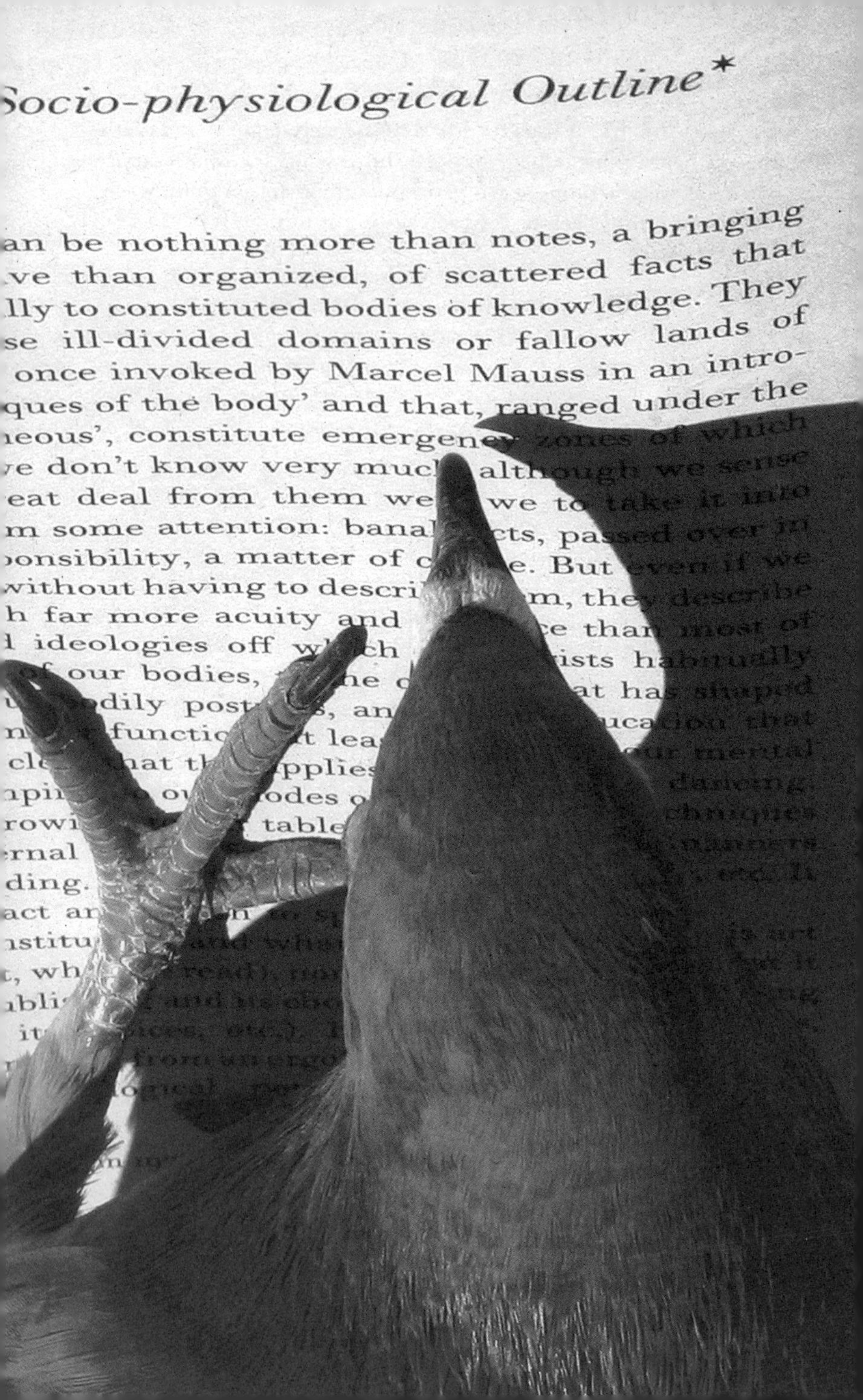
Socio-physiological Outline*
an be nothing more than notes, a bringing
ve than organized, of scattered facts that
lly to constituted bodies of knowledge. They
se ill-divided domains or fallow lands of
once invoked by Marcel Mauss in an intro-
ques of the body' and that, ranged under the
eous', constitute emergency zones of which

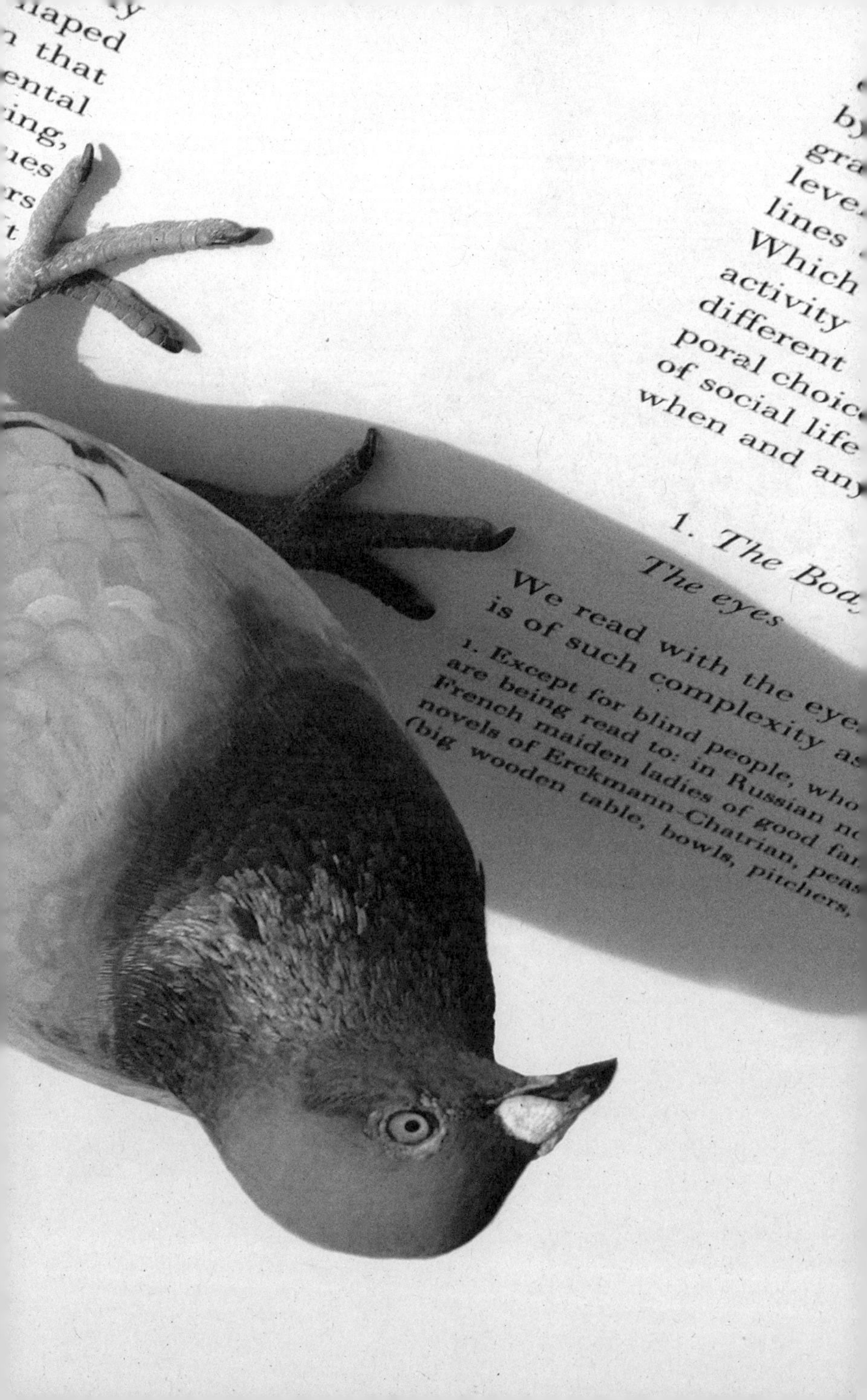

haped
n that
ental
ing,
by
gra
leve
lines
Which
activity
different
poral choic
of social life
when and any
1. The Bod
The eyes
We read with the eye
is of such complexity as
1. Except for blind people, who
are being read to: in Russian no
French maiden ladies of good fa
novels of Erckmann-Chatrian, peas
(big wooden table, bowls, pitchers,

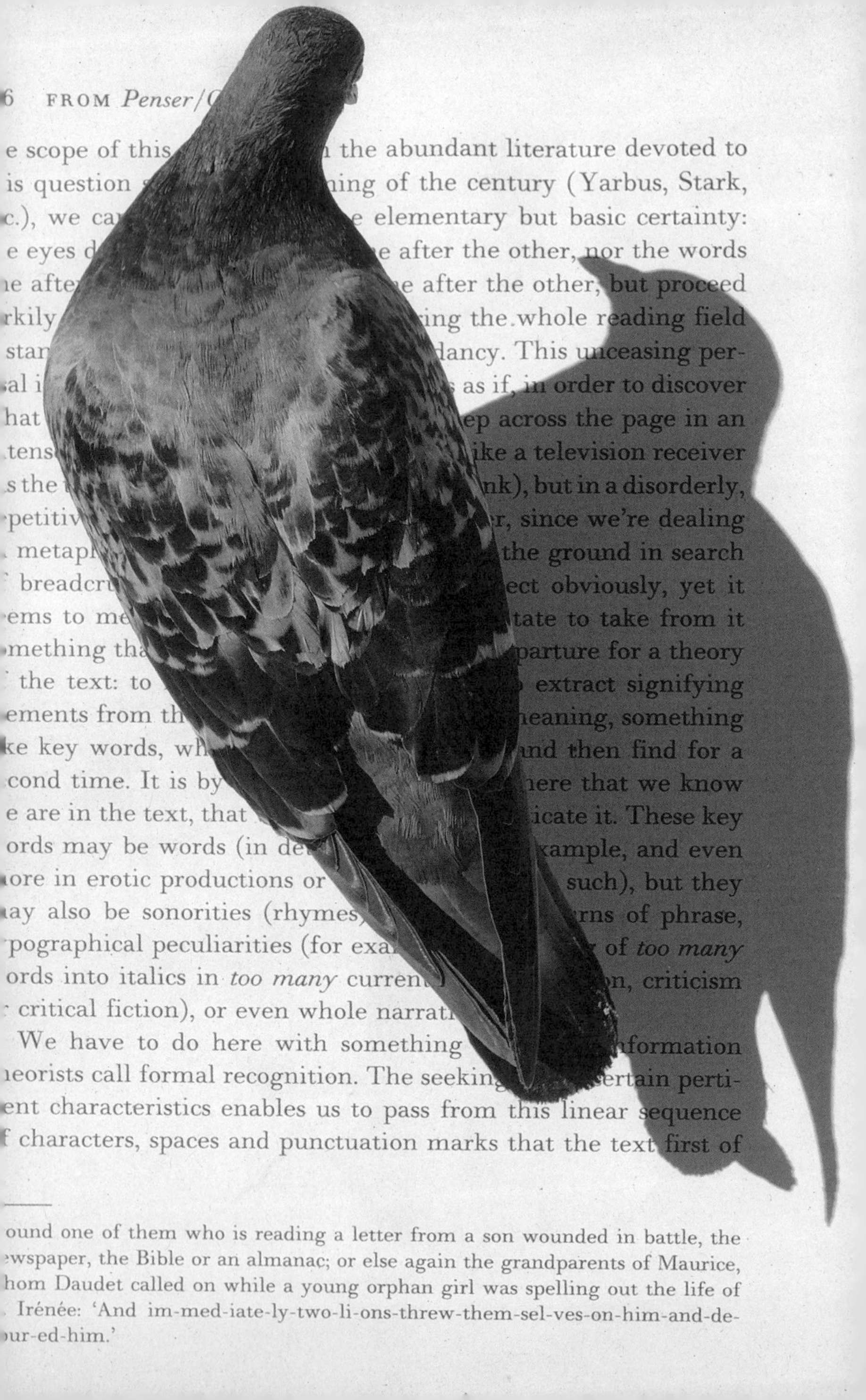
6 FROM Penser/C
e scope of this
n the abundant literature devoted to
is question
ning of the century (Yarbus, Stark,
c.), we ca
e elementary but basic certainty:
e eyes d
e after the other, nor the words
ne afte
e after the other, but proceed
rkily
ing the whole reading field
star
dancy. This unceasing per-
al i
as if, in order to discover
hat
ep across the page in an
tens
ike a television receiver
s the
nk), but in a disorderly,
petitiv
r, since we're dealing
metap
the ground in search
breadcr
ect obviously, yet it
ems to me
tate to take from it
mething tha
parture for a theory
the text: to
extract signifying
ements from th
eaning, something
ke key words, wh
nd then find for a
cond time. It is by
here that we know
e are in the text, that
icate it. These key
ords may be words (in de
xample, and even
ore in erotic productions or
such), but they
ay also be sonorities (rhymes,
rns of phrase,
pographical peculiarities (for exa
of too many
ords into italics in too many current
n, criticism
critical fiction), or even whole narrati
We have to do here with something
formation
eorists call formal recognition. The seekin
ertain perti-
ent characteristics enables us to pass from this linear sequence
f characters, spaces and punctuation marks that the text first of
ound one of them who is reading a letter from a son wounded in battle, the
ewspaper, the Bible or an almanac; or else again the grandparents of Maurice,
hom Daudet called on while a young orphan girl was spelling out the life of
Irénée: 'And im-med-iate-ly-two-li-ons-threw-them-sel-ves-on-him-and-de-
our-ed-him.'

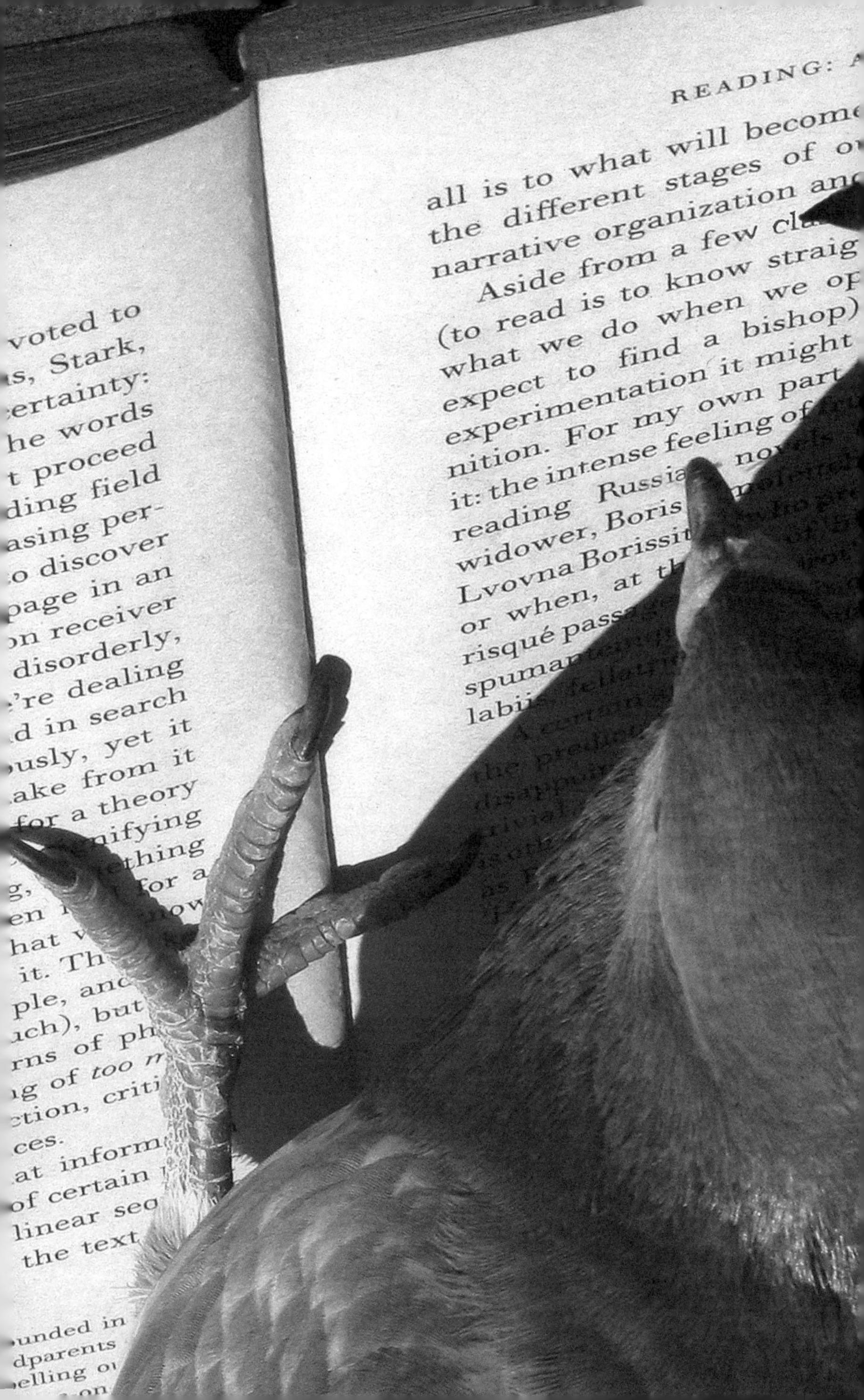
READING: A
all is to what will become
the different stages of o
narrative organization an
Aside from a few cl
(to read is to know straig
what we do when we op
expect to find a bishop)
experimentation it might
nition. For my own part
it: the intense feeling of
reading Russia
widower, Boris
Lvovna Borissit
or when, at th
risqué passa
voted to
s, Stark,
ertainty:
he words
t proceed
ding field
asing per-
o discover
page in an
on receiver
disorderly,
're dealing
d in search
ously, yet it
ake from it
for a theory
ces.
of certain
linear se
the text
unded in
dparents

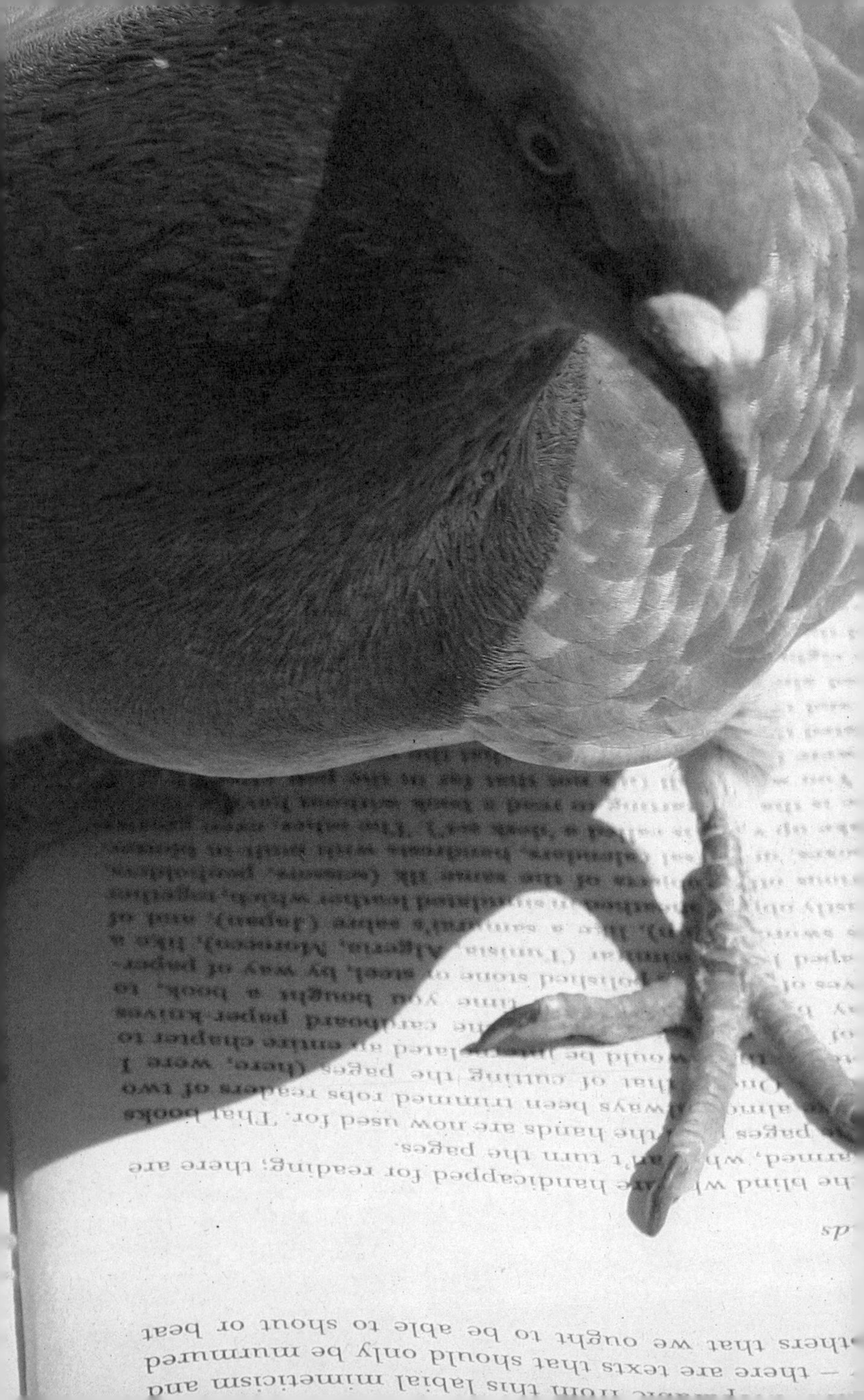
there are texts that should only be murmured
thers that we ought to be able to shout or beat
handicapped for reading; there are
turn the pages.
the hands are now used for. That books
been trimmed robs readers of two
that of cutting the pages (there, were I
would be interpolated an entire chapter to
cardboard paper-knives
time you bought a book, to
polished stone or steel, by way of paper-
(Tunisia, Algeria, Morocco), like a
like a samurai's sabre (Japan), and of

Bodily posture

The posturology of reading is obviousl
mental conditions (which I shall look
possible to envisage it as a subject in i
be a fascinating topic for research, intrins
of the body that it might be thought su
anthropologist has troubled to undertak
Marcel Mauss's that I mentioned at the st
absence of any systematic study I can only
enumeration:

reading standing up (this is the best way of co
reading sitting down, but there are so many
touching the ground, feet higher than the se
backwards (armchair, settee), elbows propp
reading lying down: lying on the back; lying
on the side, etc.;
reading kneeling (children looking through a
Japanese?);
eading squatting (Marcel Mauss: 'The squattin
my opinion, an interesting position that may
children. The greatest mistake is to deprive th
the exception of our own societies, the whole of th
has preserved it');
ding walking: one thinks especially of the pries
esh as while reading his breviary. But there is als
olling in a foreign town, street map in hand, or
tures in a gallery while reading the description
en in the guide book. Or else walking in the co
k in hand, reading out loud. That seems to be
e and more uncommon.

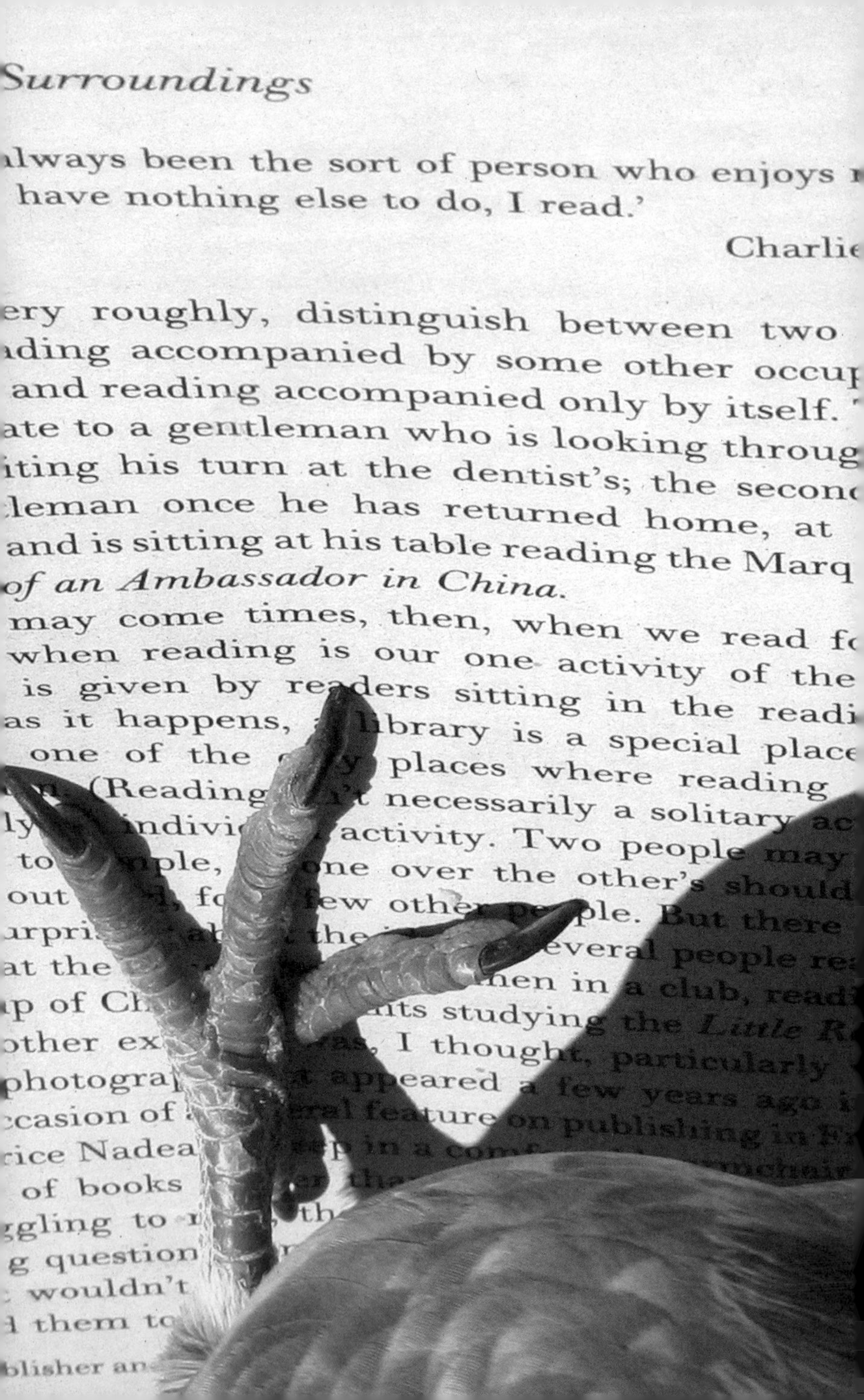
Surroundings
lways been the sort of person who enjoys
have nothing else to do, I read.'
Charli
ery roughly, distinguish between two
ading accompanied by some other occu
and reading accompanied only by itself.
ate to a gentleman who is looking throug
iting his turn at the dentist's; the secon
leman once he has returned home, at
and is sitting at his table reading the Marq
of an Ambassador in China.
may come times, then, when we read f
when reading is our one activity of the
is given by re ders sitting in the readi
as it happens, library is a special place
one of the places where reading
necessarily a solitary ac
activity. Two people may
one over the other's should
few other people. But there
several people re
en in a club, readi
ip of Ch
studying the Little R
other ex
I thought, particularly
photogra
appeared a few years ago i
casion of a
eral feature on publishing in F
rice Nadea
of books
ggling to
g question
wouldn't
them to
lisher an

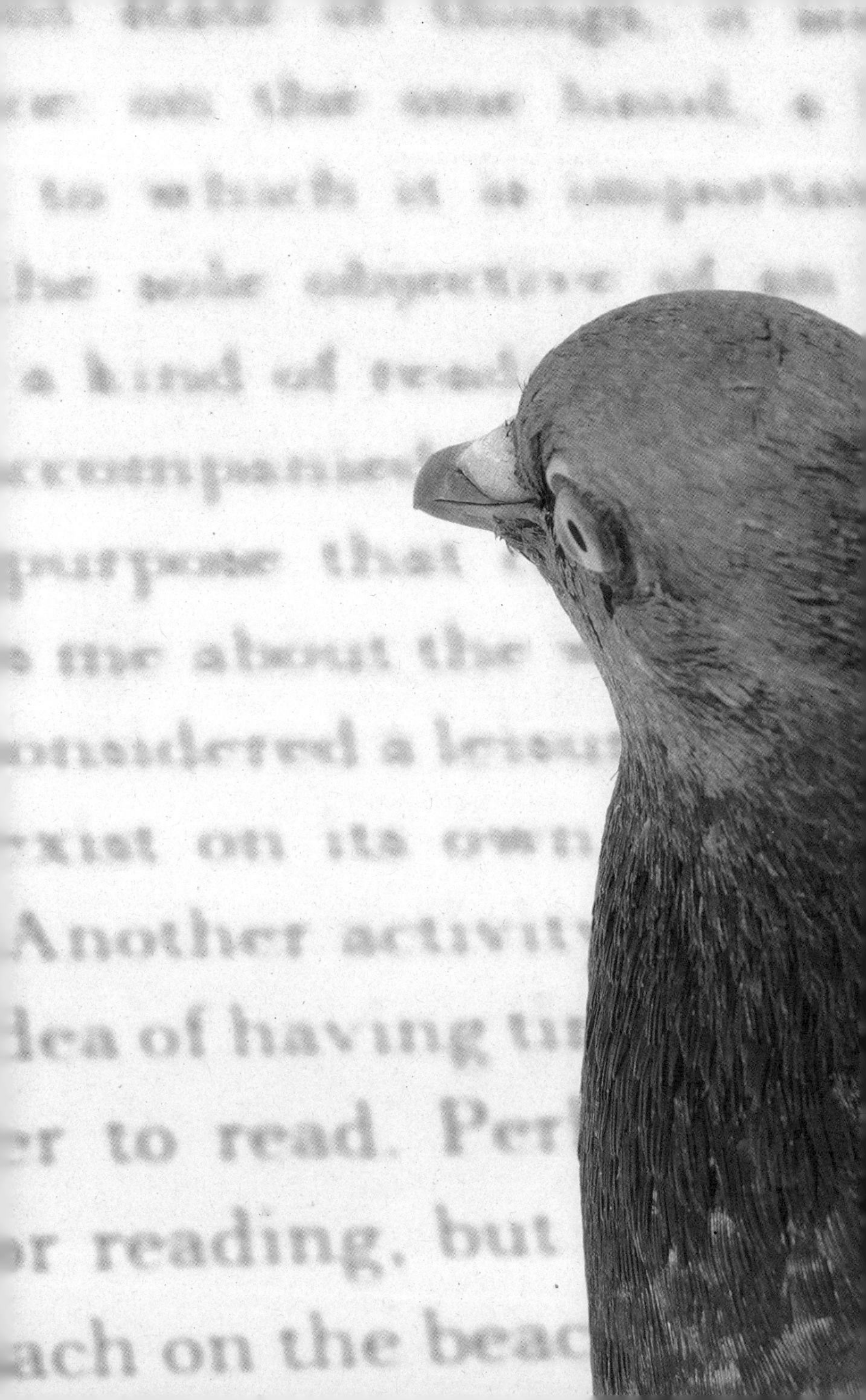

Another activ
dea of having
er to read. Per
or reading. but
ach on the beac

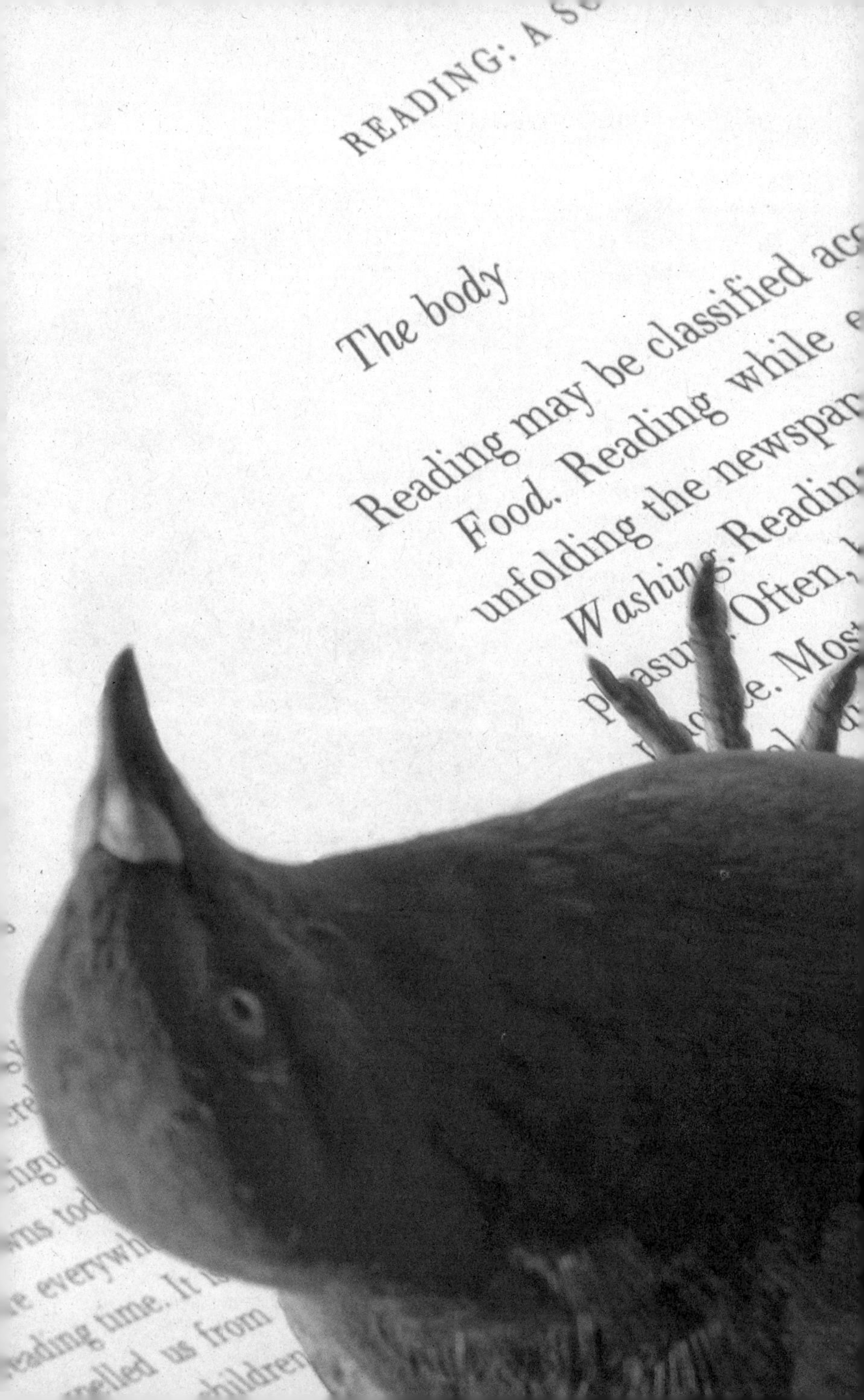

READING: A
The body
Reading may be classified
Food. Reading while
unfolding the
Washing.
Often,
everywh
reading time. It
pelled us from

cial space
ely read while working, except of course when
s of reading.
thers read in town squares while watching the
Loafers hang about round the second-hand bo
the quays, or go and read the daily papers posted
ditorial offices. Drinkers read their evening pa
ng an apéritif on the terrace of a café.
Transport
read a lot going to or coming back from our wo
ay be classified according to the means of transpo
aches are no use (reading gives you a headache); bus
ited, but have fewer readers than you might have
oubt because of all there is to see in the street.
The place to read in is the Métro, almost by de
urprised that the Minister of Culture, or the Secre
for the universities has never yet exclaimed: 'Sto
money for libraries, Messieurs. The true library of
the Métro

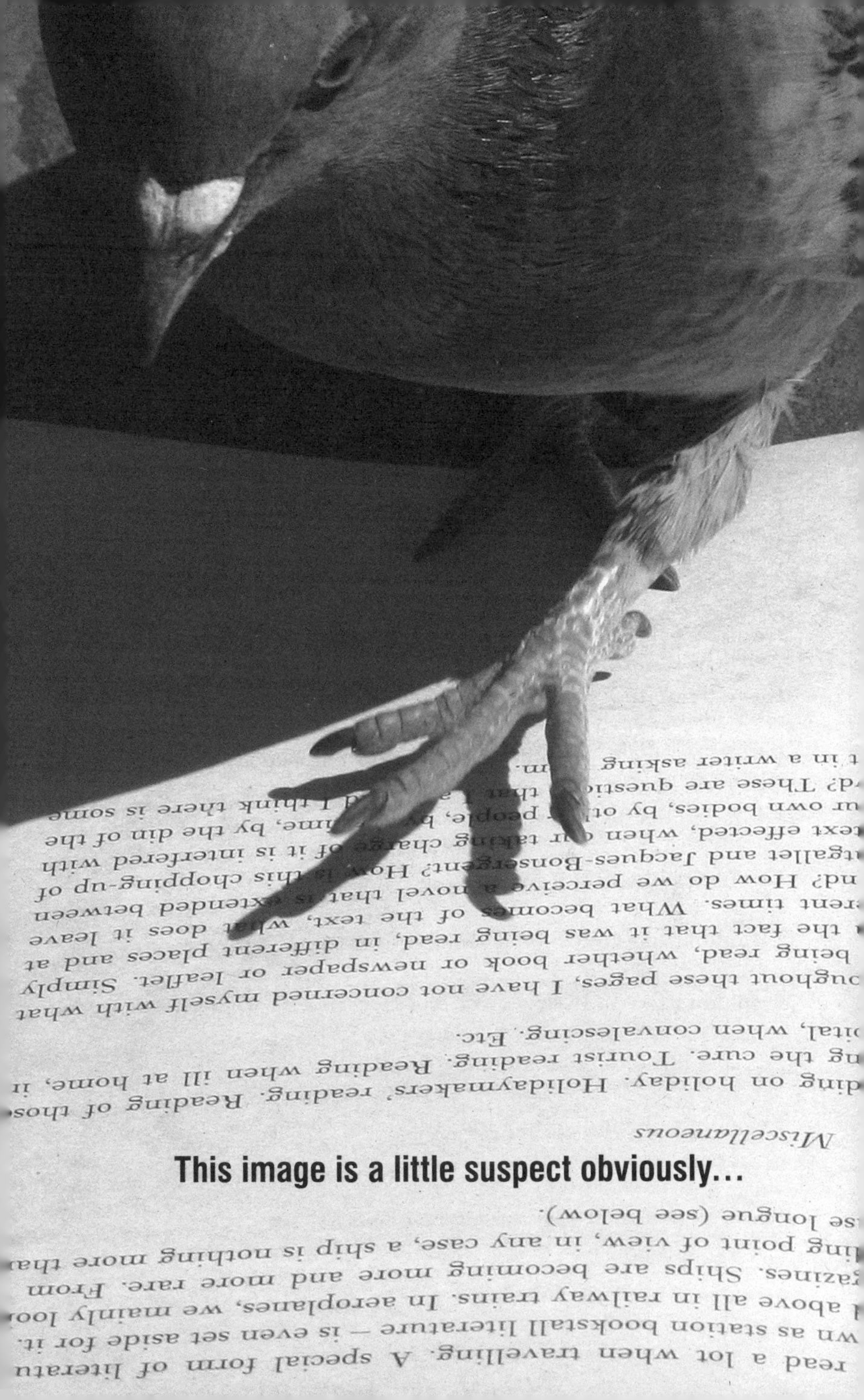

This image is a little suspect obviously…

*On the Difficulty of Imagining an Ideal City**

I wouldn't like to live in America but sometimes I would

I'd love to live on the Boulevard St-Germain but sometimes I wouldn't

I wouldn't like to live on a coral reef but sometimes I would

I wouldn't like to live in a dungeon but sometimes I would

I wouldn't like to live in the East but sometimes I would

I love living in France but sometimes I don't

I'd love to live in Greenland but not for too long

I'd like to live to a hundred but sometimes I wouldn't

I wouldn't like to live in Issoudun but sometimes I would

I wouldn't like to live on a junk but sometimes I would

I wouldn't like to live in a ksar but sometimes I would

I'd have loved to go in a lunar module but it's a bit late

I wouldn't like to live in a monastery but sometimes I would

*First published in the *Quinzaine Littéraire* in August 1981.

I wouldn't like to live at the Hôtel Negresco but sometimes I would

I wouldn't like to live in the open air but sometimes I would

I love living in Paris but sometimes I don't

I wouldn't like to live in Quebec but sometimes I would

I wouldn't like to live by my own resources but sometimes I would

I wouldn't like to live in a submarine but sometimes I would

I wouldn't like to live in a tower but sometimes I would

I wouldn't like to live with Ursula Andress but sometimes I would

I wouldn't like to live in a village but sometimes I would

I wouldn't like to live in a wigwam but sometimes I would

I'd love to live in Xanadu but not for ever

I wouldn't like to live in the Yonne but sometimes I would

I wouldn't like us all to live in Zanzibar but sometimes I would

*'Think/Classify'**

D. Summary

Summary – Methods – Questions – Vocabulary exercises – The world as puzzle – Utopias – Twenty Thousand Leagues Under the Sea – Reason and thought – Eskimos – The Universal Exposition – The alphabet – Classifications – Hierarchies – How I classify – Borges and the Chinese – Sei Shonagon – The ineffable joys of enumeration – The Book of Records – Lowness and inferiority – The dictionary – Jean Tardieu – How I think – Some aphorisms – 'In a network of intersecting lines' – Miscellaneous –?

A. Methods

At the different stages of preparation for this essay – notes scribbled on notebooks or loose sheets of paper, quotations copied out, 'ideas', see, cf., etc. – I naturally accumulated small piles: lower-case b, CAPITAL I, thirdly, part two. Then, when the time came to bring these elements together (and they certainly needed to be brought together if this 'article' was finally one day to cease from being a vague project regularly put off until a less fraught tomorrow), it rapidly became clear that I would never manage to organize them into a discourse.

It was rather as if the images and ideas that had come to me – however shiny and promising they may at first have seemed, one by one, or even when opposed in pairs – had distributed themselves from the outset across the imaginary space of my as yet unblackened sheets of paper like the noughts (or the crosses) that a not very skilful player of noughts and crosses spreads

*First published in *Le Genre humain* in 1982.

over his grid without ever managing to have three together in a straight line.

This discursive deficiency is not due simply to my laziness (or my feebleness at noughts and crosses); it's connected rather with the very thing I have tried to define, if not to take hold of, in the topic I have been set here. As if the interrogation set in train by this 'THINK/CLASSIFY' had called the thinkable and the classifiable into question in a fashion that my 'thinking' could only reflect once it was broken up into little pieces and dispersed, so reverting endlessly to the very fragmentation it claimed to be trying to set in order.

What came to the surface was of the nature of the fuzzy, the uncertain, the fugitive and the unfinished, and in the end I chose deliberately to preserve the hesitant and perplexed character of these shapeless scraps, and to abandon the pretence of organizing them into something that would by rights have had the appearance (and seductiveness) of an article, with a beginning, a middle and an end.

Perhaps this is to answer the question put to me, before it was put. Perhaps it is to avoid putting it so as not to have to answer it. Perhaps it is to use, and abuse, that old rhetorical figure known as the *excuse* whereby, instead of confronting the problem needing to be resolved, one is content to reply to questions by asking other questions, taking refuge each time behind a more or less feigned incompetence. Perhaps also it is to designate the question as in fact having no answer, that is, to refer thinking back to the unthought on which it rests, and the classified to the unclassifiable (the unnameable, the unsayable) which it is so eager to disguise.

N. Questions

Think/classify

What does the fraction line signify?

What am I being asked precisely? Whether I think before I classify? Whether I classify before I think? How I classify what I think? How I think when I seek to classify?

S. Vocabulary exercises

How could one classify the following verbs: arrange, catalogue, classify, cut up, divide, enumerate, gather, grade, group, list, number, order, organize, sort? They are arranged here in alphabetical order.

These verbs can't all be synonymous: why would we need fourteen words to describe just one action? They are different, therefore. But how to differentiate between them all? Some stand in opposition to one another even though they refer to an identical preoccupation: *cut up*, for example, evokes the notion of a whole needing to be divided into distinct elements, while *gather* evokes the notion of distinct elements needing to be brought together into a whole.

Others suggest new verbs (for example: subdivide, distribute, discriminate, characterize, mark, define, distinguish, oppose, etc.), taking us back to that original burbling in which we can with difficulty make out what might be called the readable (what our mental activity is able to read, apprehend, understand).

U. The world as puzzle

> 'Plants are divided into trees, flowers and vegetables.'
>
> Stephen Leacock

So very tempting to want to distribute the entire world in terms of a single code. A universal law would then regulate phenomena as a whole: two hemispheres, five continents, masculine and feminine, animal and vegetable, singular plural, right left, four seasons, five senses, six vowels, seven days, twelve months, twenty-six letters.

Unfortunately, this doesn't work, has never even begun to work, will never work. Which won't stop us continuing for a long time to come to categorize this animal or that according to whether it has an odd number of toes or hollow horns.

R. Utopias

All utopias are depressing because they leave no room for chance, for difference, for the 'miscellaneous'. Everything has been set in order and order reigns. Behind every utopia there is always some great taxonomic design: a place for each thing and each thing in its place.

E. Twenty Thousand Leagues Under the Sea

Conseil knew how to classify (*classer*) fish.
Ned Land knew how to hunt (*chasser*) fish.
Conseil draws up annotated lists of the fish that Ned Land draws up out of the sea.*

L. Reason and thought

What in fact is the relationship between reason and thought (aside from the fact that *Raison* and *Pensée* were the titles of two philosophical journals in France)? The dictionaries aren't much help in supplying an answer. In the *Petit Robert*, for example, a thought = whatever affects the consciousness, while reason = the thinking faculty. We would find a relationship or a difference between the two terms more easily, I fancy, by studying the adjectives they may be graced by: a thought can be kind, sudden, trite or delightful; reason can be pure, sufficient, good, or sovereign.

I. Eskimos

Eskimos, I am assured, have no *generic* name for denoting ice. They have several words (I've forgotten the exact number, but I

*Conseil and Ned Land are characters in Jules Verne's *Twenty Thousand Leagues Under the Sea*.

believe it's a lot, something like a dozen) which denote specifically the various aspects that water takes between its wholly liquid state and the various manifestations of its more or less intense frozenness.

It is hard, obviously, to find an equivalent example in French. It may be that Eskimos have only one word to denote the space that separates their igloos, whereas we, in our towns, have at least seven (*rue*, *avenue*, *boulevard*, *place*, *cours*, *impasse*, *venelle*), and the English at least twenty (street, avenue, crescent, place, road, row, lane, mews, gardens, terrace, yard, square, circus, grove, court, green, houses, gate, ground, way, drive, walk); but we do all the same have a noun (*artère*, for example) that subsumes all of these. Similarly, if we talk to a pastry-cook about cooking sugar, his answer will be that he can't understand us unless we specify what degree of cooking we want (thread, ball, crack, etc.), but then for him the notion of 'cooking sugar' is already firmly established.

G. The Universal Exposition

The objects displayed at the great Exposition of 1900 were divided into eighteen Groups and 121 Classes. 'The products must be offered to visitors in a logical sequence,' wrote M. Picard, the Chief Commissioner of the Exposition, 'and their classification must answer to a simple, clear and precise conception bearing its own philosophy and justification within it, so that the overall idea may be easily grasped.'

Read the programme drawn up by M. Picard and it appears that this overall idea was inadequate. A trite metaphor justifies the leading place given to Education and Teaching: 'It is by this that man *enters* on to life.' Works of Art come next because their 'place of honour' must be preserved. 'Reasons of this same kind' mean that the 'General Instruments and Procedures of Literature and the Fine Arts' occupy third place. In the 16th Class of which, and I wonder why, one finds Medicine and Surgery (straitjackets, invalid beds, crutches and wooden legs, army medical kits, Red Cross emergency equipment, lifesaving devices for the drowning and asphyxiated, rubber devices from the firm of Bognier & Burnet, etc.).

Between the 4th and 14th Groups, the categories follow one another without revealing any obvious idea of system. One can still see fairly easily how Groups 4, 5 and 6 are arranged (Machinery; Electricity; Civil Engineering and Means of Transport), and Groups 7, 8 and 9 (Agriculture; Horticulture and Arboriculture; Forests, Hunting and Fishing), but then we really do go off in all directions: Group 10, Foodstuffs; Group 11, Mining and Metallurgy; Group 12, Furniture and Interior Design for Public Buildings and Private Dwellings; Group 13, Clothing, Spun and Woven Fabrics; Group 14, Chemical Industry.

Group 15 is rightly given over to whatever hasn't found a place among the other fourteen, i.e. to 'Miscellaneous Industries' (paper-making; cutlery; goldsmithery; gems and jewellery-making; clock-making; bronze, cast iron, ornamental ironwork, chased metals; brushes, leatherwork, fancy goods and basketry; leather and guttapercha; knickknackery).

Group 16 (Social Economy, with the addition of Hygiene and Public Assistance) is there because it (Social Economy) 'must follow on *naturally* [my italics] from the various branches of artistic, agricultural and industrial production as being at once their resultant and their philosophy.'

Group 17 is devoted to 'Colonization'. This is a new grouping (relative to the Exposition of 1889) whose 'creation has been amply justified by the need for colonial expansion felt by all civilized peoples'.

The last place, finally, is occupied quite simply by the Army and Navy.

The division of products within these Groups and their Classes contains innumerable surprises which it isn't possible to go into in detail here.

T. The alphabet

I have several times asked myself what logic was applied in the distribution of the six vowels and twenty consonants of our alphabet. Why start with A, then B, then C, etc.? The fact that there is obviously no answer to this question is initially reassuring. The order of the alphabet is arbitrary, inexpressive and therefore neutral. Objectively speaking, A is no better than B, the ABC is not a sign of excellence but only of a beginning (the ABC of one's métier).

But the mere fact that there is an order no doubt means that, sooner or later and more or less, each element in the series becomes the insidious bearer of a qualitative coefficient. Thus a B-movie will be thought of as 'less good' than another film which, as it happens, no one has yet thought of calling an 'A-movie'. Just as a cigarette manufacturer who has the words 'Class A' stamped on his packets is giving us to understand that his cigarettes are superior to others.

The qualitative alphabetical code is not very well stocked. In fact, it has hardly more than three elements: A = excellent; B = less good; Z = hopeless (a Z-movie). But this doesn't stop it being a code and superimposing a whole hierarchical system on a sequence that is by definition inert.

For reasons that are somewhat different but still germane to my purpose, it may be noted that numerous companies go out of their way, in their corporate titles, to end up with acronyms of the 'AAA', 'ABC', 'AAAC', etc. kind so as to figure among the first entries in professional directories and phone books. Conversely, a schoolboy does well to have a name whose initial letter comes in the middle of the alphabet, because he will then stand a better chance of not being asked a question.

C. Classifications

Taxonomy can make your head spin. It does mine whenever my eyes light on an index of the Universal Decimal Classification (UDC). By what succession of miracles has agreement been reached, practically throughout the world, that 668.184.2.099 shall denote the finishing of toilet soap, and 629.1.018–465 horns on refuse vehicles; whereas 621.3.027.23, 621.436:382, 616.24–002.5–084, 796.54, and 913.15 denote respectively: tensions not exceeding 50 volts, the export trade in Diesel motors, the prophylaxy of tuberculosis, camping, and the ancient geography of China and Japan!

O. Hierarchies

We have undergarments, garments and overgarments, but without thinking of them as forming a hierarchy. But if we have managers and undermanagers, underlings and subordinates, we practically never have overmanagers or supermanagers. The one example I have found is 'superintendent', which is an ancient title. More significantly still, in the prefectorial body in France we have sub-prefects, and above the sub-prefects prefects, and above the prefects, not over-prefects or superprefects, but IGAMEs (= Inspecteur Général de l'Administration en Mission Extraordinaire), whose barbaric acronym has apparently been chosen in order to indicate that here we are dealing with big shots.

At times the underling persists even after the ling has changed his name. In the corps of librarians, for example, there aren't exactly any librarians any more; they are called curators and are classified by classes or under headings (curators second class, first class, special curators, head curators). Conversely, on the floors below, they continue to employ under-librarians.

P. How I classify

My problem with classifications is that they don't last; hardly have I finished putting things into an order before that order is obsolete. Like everyone else, I presume, I am sometimes seized by a mania for arranging things. The sheer number of the things needing to be arranged and the near-impossibility of distributing them according to any truly satisfactory criteria mean that I never finally manage it, that the arrangements I end up with are temporary and vague, and hardly any more effective than the original anarchy.

The outcome of all this leads to truly strange categories. A folder full of miscellaneous papers, for example, on which is written 'To be classified'; or a drawer labelled 'Urgent 1' with nothing in it (in the drawer 'Urgent 2' there are a few old photographs, in 'Urgent 3' some new exercise-books). In short, I muddle along.

F. Borges and the Chinese

'(a) belonging to the Emperor, (b) embalmed, (c) domesticated, (d) sucking pigs, (e) sirens, (f) fabulous, (g) dogs running free, (h) included in the present classification, (i) which gesticulate like madmen, (j) innumerable, (k) drawn with a very fine camel-hair brush, (l) etcetera, (m) which have just broken the pitcher, (n) which look from a distance like flies.'

Michel Foucault has hugely popularized this 'classification' of animals which Borges in *Other Inquisitions* attributes to a certain Chinese encyclopedia that one Doctor Franz Kuhn may have held in his hands. The abundance of intermediaries and Borges's well-known love of an ambiguous erudition permit one to wonder whether this rather too perfectly astonishing miscellaneity is not first and foremost an effect of art. An almost equally mind-boggling enumeration might be extracted simply enough from government documents that could hardly be more official :

(a) animals on which bets are laid, (b) animals the hunting of which is banned between 1 April and 15 September, (c) stranded whales, (d) animals whose entry within the national frontiers is subject to quarantine, (e) animals held in joint ownership, (f) stuffed animals, (g) etcetera (this etc. is not at all surprising in itself; it's only where it comes in the list that makes it seem odd), (h) animals liable to transmit leprosy, (i) guide-dogs for the blind, (j) animals in receipt of significant legacies, (k) animals able to be transported in the cabin, (l) stray dogs without collars, (m) donkeys, (n) mares assumed to be with foal.

H. Sei Shonagon

Sei Shonagon does not classify; she enumerates and then starts again. A particular topic prompts a list, of simple statements or anecdotes. Later on, an almost identical topic will produce another list, and so on. In this way we end up with series that can be regrouped. 'Things' that move one, for example (things that cause the heart to beat faster, things sometimes heard with a greater than usual emotion, things that move one deeply). Or else, in the series of disagreeable 'things':

upsetting things
hateful things
frustrating things
troublesome things
painful things
things that fill one with anxiety
things that seem distressing
disagreeable things
things disagreeable to the eye

A dog that barks during the day, a delivery room in which the baby is dead, a brazier without any fire, a driver who hates his ox, these are some of the upsetting things. Among the hateful things are to be found: a baby that cries at the very moment when you would like to listen to something, crows that flock together and caw when their flight paths cross, and dogs that go on and on howling, in unison, on a rising note. Among the things that seem distressing: a baby's wetnurse who cries during the night. Among the things disagreeable to the eye: the carriage of a high dignitary whose interior curtains appear dirty.

V. The ineffable joys of enumeration

In every enumeration there are two contradictory temptations. The first is to list *everything*, the second is to forget something. The first would like to close off the question once and for all, the second to leave it open. Thus, between the exhaustive and the incomplete, enumeration seems to me to be, before all thought (and before all classification), the very proof of that need to name and to bring together without which the world ('life') would lack any points of reference for us. There are things that are different yet also have a certain similarity; they can be brought together in series within which it will be possible to distinguish them.

There is something at once uplifting and terrifying about the idea that nothing in the world is so unique that it can't be entered on a list. Everything can be listed: the editions of Tasso, the islands on the Atlantic Coast, the ingredients required to make a pear tart, the relics of the major saints, masculine substantives with a feminine plural (*amours*, *délices*, *orgues*), Wimbledon finalists, or alternatively, here restricted arbitrarily to ten, the sorrows of Mr Zachary McCaltex:*

Made to feel giddy by the scent of 6,000 dozen roses
Gashes his foot on an old tin
Half eaten by a ferocious cat
Post-alcoholic para-amnesia
Uncontrollable sleepiness
All but knocked down by a lorry
Sicks up his meal

*A character in *The Sinking of the Odradek Stadium*, a novel by Perec's American friend and collaborator, Harry Mathews, which Perec translated into French in 1980.

Five-month stye on his eye
Insomnia
Alopecia

M. The Book of Records

The preceding list is not ordered, either alphabetically, or chronologically, or logically. As bad luck would have it, most lists these days are lists of winners: only those who come first exist. For a long time now books, discs, films and television programmes have been seen purely in terms of their success at the box-office (or in the charts). Not long ago, the magazine *Lire* even 'classified thought' by holding a referendum to decide which contemporary intellectuals wielded the greatest influence.

But if we are going to list records, better to go and find them in somewhat more eccentric fields (in relation to the subject that concerns us here): M. David Maund possesses 6,506 miniature bottles; M. Robert Kaufman 7,495 sorts of cigarette; M. Ronald Rose popped a champagne cork a distance of 31 metres; M. Isao Tsychiya shaved 233 people in one hour; and M. Walter Cavanagh possesses 1,003 valid credit cards.

X. Lowness and inferiority

By virtue of what complex have the departments of the Seine and the Charente insisted on becoming '*maritime*' so as not to be '*inférieure*' any longer? In the same way, the '*basses*' or 'low' Pyrénées have become '*atlantiques*', the '*basses*' Alpes have become 'de Haute-Provence', and the Loire '*inférieure*' has become '*atlantique*'. Conversely, and for a reason that escapes me, the '*bas*' Rhin has still not taken offence at the proximity of the '*haut*' or 'high' Rhin.

It will be observed, similarly, that the Marne, Savoie and Vienne have never felt humiliated by the existence of the Haute-Marne, the Haute-Savoie and the Haute-Vienne, which ought to tell us something about the role of the marked and unmarked in classifications and hierarchies.

Q. The dictionary

I possess one of the world's most peculiar dictionaries. It is entitled *Manuel biographique ou Dictionnaire historique abrégé des grands hommes depuis les temps les plus reculés jusqu'à nos jours* ('Biographical Handbook or Concise Historical Dictionary of Great Men from the Most Distant Times up until Our Own Day'). It dates from 1825.

The dictionary is in two parts, totalling 588 pages. The first 288 pages are devoted to the first five letters of the alphabet; the second part, of 300 pages, to the remaining 21 letters. The first five letters are each entitled on average to 58 pages, the last 21 to only 14. I am well aware that letter frequency is far from being uniform (in the *Larousse du XXe siècle*, A, B, C and D alone take up two volumes out of the six), but the distribution here is really too unbalanced. If you compare it, for example, with that in Lalanne's *Biographie Universelle* (Paris, 1844), you will find that the letter C takes up proportionately three times as much space, and A and E twice as much, whereas M, R, S, T and V are entitled to roughly two times less space.

It would be interesting to look more closely at what influence this inequity has had on the entries: have they been shortened, and if so how? Have they been suppressed, and if so which ones and why? By way of an example, Anthemius, a sixth-century architect to whom we owe (in part) Santa-Sophia in Istanbul, is entitled to an entry of 31 lines, whereas Vitruvius gets only six; Anne de Boulen or Boleyn also gets 31 lines, but Henry the Eighth a mere 19.

*B. Jean Tardieu**

In the sixties they invented a device that enabled the focal length of a film camera lens to be varied continuously, so simulating (rather crudely in the event) an effect of movement without the camera actually having to be moved. The device is known as a 'zoom' lens and the corresponding verb in French is *zoomer*. Although this hasn't as yet been admitted to the dictionaries, it very soon imposed itself on the profession.

This isn't always the case. In most motor vehicles, for example, there are three pedals, each of which has its specific verb: *accélérer*, *débrayer*, *freiner* (to accelerate, to declutch, to brake). But there is no verb, to my knowledge, corresponding to the gear lever. We have to say *changer de vitesse* ('change gear'), *passer en troisième* ('get into third'), etc. Similarly, there is a verb in French for shoelaces (*lacer*) and for buttons (*boutonner*), but no verb for zip fasteners, whereas the Americans have *to zip up*.

The Americans also have a verb that means 'to live in the suburbs and work in the town': *to commute*. But they don't, any more than we do, have one which would mean: 'drink a glass of white wine with a friend from Burgundy, at the Café des Deux-Magots, around six o' clock on a rainy day, while talking about the non-meaningfulness of the world, knowing that you have just met your old chemistry teacher and that next to you a young woman is saying to her neighbour: "You know, I showed her some in every colour!"'.

(from Jean Tardieu: *Un Mot pour un autre*, 1951)

J. How I think

How I think when I'm thinking? How I think when I'm not thinking? At this very moment, how I think when I'm thinking

*A French poet and radio dramatist, born in 1903, whose black humour and obsession with language were much appreciated by Perec.

about how I think when I'm thinking? The words '*penser/classer*', for example, make me think of '*passer/clamser*', or alternatively '*clapet sensé*', or even '*quand c'est placé*'.* Is this called 'thinking'?

I rarely get thoughts about the infinitely small or about Cleopatra's nose, about the holes in gruyère or about the Nietzschean sources of Maurice Leblanc and Joe Shuster.† It is much more of the order of a scribbling down, of a jogging of the memory or a truism.

Yet how, all the same, when 'thinking' (reflecting on?) about this essay, did I come to 'think' about the game of noughts and crosses, Leacock, Jules Verne, Eskimos, the 1900 Exposition, the names streets have in London, IGAMEs, Sei Shonagon, Anthemius and Vitruvius? The answer to these questions is sometimes obvious and sometimes wholly obscure. I would have to speak of feeling my way, of flair, of inklings, of chance, of encounters that are fortuitous or prompted or fortuitously prompted: of meandering in the midst of words. I'm not thinking but I am searching for my words. In the heap there must surely be one that will come to clarify this drifting about, this hesitation, this agitation which, later, is going to 'mean something'.

It is a matter also, and above all, of montage, of distortion, of contortion, of detours, of a mirror, indeed of a formula, as the paragraph that follows will demonstrate.

K. Some aphorisms

Marcel Benabou of the OuLiPo has thought up a machine for manufacturing aphorisms. It consists of two parts, a grammar and a vocabulary.

The grammar lists a certain number of formulas commonly

*These are phrases sounding rather like *penser/classer* in French. *Clamser* is a slang verb for 'to kick the bucket'; *clapet* is a word meaning 'a valve', used familiarly in such phrases as '*ferme ton clapet!*', meaning 'shut your gob!'; *quand c'est placé* would simply mean 'when it's placed'.

†Maurice Leblanc was a writer of crime novels; Joe Shuster was one of the originators of the Superman character in the United States.

used in a majority of aphorisms. For example: A is the shortest route from B to C. A is the continuation of B by other means. A little A carries us away from B, a lot brings us closer. Little As make big Bs. A wouldn't be A if it wasn't B. Happiness is in A not B. A is a malady for which B is the cure. Etc.

The vocabulary lists pairs of words (or trios, or quartets) which may be false synonyms (sentiment/sensation, knowledge/science), antonyms (life/death, form/content, remember/forget), words that are phonetically close (belief/relief, love/leave), words grouped together by usage (crime/punishment, hammer/sickle, science/life). Etc.

The injection of the vocabulary into the grammar produces *ad lib* a near-infinite number of aphorisms, each one of them bearing more meaning than the last. Whence a computer program, devised by Paul Braffort, which can turn out on demand a good dozen within a few seconds:

Remembering is a malady for which forgetting is the cure
Remembering wouldn't be remembering if it weren't forgetting
What comes by remembering goes by forgetting
Small forgettings make big rememberings
Remembering adds to our pains, forgetting to our pleasures
Remembering delivers us from forgetting, but who will deliver us from remembering?
Happiness is in forgetting, not in remembering
Happiness is in remembering, not in forgetting
A little forgetting carries us away from remembering, a lot brings us closer
Forgetting unites men, remembering divides them
Remembering deceives us more often than forgetting
Etc.

Where is the *thinking* here? In the formula? In the vocabulary? In the operation that marries them?

W. 'In a network of intersecting lines'

The alphabet used to 'number' the various paragraphs of this text follows the order in which the letters of the alphabet appear in the French translation of the seventh story in Italo Calvino's *If on a Winter's Night a Traveller . . .*

The title of this story, '*Dans un réseau de lignes entrecroisées*', contains this alphabet up to its thirteenth letter, O. The first line of the text enables us to go up to the eighteenth letter, M, the second gives us X, the third Q, the fourth nothing, the fifth B and J. The last four letters, K, W, Y and Z, are to be found, respectively, in lines 12, 26, 32 and 41 of the story.

From which it may easily be deduced that this story (at least in its French translation) is not lipogrammatic. It will be found similarly that three letters of the alphabet thus formed are in the same place as in the so-called normal alphabet: I, Y and Z.

Y. Miscellaneous

Interjections as classified by a (very second-rate) crossword dictionary (extracts):

Of admiration: *eh*
Of anger: *bigre*
Of scorn: *beuh*
Used by a carter in order to go ahead: *hue*
Expressing the sound of a falling body: *patatras*
Expressing the sound of a blow: *boum*
Expressing the sound of a thing: *crac, cric*
Expressing the sound of a fall: *pouf*
Expressing the cry of bacchantes: *evohé*
To urge on a pack of hounds: *taiaut*
Expressing a disappointed hope: *bernique*
Expressing an oath: *mordienne*
Expressing a Spanish oath: *caramba*

Expressing King Henri IV's favourite oath:
ventre-saint-gris
Expressing an oath expressing approval: *parbleu*
Used for getting rid of someone: *oust*, *ouste*

from *L'Infra-ordinaire* (1989)

*Approaches to What?**

What speaks to us, seemingly, is always the big event, the untoward, the extra-ordinary: the front-page splash, the banner headlines. Railway trains only begin to exist when they are derailed, and the more passengers that are killed, the more the trains exist. Aeroplanes achieve existence only when they are hijacked. The one and only destiny of motor-cars is to drive into plane trees. Fifty-two weekends a year, fifty-two casualty lists: so many dead and all the better for the news media if the figures keep on going up! Behind the event there has to be a scandal, a fissure, a danger, as if life reveals itself only by way of the spectacular, as if what speaks, what is significant, is always abnormal: natural cataclysms or historical upheavals, social unrest, political scandals.

In our haste to measure the historic, significant and revelatory, let's not leave aside the essential: the truly intolerable, the truly inadmissible. What is scandalous isn't the pit explosion, it's working in coalmines. 'Social problems' aren't 'a matter of concern' when there's a strike, they are intolerable twenty-four hours out of twenty-four, three hundred and sixty-five days a year.

Tidal waves, volcanic eruptions, tower-blocks that collapse, forest fires, tunnels that cave in, the Drugstore des Champs-Elysées burns down. Awful! Terrible! Monstrous! Scandalous! But where's the scandal? The true scandal? Has the newspaper told us anything except: not to worry, as you can see life exists, with its ups and its downs, things happen, as you can see.

The daily papers talk of everything except the daily. The papers annoy me, they teach me nothing. What they recount doesn't concern me, doesn't ask me questions and doesn't answer the questions I ask or would like to ask.

What's really going on, what we're experiencing, the rest, all

*First published in *Cause Commune* in February 1973.

the rest, where is it? How should we take account of, question, describe what happens every day and recurs every day: the banal, the quotidian, the obvious, the common, the ordinary, the infra-ordinary, the background noise, the habitual?

To question the habitual. But that's just it, we're habituated to it. We don't question it, it doesn't question us, it doesn't seem to pose a problem, we live it without thinking, as if it carried within it neither questions nor answers, as if it weren't the bearer of any information. This is no longer even conditioning, it's anaesthesia. We sleep through our lives in a dreamless sleep. But where is our life? Where is our body? Where is our space?

How are we to speak of these 'common things', how to track them down rather, flush them out, wrest them from the dross in which they remain mired, how to give them a meaning, a tongue, to let them, finally, speak of what is, of what we are.

What's needed perhaps is finally to found our own anthropology, one that will speak about us, will look in ourselves for what for so long we've been pillaging from others. Not the exotic any more, but the endotic.

To question what seems so much a matter of course that we've forgotten its origins. To rediscover something of the astonishment that Jules Verne or his readers may have felt faced with an apparatus capable of reproducing and transporting sounds. For that astonishment existed, along with thousands of others, and it's they which have moulded us.

What we need to question is bricks, concrete, glass, our table manners, our utensils, our tools, the way we spend our time, our rhythms. To question that which seems to have ceased forever to astonish us. We live, true, we breathe, true; we walk, we open doors, we go down staircases, we sit at a table in order to eat, we lie down on a bed in order to sleep. How? Where? When? Why?

Describe your street. Describe another street. Compare.

Make an inventory of your pockets, of your bag. Ask yourself about the provenance, the use, what will become of each of the objects you take out.

Question your tea spoons.

What is there under your wallpaper?

How many movements does it take to dial a phone number? Why?

Why don't you find cigarettes in grocery stores? Why not?

It matters little to me that these questions should be fragmentary, barely indicative of a method, at most of a project. It matters a lot to me that they should seem trivial and futile: that's exactly what makes them just as essential, if not more so, as all the other questions by which we've tried in vain to lay hold on our truth.

*The Rue Vilin**

1
Thursday 27 February 1969, around 4 p.m.

The Rue Vilin starts level with No 29 in the Rue des Couronnes, opposite some new blocks of council flats, recently built but with something old about them already.

On the right (even numbers), a building with three faces: one fronting on the Rue Vilin, another on the Rue des Couronnes, a third, narrow, one describing the slight angle the two streets make between them. On the ground floor, a café-restaurant with a sky-blue shopfront and yellow trimmings.

On the left (odd numbers), No 1 has been recently done up. I've been told it's the building where my mother's parents lived. There are no letter boxes in the tiny entrance lobby. On the ground floor, a shop, in the old days for furniture (traces of the lettering MEUBLES are still visible), which may be being set up again as a haberdashery to judge by the articles to be seen in the shop window. The shop is closed, and unlit.

From No 2, the sound of jazz: New Orleans revival (Sidney Bechet? More Maxim Saury†).

On the odd-number side: a paint shop
the building at No 3, recently done up
AU BON TRAVAIL, Ready-to-wear, Hosiery
A dairy, LAITERIE PARISIENNE

*First published in the Communist newspaper *L'Humanité* in November 1977. This was the street in north-east Paris where Georges Perec spent the first five years of his life.

†Maxim Saury was one of the French jazzmen who imitated the New Orleans style (as exemplified by Sidney Bechet) after the Second World War.

From No 3 on, the buildings are no longer being done up.

At No 5, a dry cleaner's, 'AU DOCTEUR DU VETEMENT', then BESNARD, Ready-to-wear.

Opposite, at No 4: a shop selling buttonholes

At No 7, a sign cut out of metal: Pumps, on the façade POMPES COUPPEZ et CHAPUIS. The shop looks to have closed long since.

Then, still with the odd numbers, a small shop, unidentifiable.

At No 9, Restaurant-Bar Marcel.

At No 6, a sanitary engineer's.

At No 6, Soprani, hairdresser.

At Nos 9 and 11, two shops, closed.

At No 11, Vilin Laundry.

Past No 11, a concrete fence forms the corner of the Rue Julien-Lacroix.

At No 10, Skins Dressed to Order.

At No 10, a former stationer cum haberdashery.

At No 12, forming the corner, H. Selibter, Trousers All Styles.

There are cars practically all the way along the pavement on the odd-number side.

The slope remains roughly the same (quite steep) all the way up the street. The street is paved. The Rue Julien-Lacroix intersects it more or less in the middle of its first – and longer – section.

At the intersection (even-number sides of both streets), a house under repair with a wrought-iron balcony on the first floor and the announcement, repeated twice

BEWARE OF THE STEPS

There is no sign of any steps; a bit later on you realize it means the steps that end the street: for a car, the Rue Vilin becomes a cul-de-sac after the Rue Julien-Lacroix.

At the intersection (odd-number side of the Rue Vilin, even-number side of the other street), a food shop stocking Vins Préfontaines (if a sign on the door is to be believed) and Vins du Postillon (according to the canvas sun-blind).

At No 19, a long single-storey house.

At No 16, a shop, closed, which could have been a butcher's.

At No 18, a residential hotel flanked by a café-bar, the Hôtel de Constantine.

At No 22, an old café, closed, without any lights; you can make out a large oval mirror at the far end. Above, on the second floor, a long wrought-iron balcony, washing hung out to dry. On the door of the café, a notice:

THIS ESTABLISHMENT IS CLOSED ON SUNDAYS

At No 24 (this is the house where I lived):

First, a single-storey building with, on the ground floor, a doorway (blocked up); all around, still traces of paintwork and above, not yet completely rubbed away, the inscription

LADIES' HAIRDRESSER

Then a low building with a doorway giving on to a long paved courtyard on several different levels (flights of two or three steps). On the right, a long single-storey building (giving in the old days on to the street through the blocked-up doorway to the hairdressing salon) with a double flight of concrete steps leading up to it (this is the building we lived in; the hairdressing salon was my mother's).

At the far end, a shapeless building. On the left, what look like rabbit hutches.

I didn't go back in.

An old man, coming from the far end, went down the three steps that led to 'our' quarters. Another old man came in with a heavy bundle (of washing?) on his back. Then, finally, a young girl.

At No 25, opposite, a house with a double porch opening on to a long, gloomy courtyard and a shop that appears closed but from which a regular sound is coming: like blows from a hammer but more 'mechanical' and not so loud. Through a dirty window-pane, you can identify a sewing machine, but no one working at it.

At No 27, a shop, closed, 'La Maison du Taleth', with signs in Hebrew still to be seen and the words MOHEL, CHOHET, BOOKS, STATIONERY, RELIGIOUS OBJECTS, TOYS, on a façade of a faded blue.

On the site of No 29, a rubblestone fence recently whitewashed. The outlines of rooms with yellow or yellowed wallpaper are visible on the side of No 31.

No 31 is a boarded-up house. The windows on the first two floors have been blocked up. There are still curtains on the third floor. On the ground floor a boarded-up shop

POWER LIGHTING

A.MARTIN

ELECTRIC COILS MOTORS

FACTORIES EQUIPPED

At No 33, a building boarded up.

The street then bends, on the right, through an angle of about 30 degrees. On the even-number side, the street stops at No 38. Next, there is a red-brick shack, then the top of a flight of steps coming from the Passage Julien-Lacroix which also starts from the Rue des Couronnes but a little lower down than the Rue Vilin. Then a large expanse of waste ground, with loose stones and bare grass.

On the odd-number side, on the left, level with No 49, the street bends for a second time, also through about 30 degrees. This gives the street the general appearance of a very elongated S (like the high-tension symbol ϟϟ).

On the odd-number side, the street ends level with Nos 53–5 in a flight of steps, or rather three flights of steps that also make roughly a double sinusoid (less an S-shape than a wrong-way-round question-mark).

No 49 is a yellow house with a zinc mansard-roof on the second storey. Two windows on the first floor. At one of them (the right-hand one for me), an old lady, staring at me. On the ground floor (in the old days?) a 'BUILDING CONTRACTOR'.

At No 47, a boarded-up house with traces of red paint on the walls. At No 45, a shop, closed, and a three-storey building that was the

HOTEL DU MONT-BLANC
Furnished Rooms and Offices

At No 34, a former Wines and Spirits.

Blind windows everywhere.

At Nos 53–5, there was a Wine and Coal Merchant 'AU REPOS DE LA MONTAGNE'. The building was split down the middle, from top to bottom, on 5–4–68 (that is the date written on the plaster). The three doorways to the three first-floor windows have been bricked up.

At the top of the steps, you come to a small road junction, leading to the Rue Piat to the left, the Rue des Envierges facing you, the Rue du Transvaal to the right. Where the Rue des Envierges intersects with the Rue du Transvaal, there is a beautiful ochre-coloured bakery. Along the balustrade by the steps, next to a street-light, is a motor scooter garishly painted in bright colours to look like the skin of a wild animal. Two Algerians are leaning there for a moment. Two blacks are coming up the steps. Although it's rather overcast, there's quite an extensive panorama to be seen: churches, tall modern blocks, the Panthéon?

On the waste ground, two children are fighting a duel with coathangers for swords.

At seven o' clock in the evening, I went back, running almost, to see what the Rue Vilin looked like after dark. There are very few windows with lights in – scarcely two per building – in the upper part of the street, but more at the start. The old café at No 22 was lit up, full of Algerians. It's also a hotel (I saw a notice 'Room Prices').

Several shops I had thought were closed for good have their lights on.

2

Thursday 25 June 1970, around 4 p.m.

The market is being set up on the Boulevard de Belleville. Roadworks continuing into the Rue des Couronnes. Building under construction on the corner of the Rue J.-P.Timbaud. A whole block of houses has been knocked down on the corner of the Rue des

Couronnes. A bit further along the Boulevard, riot police buses (recent incidents between Jews and Arabs).

The Rue Vilin is one-way; you can't go up it. The cars are parked on the odd-number side.

Nos 1 and 3 have been done up. At No 1, a food shop, closed, and a haberdashery, still open. On the second floor, a man is at his window.

At No 3, a paint shop and a hosiery. The woman in the paint shop takes me for an official:

'So, you've come to knock us down?'

At No 2, a café-restaurant, at No 4, a shop selling buttonholes. Roadworks: putting in natural gas.

At No 5, the dairy, Laiterie Parisienne, Au Docteur du Vêtement, Dry Cleaners Mending Done. Besnard Ready-to-Wear.

You can hear Arab music coming from higher up.

At No 6, Sanitary Engineer. A. Soprani, Hairdresser, Late Opening Thursdays (the shop looks newly refurbished).

At No 7, Couppez, Pumps (closed): two storeys out of three are bricked up. Another closed shop. A small notice in felt pen, worn away except for the red:

I sell   on Tuesdays and Wednesdays.

No 8 is a house of three storeys, with two women at the windows. At No 9, the restaurant-bar Marcel and a shop, closed. At No 10, closed, Skins Dressed to Order, and also closed, a stationer-cum-haberdashery. At No 11, a shop, closed. At No 13, a laundry with a faded blue façade. On the second floor, an apartment has been bricked up. No 12 is a building of five storeys. On the ground floor, Selibter, Trousers All Styles. At No 14, a boarded-up house, also at No 15 (intersection with the Rue Julien-Lacroix). At No 16, a former butcher's? At No 17, a former food shop has become a bar-café (BAR-CAFE has been painted in white on the door). At No 18, Hôtel de Constantine, Furnished Rooms Café-Bar. Nos 19, 21 and 23 are houses of a single storey, dilapidated. No 20 is a four-storey house, dilapidated, the fourth floor seems to have been boarded up. At No 22, a café-hotel? At No 24, in the little courtyard, a cat on a coal bunker. The inscription LADIES' HAIRDRESSER is still visible. Communist Party posters. At No 25, a shop, closed.

At No 26, a boarded-up ground floor. At No 27, a shop, closed. Then, as far as No 41, a cement fence. At No 30, a two-storey house, partly bricked up; a fashion shop. At No 32, boarded up shops (Wines and Spirits). No 34 has been almost entirely bricked up. Past No 36 the waste ground begins.

From No 41 to No 49, almost all the buildings have been bricked up, among them, at No 45, the HOTEL DU MONT-BLANC. At No 49, a yellow house, formerly a builder's, a lady at the first-floor window. Nos 51, 53 and 55 are survivors (A LA MONTAGNE, Wines & Spirits).

3
Wednesday 13 January 1971

Dry cold. Sunshine.

There's a triangular pediment above the door to No 1. The left-hand shop, painted blue, with a torn red awning hanging down, is closed. The right-hand shop sells tailoring materials maybe. At No 3, a paint shop and 'Au Bon Accueil', Ready to Wear, Hosiery. At No 2, café-restaurant. At No 4, buttonholes. At No 5, Laiterie Parisienne and Au Docteur du Vêtement, Dyeing, Pressing, Besnard, Ready-to-Wear. At No 7, a building that has been demolished, and a fence with *La Cause du Peuple* posters. At No 6, Sanitary Engineer and Hairdresser. At No 9, a café-restaurant bar: MARCEL'S, and a shop, closed. At No 11, a shop, closed, and VILIN Laundry (on the corner of the Rue Julien-Lacroix):

Compulsorily purchased
Closing Down
24 December

At No 10, Skins Dressed to Order and stationer-cum-haberdashery, closed. At No 12, Trousers All Styles. At No 14, a house, closed, and at No 15, a house, demolished. At No 17, Bar Cellar; on the awning CHEZ HADDADI FARAD; on the door:

Novo Otvoren
Jugoslovenski
Cafe-restoran
Kod Milene

The green butcher's shop is closed, as is another shop. At No 18, HOTEL DE CONSTANTINE, café-bar. At No 22, a hotel-café. At Nos 19 and 21, houses boarded up? At No 26? At No 24, ladies' hairdresser (not the shop, simply traces of the shop sign painted on the wall). In the courtyard of No 24, metal girders; workmen opposite are repairing a roof (of a building in the Rue des Couronnes?). Cranes in the distance.

Nos 25, 27, shops, closed. Starting at No 27, fences. At No 28, a house still lived in. At No 30, a fashion shop with the inscription MODES EN ANGLAISES. At No 32, Wines and Spirits, closed. Nos 34 and 36 are slums. A woman comes out from No 36; she has lived there for 36 years. She had only come for three months; she has a clear memory of the hairdresser at No 24:

'She didn't stay very long.'

Nos 41, 43, 45 (Hôtel du Mont-Blanc) and 47 are buildings that have been blocked up. Then fences.

Cars right the way along the street. A few passers-by.

At No 49, a lady coughing at the window. No 51 is a house that has been boarded up. Nos 53–5 (The Repos de la Montagne, Wines) is closed. Right at the top, waste ground. A shed with a brand-new notice:

PLASTIC APPLIANCES

4

Sunday 5 November 1972 around 2 p.m.

No 1 is still there. No 2, No 3, paint and ready-to-wear 'Au Bon Accueil'. No 4, buttonholes, closed. No 5, dairy now a plumber's? No 6, hairdresser. No 7, knocked down. Nos 8, 9? No 10, skins dressed. No 11, knocked down. No 12, Selibter. No 13, knocked down. No 14, a building knocked down, a shop still standing. No 15, totally demolished. No 16? No 17, bar-cellar. No 18, Hôtel de Constantine. Nos 19? 20? 21, knocked down. No 22, hotel-café. No 23? No 24, still intact. No 25, a shop, closed. No 26, windows bricked up, No 27, bricked up, Nos 28, 30, 36, still standing.

A tabby cat and a black cat in the courtyard of No 24.

After No 27, on the odd-number side, nothing any longer; after No 36, on the even-number side, nothing any longer. On the building at No 30, Johnny Halliday posters.

Right at the top, PLASTIC APPLIANCES.

On the waste ground, a demolition site.

Pigeons, cats, car bodies.

I met a little boy of ten; he was born in the 16th arrondissement.* He is leaving for his own country, Israel, in eight weeks' time.

5
Thursday 21 November 1974, around 1 p.m.

The council blocks at the bottom of the Rue des Couronnes are finished.

The lower part of the Rue Vilin seems still just about alive: piles of rubbish, washing hanging in the windows.

No 1 is still intact. At No 7, there is a fence and some waste ground. Besnard, Ready-to-Wear, at No 5, is closed. At No 9, the restaurant bar MARCEL'S is closed. At No 6, there is one shop (a hairdresser's) open and one shop closed. At No 4, buttonholes?

At the intersection of the Rue Vilin and the Rue Julien-Lacroix, all that's still standing is Selibter, Trousers. The other three corners are occupied, two by waste ground, the other by a building entirely bricked up.

Nos 18 and 22 are café-hotels still standing, as are Nos 20 and 24.

On the odd-number side, No 21 is being demolished (you can

*In which GP himself lived at the age of ten, after the war.

see bulldozers, diggers, fires), Nos 23 and 25 have been gutted. Past No 25, nothing any longer.

Where No 26 stood, a small trailer fitted out as a shack. Car bodies.

Mounds of uncollected rubbish (in the Rue Julien-Lacroix, army conscripts have replaced the striking refuse men).

A dead sparrow in the middle of the roadway.

At No 30, a small poster:

> Official Notice. City of Paris
> 25 – 26 – 27 August 1974
> Compulsory Purchase Order, Nos 28 and 30
> Creation of a public open space in Paris 20e.

Nothing beyond No 30. Fencing, waste ground where car breakers are busy. Election posters on the fences.

6

27 September 1975, around 2 a.m.

Almost the whole of the odd-number side has been covered with cement fences. On one of them a graffito:

> WORK = TORTURE

*Two Hundred and Forty-three Postcards in Real Colour**

For Italo Calvino

We're camping near Ajaccio. Lovely weather. We eat well. I've got sunburnt. Fondest love.

We're at the Hôtel Alcazar. Getting a tan. Really nice! We've made loads of friends. Back on the 7th.

We're sailing off L'Ile-Rousse. Getting ourselves a tan. Food admirable. I've gone and got sunburnt! Love etc.

We've just done Dahomey. Superb nights. Fantastic swimming. Excursions on camel-back. Will be in Paris on the 15th.

We've finally landed in Nice. Lots of lazing about and sleep. Really nice (despite the sunburn). Love.

A quick line from Urbino. Weather good. Long live scampi fritti and fritto misto! Not forgetting Giotto e tutti quanti. Friendly regards.

We're at the Hôtel Les Jonquilles. Marvellous weather. We go to the beach. Have got to know loads of delightful people. A hug and a kiss.

We're at the Hôtel des Quatre-Sergents. Sunbathing. Footy! Sunburn. Thinking of you all the time.

Greetings from Hellénie. Sunning ourselves. Super! We've made heaps of friends. Many regards.

Visiting the Channel. Very restful. Lovely beaches. I've got sunburnt. Love.

*First published in *Le Fou parle* in October 1978.

Here we are in Fréjus. Doing nothing all day except relax. Really nice. I go aquaplaning. Back as planned.

We're camping next to Formentera. Weather good. Vast beach. My shoulders are roasted. Fond love to all the boys and girls.

We're at the Hôtel Beau-Rivage. Lovely weather. We go to the beach. I've been playing boules. It all comes to an end on Tuesday, alas.

Arrived without incident. We're at the Versailles Motel. Food excellent. Interesting acquaintances. Love and kisses.

We're touring around Cyprus. The sun's come along with us. We're red as roosters but great all the same. Hope to see you when we get back.

We're really covering the Costa Esmeralda. Very interesting. Typical cuisine. Locals a delight. Many regards.

We're camping near Wood's Hole. Sunning ourselves. Lobster at every meal. I've caught a salmon. Many regards.

Here we are at Knightsbridge. Weather good. Swimming and golf. Back on the 3rd.

We're at the Hôtel Obelisk. Lots of lazing about. Gorgeous. Have got to know several delightful people. All our regards.

We're staying at the Carlton. Getting ourselves a tan. Sublime meals. Terrible nights in the nightclubs. Back on the 11th.

We're exploring the Quatre-Cantons. Lovely weather. The shorelines are superb. People friendly and open. Love and kisses.

We're travelling through the Balearics. Beautiful and we're stuffing ourselves into the bargain. I've got sunburnt. Expect to be back a week on Monday.

On holiday in Guernsey. We live well. Terrific food. We've made loads of friends. Hugs all round.

A letter from Etretat. Weather good. Having a nice time. My asthma is better. Many regards to all four of you.

We're at the Roma. Service impeccable. We live like kings. I'm being introduced to the subtle art of cocktails. Fondest love.

We're at the Hôtel Nadir. Sunning ourselves on the beach with all the group. Kind thoughts.

We're somewhere in the Persian Gulf. Weather ideal. Exotic food. Underwater fishing. Kind regards and many of them.

Swiss hotels are still the world's best. And the panoramic views are spectacular. A hug and a kiss.

A letter from La Marsa. What a beach! I nearly got sunstroke. Leaving again on Saturday evening for Sicily and Italy.

Here we are in St-Trop! Heavenly weather. There's a whole gang of us. Perfect! Love.

We're at the Hôtel Dardanella. Noshing and lazing about. I'm getting fat. Back beginning of September.

We're at the King and Country. Select beach. We're getting a tan. Tennis and squash. Love and kisses to all.

We're touring around Malta. Lovely weather. We share our meals with some very correct English people. Back around the 10th.

Fond greetings from Hungary. We've been getting a tan on Lake Balaton and been horse-riding. Friendly regards.

We've pitched our camp near Fécamp. Basking on the beach with a whole gang of friends. Thinking of you.

A big hello from Jerez. Room very comfortable. Good simple food. I've put two kilos back on. Back on the 22nd.

We're at the Bella Vista. Ultra-comfortable. Gastronomic specialities. Canasta every evening! We haven't forgotten you.

We're staying at the Negresco. Sublime weather. Everything perfect. My cold's gone. Back on the 17th.

We're cruising off the Yucatan. Ideal weather. Everything just right. I caught a baby shark, 30 kilos! Love.

On holiday in Ulster. Very beautiful beaches. The Irish are wonderful. Reckon to be in Strasbourg on the 4th.

A big hello from Biarritz. So nice letting yourself go brown in the sun. I've done a bit of sailing. Love.

We've landed in Deauville. I'm having a good rest but the meals are too big. The guests in the hotel are very friendly. Many regards.

We're at the Hilton. Lazing in the sun all day beside the pool. Love to all.

We're at the Louis XIV. Very select. Very good weather, too. I go riding to keep my figure. Love.

We're crossing Ireland. Lovely weather. Adorable. Thinking about your sunburn!!!

We're sailing in Zealand. Sunbathing on deck. The cook's a chef! I've learnt to tell fortunes. Fondest love.

Here I am in Knokke-Le Zoute. We pack into the nightclubs. Having a super time. Be with you again on the 12th as expected.

A brief line from Ars-en-Ré. It's very beautiful. We go to the beach. I've been playing tennis. Fondest love.

We're at the Hôtel Zircone. It's very warm. We eat *so* well! I've got sunburnt. Kissy-wissies.

We've pitched the tent near Utica. Lots of lazing about and sleep. We go to the beach. I've made stacks of friends. Fondest love.

We're at the Hôtel Unterwald. Weather good. We eat well. I've been on some outings. Back on Sunday week.

We're staying at the Intercontinental. Sauna. Solarium. Smashing! Birds galore. Much love.

We're crossing Sardinia. Getting a tan all over. Sunburn! Pasta prima! Expect to be back Wednesday next.

We're travelling through Greece. Gorgeous siestas beside the sea. Have met loads of very friendly people. We think of you often.

Here we are in Jacksongrad. We're recuperating. It's ideal. I've managed to get sunburnt all the same! It had to happen! All my regards to you.

News from Quichua. Constant sunshine. Exotic cuisine. I've been riding. Back on the 27th.

We've managed to get in at the Pension Esmeralda. Weather good. We go to the beach. Lots of friends, male and female. Thinking of you.

Hôtel Trianon. Every comfort. Really nice. Gee-gees every morning. Back home Sunday evening.

We're exploring the St Trop coast. Sunning ourselves. So good to be in a bikini! I've made loads of friends. A hug and a kiss.

We're being tourists in Roussillon. Lovely long days on the beaches, but you have to watch out not to get burnt. We'll be back in Tours on the 23rd.

The latest from Bastia: relaxation Corsican-style, the good life. Friends galore. Hugs and kisses all round.

We've set the tent up in Vertbois. Weather good. All day on the beach. I've got sunburnt. All my regards.

We're at the Pfisterhof. Lovely days beside the lake. We do some sailing. A hug for you all.

We're staying at the Stella Matutina. Long sunbathing sessions. Very good simple food. We play cards with the people at the next table. Many regards.

We're crossing the Vaucluse. Weather magnificent. Swimming in the Rhône. I go riding. Fond regards.

Covering every inch of Oregon. Admirable scenery. Food fit for trappers. The Yanks are great. Love.

A letter from Nouméa. We sunbathe, stuff ourselves, sunbathe again and even get roasted. Reckon to come home on the 2nd.

A big hello from Calvi. Weather good. The whole day on the beach with our friends. Much love.

We've got a room at the Lion d'Or. And talk about sleeping! It's doing us good. We're recuperating. Will be in Saint-Etienne on the 14th.

We're at the Hôtel Quirinal. Long siestas on the terrace. Food fit for princes. A spot of baccarat in the evenings. Love.

On holiday in Denmark. Weather good. Very beautiful beaches. Danish girls are quite something! Back on the 6th.

We're in Martinique. Beautiful, super and blue! We've been deep-sea fishing. Fondest regards.

We've set down our back-packs near Ragusa. Sunning ourselves. Decent food. I've managed to lose two kilos all the same. Thinking of you.

A brief line from Ostend. Weather good. Very comfortable. I've caught masses of shrimps. Back on the 19th.

We're at the Hôtel Alhambra. We live like princes, life in the big house. The museum is very fine. Many regards.

We're staying at the Cheval d'Or, but rather missing the beach (not the sunburn though). Back in a fortnight.

We're roaming around the Troad. Unforgettable scenery. Weather good. Food sometimes strange. Much love.

We're doing *our* cruising in the Massif Central. Long cross-country walks with the whole outfit. Smashing! Will be in Paris on the 31st.

Here we are in Draguignan. We go to the sea every day to get brown. I play miniature golf. Lots of big fat kisses.

We've landed in Kerkennah. Weather good. There's a whole gang of us taking it easy. We think of you often.

We're at the Hôtel Xanadu. Luxury, peace, sheer sensuality! Exquisite food. Dad's putting on weight. Much love.

We're at the Hôtel des Pins. We sunbathe on the beach and play Scrabble. Many fond regards.

On holiday in Zanzibar. The sun's scorchingn but the food is exquisite. Think of you a lot.

We're crossing Sicily. Sunning ourselves. Rambles on donkey-back. Much love.

A brief line from Brighton. Getting a tan in the English sun. Have met lots of really friendly folk. Will phone when I get back end of August.

Holidays in Narbonne. Heavenly peace, home-made cassoulet. A spot of boules to take care of the figure. Love.

We're staying at the Hôtel Jugurtha. A lot of lying around and going to the beach. We've made some friends. Reckon to be home around the 8th or 9th.

We're at the Yoyo Motel. Colour telly, and all that! Fantastic! Love to all.

We're on our way back from the Ardennes. Weather's been very good. It was perfect. We've done a lot of riding. We'll be in Paris this Sunday.

We're doing Judea. We're as red as tomatoes from the sun. Many friendly regards.

Here we are in Houlgate at last. Getting ourselves a tan. True happiness! I won 32 francs at lotto! Friendly regards.

Here we are in Le Lavandou. It's beautiful. We eat really well. I've made loads of friends. Back on the 25th.

We're at the Hôtel O'Connor. Lots of lazing about on the beach. I've caught sunburn. Many regards.

We're putting up at the Yalta. Lovely weather. Good simple food. Atmosphere very francophile. Back on the 29th.

We're really covering Venezia. Weather very good. Really nice! I've got sunburnt. Kisses.

We're exploring the Gironde from top to bottom. We live well. Vintage châteaux and vintage everything else. I've been clay pigeon shooting. Back on the 21st.

We're camping near Zoug. Peaceful, relaxing, the beach is really lovely. I go surfing. Thinking of you.

A big hello from Ipanema. Extraordinarily beautiful. Fiesta under the coconut trees! I have to be back on the 5th, alas.

We're in England. Peaceful and relaxing. We go to the beach. I go riding. Thinking of you.

A big hello from Inverness! Weather good for the time of year. Decent nosh. Good for the calf muscles. Many regards.

The Pension Riva Bella is just the job. Weather good. Nosh good. I go water-skiing. Kisses.

We're at the Hôtel des Dunes. Long sunbathing sessions. Comfortable. Bopping every evening in a crowded nightclub. Many regards to the gals that stayed behind in Paris!

Ploughing the North Sea. We're not getting a tan but nice all the same. The fish are biting. Fond regards.

Fondest love from Russia! The explorers are letting themselves go on the beaches of the Black Sea. Have met loads of exciting people.

We're camping near Exeter. Lots of lazing about. It's really great. I've got sunburnt. Back soon.

We've landed near Tropea. Magnificent weather and dinner by candlelight. There's a good dozen of us here. Love.

We're at the Pension Hegel und Sein. Ideal weather for the time of year. Magnificent beach. The sun beats down. We'll be home as planned at the end of the month.

Everything's perfect at the Hôtel de la Mer. We go to the casino. Love.

Crossing Finland you tan in the midnight sun. Very interesting contacts with the local population. Reckon to come back in the middle of the month.

We're in Finistère. Siestas and gastronomy. A few visits to châteaux. Thinking of you.

Here we are in Port-Cros. Lots of lazing about. Sublime, and all that. We've met the Douglases and a whole gang of people. Think of you a lot.

A letter from Les Sables d'Olonne. Weather good. We go to the beach. I've got sunburnt. Back on the 28th.

We're at the Hôtel de la Croisette. Weather good. We go to the beach. I won a ping-pong tournament. We think of you often.

We're putting up at the Engadiner. Staff very well-trained. Ample nosh. I'm watching my waistline. Back next week.

We're in the heart of the Black Forest. Seasonal weather. Splendid excursions. A bit of fly fishing. Love.

Travelling through the Cotentin, taking it easy! Gastro- – but not eco- – nomic stops. We've bumped into quite a few friends. Plan to return the 16th.

We've landed in Menton. Getting ourselves a tan. We eat well. I've been playing miniature golf. Fondest love.

Here we are in Quimper. Weather good. We go to the beach with loads of friends. Thinking of you.

The Quentin Durward is a hotel like no other. We sleep like dormice. It's heavenly. I'm becoming healthy again. Love.

We're at the Hôtel de la Baie. Siestas. Blow-outs. I play a lot of tennis. Thinking of you.

We're doing the Gulf of Lions. Superb weather. We go swimming. I've got sunburnt. Many regards.

We're really covering the Everglades. Well worth the trip. Sublime. I'm getting to be a champion water-skier. Love.

Here we are in Antibes. Sunning ourselves. Small restaurants quite cheap. The local girls aren't too dear either! We'll be in Paris next Tuesday.

A big hello from Cadaquès. Not a cloud in the sky. Really nice. I go water-skiing. Fondest love.

We're living in the Hôtel de la Plage. Lots of lazing about. Monstrous meals with our friends. Back in Brive on the 13th.

We're at the Worcester Hotel. Doing the beach. Sunshine and sunburn. Ouch! Kisses.

We're doing the Lubéron. Lovely weather. We eat divinely well. I play boules. Back around the end of the month.

We've crossed the North Cape. Midnight sun, and all that! Well worth the effort. Many regards.

Dropping you a brief line from Xenos while sunbathing on the beach between two spells of underwater fishing. Many regards.

We're camping near Positano. Loads of friends. Weather good. It's great. Back on the 20th.

We're at the Pension Mimosa. Lots of lazing about, sleeping and snacking. I've got sunburnt. Many fond regards.

Greetings from the Hôtel des Hortensias. Magnificent weather. Everyone's happy. We'll be back in Loches on the 18th.

We're visiting Florida. Sublime weather. Heavenly hamburgers. A bit homesick all the same. Love.

We're roaming around in Württemberg. Better than a lot of silly sunbathing. I go riding. We'll be in Paris on the 1st.

Here we are in Jersey. Really nice. I've even got sunburnt!! Kisses.

We've pitched our camp near the legendary Ys. Lots of lazing about and sleep. We eat well. I go sailing. Many regards to you all.

We're staying at the York et Mayence. Very smart. Private beach. Select clientèle. Love.

We're at the Hôtel de l'Union. Weather good. We're having a heavenly rest. Marc has completely recovered. Kind regards.

We're roaming about in Calabria with all the clan. You should see the fun we're having! Many sunny regards.

We're really covering Morocco. Fantastic beaches. Nothing but sunburn! Love.

We're camping near Ostia. Sunbathing. Just the job! I've learnt to play bridge. Back on the 26th.

Am at the Berghof. It's magnificent. A bit of swimming and lots of siestas in the sun. Shall be back in a fortnight's time.

We're at the Hôtel Ingres et de la Poste. It's very beautiful. I go riding on the beach. Back on the 8th.

A brief line from Girolata. Long siestas on the beach. I've got sunburnt. Back on the 24th.

We're staying at the Kandahar. Long siestas beside the lake, games of tennis, bridge in the evenings. Many regards.

We're at the Adriatica. Weather good. We eat very well. I've got sunburnt. We'll be in Paris on Monday.

We're visiting the USA. Letting ourselves go. Food not so bad. I've got sunburnt. Our regards to you.

The latest from Reggio di Calabria! Lots of lazing about on the beach. There's a whole gang of us. You're not forgotten.

A letter from Djerba. Superb weather. Couscous I love you. I'm as red as a crayfish. Home at the end of August.

I recommend the Soleil d'Or. Terraces in the sun. Food top class. Bridge every evening. Thought of you when I made six NT redoubled!!!

Our address: Motel des Géraniums. We're roasting in the sun! Super! Back soon.

We're travelling round Java. Skin like leather from the sun, long cross-country trips by Land-Rover. Heavenly! Much love.

We're cruising off New Caledonia. Lots of lazing about. Beaches. Loads of friends. We return early October.

A letter from Hendaye. Lots of lazing about and sleep. Really nice! I go surfing. Lots and lots of love.

We've pitched our camp near La Ciotat. Weather superb. And how we eat! Veritable banquets with twenty-five or thirty people! Thinking of you all the same, as the card proves!

We're putting up at the Hôtel des Troglodytes. Weather good. We go to the sea every day. I've got sunburnt. Much love.

We're at the Hôtel Ronceray. We go sunbathing. Super! Lots of volleyball. Thinking of you.

We're sailing close to the Belgian coast. We tan ourselves in the sea breezes. Not so disagreeable. I got stung by a jellyfish. Friendly regards.

We're visiting the Var. A lot of good rest and good food and a spot of walking. Much love.

A big hello from Cargèse. We're taking it easy. It's heavenly. I've made loads of friends. Home at the end of the month.

We've fetched up in Enghien. Weather good. Canoeing on the lake. Nights in the casino. Fondest love.

We have a room at the Villa Blanche. Lots of lazing about and sleep. Really nice. We've got to know a very charming old couple. Back as expected on the 30th.

I'm staying at the Hôtel Odradek. They can't do too much for me. Very good simple food. Their sauna's lovely. A hug and a kiss for you all.

We're doing the Normandy coast. Weather good. We go to the beaches. I've taken lots of pictures of pillboxes. Will be in Toulouse on the 23rd.

We're touring around Corsica. Long siestas and samplings of regional specialities. We're putting on weight. Many regards.

A brief line from Quimperlé! We're sunning ourselves. Seafood galore. I've learnt to make crêpes. Many regards.

Here we are in Berck. Weather good. We go to the beach. We've made loads of friends. Home on the 14th in the evening.

We're at the Albergo della Francesca. Lots of lazing about and museums. Out of this world! I'm taking lots of photos. Many regards.

We're at the Hôtel du Midi. We sunbathe on the beach. We've made loads of friends. Return around the 2nd or 3rd.

We're visiting Romania. Magnificent weather. Their beaches are superb. I've got sunburnt. Hugs and kisses.

We're exploring Oléron. Charming. Long treks on horseback. Have to leave in 3 days' time, alas!

We're camping not far from Perros-Guirec. I've got sunburnt from staying on the beach. Love.

We've set up our tent near Winterthur. Weather warm. Really nice. We go on excursions. Friendly regards.

Our motel's name is La Tagada. Peace and quiet, and all that. There's a two-star place not far away where the guests are a bit much, boo-sucks! Kisses.

We're at the Hôtel Xanthippe. The sun's scorching on the beach. Many regards to all at the office.

We're travelling through Dalmatia. Heavenly weather. We've met stacks of French people! We eat remarkably good cheese. Fond regards.

We're really covering the Basque coast. Très intéressant. Really nice. Love.

A big greeting from Minorca. We sunbathe on the beach. I go skiing on the water. Home as late as possible!

We're camping near Huelva. We're relaxing like mad and gorging ourselves. I've got sunburnt. Fondest love.

We're at the Zimmerhof. Absolute peace. Sumptuous meals. The art gallery is wonderful. Will be in Paris for Louise's birthday.

Our hotel is called Les Sables d'Or. Weather good. Really comfortable! The people are very nice. Love.

We're exploring the Costa Brava. Weather good. We eat well. I've got sunburnt. Expect to return morning of the 17th.

We're visiting the Normandy islands. We sunbathe a bit on the beaches. We've made quite a few friends. Friendly regards.

News from the island of Yeu! I stayed a bit too long in the sun. But really nice all the same! Thinking of you.

A letter from Utrecht. It's very beautiful. We eat Indonesian. Super old houses! We'll be back on the 5th.

We have a room in the Pension Xenophilos. Lots of lazing about on the beach. Have made stacks of girl-friends. Will introduce them to you!

We're crossing Haiti. Weather ideal. Everything perfect. The people are very welcoming. Love.

We're travelling through the Lake District. Très romantique, but no risk of getting sunburnt. Home on the 19th.

Here we are in Ios. Heaps of us sunbathing all together. Really nice. Kisses.

We're ploughing the waters off York Island. We sunbathe on deck. Fish at every meal. I'm being introduced to sailing. Many regards to all, boys and girls.

On holiday in Varna. Out of this world! We're sunning ourselves. There's a fun bunch of lads here. Regards.

I'm at the Zauberberg. Weather good. We eat very well. We've met loads of interesting people. Hugs and kisses.

We're travelling along the Casamance Coast. Weather superb. I've got sunburnt, but it's super all the same! Back on the 4th.

There's a whole gang of us in southern Tunisia. The good life, barbecuing a whole sheep, and all the rest of it. Love.

We're roaming around in the Greek Islands. All the sea urchins we're eating! The people are being really nice to us. Yippee! And to think we've got to come home!

Taking a leisurely tour of Illyria. Beautiful beaches. Treks on mule-back. Much love.

Here we are at Sables-d'Or-les-Pins. It's so pleasant not doing anything! Long siestas on the beaches. Full of friendly types. We leave the day after tomorrow, alas.

Here we are in Gijón. Not a cloud in the sky. Paella every day. Lovely excursions. Fondest love.

We're at the Hôtel Napoli. Superb weather. We're on the beach all day long. I've made loads of girl-friends. Heading back to Armentières on the 22nd in the evening.

At the Pension Umberto our spirits are set fair. I've gone and got sunburnt! Kissy-wissies.

We're in the Aegean. Getting ourselves a tan. I go water skiing. It's smashing. Expect to return on the 11th.

Ploughing the Gulf of Taranto. La Dolce Vita! Beaches of fine sand. I've got sunburnt, worse luck. Thinking of you a lot.

A brief line from Tahiti. Lazing about and playing the ukulele. Paradise! I go riding. Friendly regards.

A brief line from Roscoff. Weather good. We eat very well. We've made some friends. Home on the 26th.

We've found a room at the Hôtel des Fleurs. Weather good. We go to the beach. You should see my sunburn! Many regards.

We're at the FitzJames. What a spread! A really cool bar. Home Monday.

We're travelling round the Peloponnese. Sun strong, I have a big hat, we're very happy. Hugs and kisses.

We're doing Senegal. Tired but enthusiastic. Nosh the only problem. We've been to a banana plantation. Will be in Paris on the 30th.

Here we are in Villablanca. We're going brown. Food very decent. I've put on weight. Hugs and kisses.

A brief greeting from Ouistreham. Weather good. Visits to the beaches. I go surfing. Thinking of you a lot.

We've found somewhere to stay at the Pension Wagner. Musical atmosphere. Exhilarating. We've met loads of very amusing people. We send you a great big kiss.

Greetings from the Karlsbad Hotel. Cure very pleasant. Exquisite food. I've lost a bit of weight. Many friendly regards.

There's a whole gang of us really covering Languedoc. Weather good. We go to the beaches. Thinking of you.

We're crossing Quiberon. Sweet inactivity. We eat very well. I'm getting a bit of a paunch. Love to you.

The latest from Dubrovnik. We're sunning ourselves. We eat chevapchitchi. I've made some pottery. Back on the 12th.

We're camping near Monastir. Gloriously sunny. Heavenly. I'm peeling. Love.

We're at the Hôtel du Golfe. Lots of lazing about and sleep. Quite a treat! I've been go-karting. Back around the 28th.

We have a room at the Etoile d'Or. Sunbathing sessions on the beach. Crowds of people, but very nice. Love to Pops and Mumsy.

We're rambling along the Côte. Ideal weather. We've discovered some cosy little calanques. Back on the 16th.

There's a whole gang of us touring around in the Cyclades. Magnificent. We're happy. Many regards.

A big hello from Trouville. Long sunbathing sessions. I'm as red as two lobsters. Many regards.

The latest from Xylos. Weather very good. Couldn't be nicer, and Jean goes riding. Home on the evening of the 12th.

Living at Louisette's. She's putting herself out for us and doing us proud with her cooking! Everyone joins with me in sending you our fond regards.

We're at the Bellevue. We stay on the beach for ever. I'm playing lots of volleyball. Back on the 20th.

Exploring the Pyrenees. Weather good. We eat very well (regional delicacies). The whole coach party send you their fondest love.

We're in Portugal. Beautiful! Really nice (despite the sunburn!). Back on the 27th.

The latest from Zarzis. There's a whole gang of us sunning ourselves on the beach. Hugs and kisses for you all.

Here we are at St-Jean-de-Monts. Lots of lazing about and eating seafood. Have got sunburnt. Many regards.

We're at the Hôtel de France. Nosh and service impeccable. I'm reading Proust. Kisses.

We're at the Hôtel Oscar Wilde. Lovely weather. The organization is perfect. The whole congress sends you its friendly regards.

We're travelling through Jutland. Weather good. Outings by horse and buggy, very nice. Thinking of you.

We're visiting Yugoslavia. There's a whole group of us. We do nothing on the beaches. Love.

A brief letter from Wingate. The sun's come along with us. It's all very very very nice. Coming back to Beauvais around the 24th.

Greetings from Juan-les-Pins. Lots of lazing about, top-notch grub and crumpet by the plateful who all send you a kiss.

We're at the Pension Le Joli Coin. Weather good. Nice. Yesterday we all went to see the caves. All the old folk from La Garenne join with me in sending you their friendly greetings.

I'm at the Continental. Impeccable. It's very hot. Tennis, riding, golf and the casino. Love.

We're in the Orkneys. It's very good. We've met lots of funny people. All very super. Back on the 10th.

We've landed near Yvetot. Lots of lazing about on the beach in the sun. Love.

News from the holidaymakers on Zyklos. Numerous and magnificent cases of sunburn consequent to overmuch basking on the sand! Many regards.

We're at the Vienna and Zimmerli. Lots of lazing about beside the lake, regattas and casino. Much love.

Weather sublime, high-quality food, delightful people. We're at the Hôtel de Gascogne. Thinking of you a lot.

We're playing at being explorers on the Atlantic Coast. Long sunbathing sessions. We eat just like the hogs we are. A thousand regards.

We're at the Pension Iglesias. The sun's shining. We eat outside even in the evenings. A thousand kind regards to you and your family.

*The Holy of Holies**

It's a long time since the word *bureau* has made us think of *bure*, or 'homespun', that rough brown woollen material from which they sometimes used to make table coverings, though it served mainly for monks' habits, and still evokes the harsh, rigorous life of Trappists and hermits at least as much as do sackcloth or hairshirts. Via a series of metonyms, we have moved from the aforesaid table-covering to the writing-table itself, then from the aforesaid table to the room it was installed in, then to the furnishings as a whole that comprised this room and finally to the activities carried out there, to the authority attaching to them, and even indeed to the services rendered there. Thus, if we explore the various usages of the term, we can speak of a *bureau de tabac* (tobacconist's shop), of a *bureau de poste* (post office), of the Deuxième Bureau (Government Intelligence Services), of a theatre playing *à bureaux fermés* (to members only), of a *bureau de vote* (polling station), of the Politburo, or quite simply of *bureaux* meaning 'offices', those uncertain places awash with badly fastened folders, die stamps, paper clips, sucked-on pencils, rubbers that no longer rub out, off-yellow envelopes, where generally surly clerks pass you on from one *bureau* to another by making you fill in forms, sign registers and await your turn.

We obviously shan't be concerned here with these anonymous offices crammed with pen-pushers, but rather with the directors' offices that are symbols of power or even of omnipotence, with the offices of the great and good, whether they be the Managing Directors of multinationals, magnates of high finance, advertising or the cinema, nabobs or Heads of State. In short, the Holy of Holies, the place barred to ordinary mortals, where those who, roughly speaking, govern us preside behind the triple rampart of

*First published in *Vogue Hommes* in September 1981.

their private secretary, their padded door and their pure wool carpeting.

In order to assume the crushing responsibilities incumbent upon them, the great and good don't really have need of much more than silence, calm and discretion. And of space perhaps, so as to be able to march up and down as they ponder deeply. And an intercom of course, on which to ask their secretary to call So-and-So, to cancel Thingummy, to remind them of their lunch with What's-his-name and the Concorde flight at five o'clock, to bring them their Alka Seltzer and to send them in Such-and-Such. Plus two or three armchairs for summit meetings. But nothing that might recall the harsh realities of Office Life or the complicated ins and outs of Bureaucracy: no typewriter, no pending files, no staplers, no pots of glue, no false cuffs (which, come to think of it, can't be so very common in our own day). For here it is a matter simply of thinking, of conceiving, deciding and negotiating, and this has nothing to do with all those subordinate tasks that the faithful carthorses will carry out scrupulously on the floors below.

It would be perfectly legitimate therefore to imagine these highly placed personages in offices that are almost empty, especially in view of the startling progress made by the still embryonic science to which the ghastly name of 'bureautique' has been given, which enables us from now on to conceive of offices without an office, where everything – or nearly everything – could be dealt with by a telephone or computer terminal plugged in anywhere at all – in a bathroom, on a yacht, or in a trapper's cabin somewhere in Alaska.

Nevertheless, the offices of MDs and other bigwigs are seldom empty. But if the furnishings, equipment, instruments and accessories they contain don't always have a lot to do with the functions that are exercised there, they still obey a profound necessity: that of incarnating, of representing the Man who inhabits them and who has selected them as the very indicators of his status, prestige and power. Before they are offices, these are the signs, the emblems, the signatures by means of which these VIPs mean effectively to signify to their interlocutors (and, if need be, to their collaborators) that they are VIPs and, as such, unique, irreplaceable and exemplary.

From this starting-point, countless variations are possible. Between the rigorously classical and the sensibly modern, the severe and the superfluous, the monastic and the lordly, the paterfamilias and the go-getter, the American look and English chic, the daddy's boy and the young wolf, the starched collar and the I-was-a-hippy-myself-once, one might begin to rough out a whole typology of superior intelligences (or ones believing themselves to be so) merely by observing their offices. One will manifest his respect for immemorial values by choosing an inlaid desk and a glass-fronted bookcase filled with bound volumes; another will play at being the genius-on-the-boil, Einstein-style, and clutter his space with punch-balls, strip cartoons, playing cards and dwarf tortoises; a third will signal his sense of boldness by entrusting the improvement of his officescape to an Italian designer mad on stands made from basalt, lava and matt anodized steel; a fourth will give you to understand that his IQ is notably higher than the average by carelessly leaving lying about a few treatises on ergodics or plagiology; a fifth will insinuate that he might well have been a Maecenas by hanging in some prominent place a canvas by Max Ernst, unless that is he puts on show the medals and diplomas won by his firm, the portrait of the grandfather who founded the business, or the 71lb barracuda he brought back from San Domingo in 1976.

There are spartan offices and debonair offices, laboratory-like offices where the 'work surface' is a huge expanse of grey metal graced by a few controls which cause James Bondish gadgets to appear as if by magic, boudoir-offices and plush offices, piously old-fashioned offices, fake-retro or false rococo, offices weighed down by age, imposing offices, welcoming offices, offices that are like refrigerators.

But whether they privilege order or disorder, the useful or the useless, the grandiose or the easy-going, all are the actual space of power of the great and good. It is from these offices of steel, glass or rare woods that the MDs will launch their decisive takeover bids, that the kings of gruyère cheese will set out to assault the ballpoint pen magnates, that the Belgian barons will swallow whole the Bavarian brewers, that CBS will buy up NBC,

TWA KLM and IBM ITT. And that will continue to be the way things are for a long time to come; unless one day, in the depths of one of these silent, padded offices, a hand presses down on a small red button and sets in train some foolish event . . .

*Attempt at an Inventory of the Liquid and Solid Foodstuffs Ingurgitated by Me in the Course of the Year Nineteen Hundred and Seventy-Four**

Nine beef consommés, one iced cucumber soup, one mussel soup.

Two Guéméné andouilles, one jellied andouillette, one Italian charcuterie, one cervelas sausage, four assorted charcuteries, one coppa, three pork platters, one figatelli, one foie gras, one fromage de tête, one boar's head, five Parma hams, eight pâtés, one duck pâté, one pâté de foie with truffles, one pâté en croûte, one pâté grand-mère, one thrush pâté, six pâtés des Landes, four brawns, one foie gras mousse, one pig's trotters, seven rillettes, one salami, two saucissons, one hot saucisson, one duck terrine, one chicken liver terrine.

One blini, one empanada, one dried beef.
Three snails.

One Belon oysters, three coquilles St-Jacques, one shrimps, one shrimp croustade, one friture, two baby eel fritures, one herring, two oysters, one mussels, one stuffed mussels, one sea-urchins, two quenelles au gratin, three sardines in oil, five smoked salmons, one tarama, one eel terrine, six tunas, one anchovy toast, one crab.

Four artichokes, one asparagus, one aubergines, one mushroom salad, fourteen cucumber salads, four cucumbers à la crème, fourteen celery rémoulades, two Chinese cabbages, one palm hearts, eleven assiette de crudités, two haricot vert salads, thirteen melons, two salades niçoises, two dandelion salads with bacon, fourteen

*First published in *Action Poétique* in 1976.

radishes with butter, three black radishes, five rice salads, one Russian salad, seven tomato salads, one onion tart.

One Roquefort croquette, five croque-monsieurs, three quiche Lorraines, one Maroilles tart, one yoghourt with cucumber and grapes, one Romanian yoghourt.

One torti salad with crab and Roquefort.

One eggs with anchovy, two boiled eggs, two eggs en meurette, one ham and eggs, one bacon and eggs, one eggs en cocotte with spinach, two eggs in aspic, two scrambled eggs, four omelettes, one sort of omelette, one soya-seed omelette, one craterellus omelette, one duck skin omelette, one confit d'oie omelette, one herb omelette, one Parmentier omelette.

Two haddocks, one sea-bass, one skate, one sole, one tuna.

One flank of sirloin, three flanks of sirloin with shallots, ten steaks, two steak au poivres, three steak and chips, one rump steak à la moutarde, five roast beefs, two ribs of beef, two top rumpsteaks, three beef grillades, two chateaubriands, one steak tartare, one rosbif, three cold rosbifs, fourteen entrecôtes, three entrecôtes à la moelle, one fillet of beef, three hamburgers, nine skirts of beef, one plate of beef.

Four pot-au-feus, one daube, one jellied daube, one braised beef, one beef mode, one beef gros sel, one beef à la ficelle.

One braised veal with noodles, one sauté of veal, one veal chop, one veal chop with pasta shells, one 'veal entrecôte', six escalopes, six escalope milanaises, three escalope à la crèmes, one escalope with morels, four blanquette de veaus.

Five andouillettes, three black puddings, one black pudding with apples, one pork cutlet, two sauerkrauts, one Nancy sauerkraut, one pork chop, eleven pairs of frankfurters, two pork grillades, seven pigs' trotters, one cold pork, three roast porks, one roast pork with pineapple and bananas, one pork sausage with haricots.

One milk-fed lamb, three lamb cutlets, two curried lambs, twelve gigots, one saddle of lamb.

One mutton cutlet, one shoulder of mutton.

Five chickens, one chicken kebab, one chicken au citron, one chicken en cocotte, two chicken basquaises, three cold chickens, one stuffed chicken, one chicken with chestnuts, one chicken aux herbes, two jellied chickens.

Seven poules au riz, one poule au pot.

One pullet au riz.

One coq au riesling, three coq au vins, one coq au vinaigre.

One duck with olives, one duck magret.

One guinea-fowl salmis.

One guinea-fowl with cabbage, one guinea-fowl with noodles.

Five rabbits, two rabbits en gibelotte, one rabbit with noodles, one rabbit à la crème, three rabbits à la moutarde, one rabbit chasseur, one rabbit à l'estragon, one rabbit à la tourangelle, three rabbits with plums.

Two young wild rabbits with plums.

One civet of hare à l'alsacienne, one hare daube, one hare stew, one saddle of hare.

One wild pigeon salmis.

One kidney kebab, three kebabs, one mixed-grill, one kidneys à la moutarde, one calves' kidneys, three têtes de veau, eleven calves' livers, one calves' tongue, one ris de veau with pommes sarladaises, one ris de veau terrine, one lamb's brains, two fresh goose livers with grapes, one goose gizzards confit, two chicken livers.

Twelve cold cuts, two assiette anglaises, *n* cold buffets, two couscous, three 'chinese', one moulakhia, one pizza, one pan bagnat, one tahina, six sandwiches, one ham sandwich, one rillette sandwich, three Cantal sandwiches.

One ceps, one kidney beans, seven haricot verts, one sweetcorn, one mashed cauliflower, one mashed spinach, one mashed fennel, two stuffed peppers, two pommes frites, nine gratin dauphinois, four mashed potatoes, one pommes dauphine, one pommes boulangère, one pommes soufflées, one roast potatoes, one sautée potatoes, four rices, one wild rice.

Four pasta, three pasta shells, one fettucini à la crème, one macaroni cheese, one macaroni, fifteen fresh noodles, three rigatonis, two raviolis, four spaghettis, one tortellini, five tagliatelle verdes.

Thirty-five green salads, one mesclun salad, one Treviso salad à la crème, two chicory salads.

Seventy-five cheeses, one ewe's milk cheese, two Italian cheeses, one Auvergne cheese, one Boursin, two Brillat-Savarins, eleven Bries, one Cabécou, four goats' milk cheeses, two crottins, eight Camemberts, fifteen Cantals, one Sicilian cheeses, one Sardinian cheeses, one Epoisses, one Murols, three fromages blancs, one fromage blanc de chèvre, nine Fontainebleaus, five mozzarellas, five Munsters, one Reblochon, one Swiss raclette, one Stilton, one Saint-Marcellin, one Saint-Nectaire, one yoghourt.

One fresh fruit, two strawberries, one gooseberries, one orange, three mendiants.

One stuffed dates, one pears in syrup, three pears in wine, two peaches in wine, one pêche de vigne in syrup, one peaches in Sancerre, one apples normande, one bananas flambées.

Four stewed fruit, two stewed apples, two stewed rhubarb and quetsch.

Five clafoutis, four pear clafoutis.

One figs in syrup.

Six fruit salads, one tropical fruit salad, two orange salads, two strawberry, raspberry and gooseberry salads.

One apple pie, four tarts, one hot tart, ten tarts Tatin , seven pear tarts, one pear tart Tatin, one lemon tart, one apple and nut tart, two apple tarts, one apple tart meringue, one strawberry tart.

Two crêpes.

Two charlottes, three chocolate charlottes.

Three babas.

One crème renversée.

One galette des rois.

Nine chocolate mousses.

Two floating islands.

One bilberry kugelhupf.

Four chocolate gâteaux, one cheese gâteau, two orange gâteaux, one Italian gâteau, one Viennese gâteau, one Breton gâteau, one gâteau au fromage blanc, one vatrushki.

Three ice-creams, one green lemon sorbet, two guava sorbets, two pear sorbets, one chocolate profiterolles, one raspberry melba, one pear belle-hélène.

Thirteen Beaujolais, four Beaujolais Nouveau, three Brouillys, seven Chiroubles, four Chenas, two Fleuries, one Juliénas, three Saint-Amours.

Nine Côtes-du-Rhônes, nine Châteauneuf-du-Papes, one Châteauneuf-du-Pape '67, three Vaqueyras.

Nine Bordeaux, one Bordeaux Clairet, one Lamarzelle '64, three Saint-Emilions, one Saint-Emilion '61, seven Château-la Pelleterie '70s, one Château-Canon '62, five Château-Négrits, one Lalande-de-Pomerol, one Lalande-de-Pomerol '67, one Médoc '64, six Margaux '62s, one Margaux '68, one Margaux '69, one Saint-Estèphe '61, one Saint-Julien '59.

Seven Savigny-lès-Beaunes, three Aloxe-Cortons, one Aloxe-Corton '66, one Beaune '61, one white Chasagne-Montrachet '66, two Mercureys, one Pommard, one Pommard '66, two Santenay '62s, one Volnay '59.

One Chambolle-Musigny '70, one Chambolle-Musigny Les Amoureuses '70, one Chambertin '62, one Romanée-Conti, one Romanée-Conti '64.

One Bergerac, two red Bouzys, four Bourgueils, one Chalosse, one champagne, one Chablis, one red Côtes-de-Provence, twenty-six Cahors, one Chanteperdrix, four Gamays, two Madirans, one Madiran '70, one Pinot Noir, one Passetoutgrain, one Pécharmant, one Saumur, ten Tursans, one Traminer, one Sardinian wine, *n* miscellaneous wines.

Nine beers, two Tuborgs, four Guinnesses.

Fifty-six Armagnacs, one Bourbon, eight Calvadoses, one cherries in brandy, six Green Chartreuses, one Chivas, four cognacs, one Delamain cognac, two Grand Marniers, one pink-gin, one Irish coffee, one Jack Daniel's, four marcs, three Bugey marcs, one marc de Provence, one plum liqueur, nine Souillac plums, one plums in brandy, two Williams pears, one port, one slivovitz, one Suze, thirty-six vodkas, four whiskies.

N coffees
one tisane
three Vichy waters

from *L.G.* (1992)

*Robert Antelme or the Truth of Literature**

The literature of the concentration camps does not get attacked. The moment a book speaks of the camps, or even, more generally, of Nazism, it's more or less assured of being everywhere received with a certain sympathy. Even those who don't like it won't want to say hard things about it. At worst it won't be spoken of at all. You might go so far as to say that it's indecent to link the world of the camps with what is called, if need be with a faint note of disdain, 'literature'.

Yet it seems that such an attitude is often ambiguous. The literature of the camps is most often seen merely as a useful or even necessary testimony, as a precious, indeed indispensable and upsetting document on the 'atmosphere' of the time: the war, the Liberation, the 'turning-point of our civilization'. But it's clear that a careful distinction is being drawn between books like these and 'real' literature. To the point where we no longer quite know whether underlying this attitude is the fact that we feel too great a respect (or have too bad a conscience) faced with the phenomenon of the camps, to the extent of believing that such expression as literature can give to it will only ever be inauthentic and ineffective, or whether we believe that the experience of a deportee is unable, in itself, to give rise to a work of art. We don't quite know whether it is literature that we look down on, in the name of the concentration camps, or the concentration camps, in the name of literature. However that may be, this twofold attitude accounts

*First published in *Partisans* in 1962. At the time when he wrote *L'Espèce humaine*, Robert Antelme was the husband of the novelist Marguerite Duras. She helped nurse him back to health but then left him for another left-wing writer, Denys Mascolo. This essay dates to a time when Perec was more political in his outlook than he subsequently became.

for more or less the totality of the actual audience and the actual impact – falsified and superficial – of camp literature.

But literature is not an activity separated from life. We live in a world of words, of language, of stories. Writing is not the privilege exclusively of the man who sets aside for his century a brief hour of conscientious immortality each evening and lovingly fashions, in the silence of his study, what others will later proclaim, solemnly, to be 'the honour and integrity of our letters'. Literature is indissolubly bound up with life, it is the necessary prolongation, the obvious culmination, the indispensable complement of experience. All experience opens on to literature and all literature on to experience, and the path that leads from one to the other, whether it be literary creation or reading, establishes this relationship between the fragmentary and the whole, this passage from the anecdotal to the historical, this interplay between the general and the particular, between what is felt and what is understood, which form the very tissue of our consciousness.

For the returning deportee, to speak, to write, is a need as strong and immediate as is his need for calcium, for sugar, sunlight, meat, sleep and silence. It's not the case that he can remain silent and forget. He has first of all to remember. He has to explain, to tell, to dominate that world whose victim he was.

'In the first days following our return,' writes Robert Antelme, 'we were all of us, I think, prey to a veritable delirium. We wanted to speak, to be heard finally. We were told that our physical appearance was sufficiently eloquent in itself. But we had just come back, we had brought our memory back with us, our living experience, and we felt a frantic desire to tell it just as it was.'

This is when the problems arise. The need is to testify as to what the world of the camps was like. But what is a testimony? At the time when Robert Antelme was sitting down to write, the contents page of just about every review contained an episode, or a document, or a testimony concerning the camps. They were being recounted and made manifest in dozens of books.

But it happens that testimony can be mistaken, or can fail. In the end, people display the same attitudes towards books about the camps as they do towards the camps themselves: they clench their fists, grow indignant, are moved. But they attempt neither to understand, nor to think more deeply about them. The Americans who liberated Robert Antelme in Dachau said 'Frightful', and left it at that. And Micheline Maurel, in *Un camp très ordinaire*, tells us that the question most frequently put to her when she came back was 'Were you raped?' That was the one question that truly interested people, the only one that fitted in with their notion of terror. Beyond that there was nothing, they didn't understand, couldn't imagine. They stopped short at a facile compassion. In every case, whether it was monotonous or spectacular, the horror numbed them. The testimonies were ineffective; stupefaction, stunned amazement or anger became the normal modes of reading. But those who wrote sought to go further than that. They didn't want to evoke pity, tenderness or revolt. It was a matter of making people understand what they couldn't understand, of expressing what was inexpressible.

'Right from the start,' writes Robert Antelme,

> it seemed to us impossible to overcome the distance we discovered between the language available to us and this experience which, for the most part, we were still continuing in our bodies. How could we resign ourselves to not trying to explain how we had reached this state? We were still in it. Yet it was impossible. The moment we began to recount we felt suffocated. Even to ourselves what we had to tell then began to appear *unimaginable*. And the passage of time only confirmed this disproportion between the experience we had lived through and the account it was possible to give of it. We had to deal indeed with one of those realities which make people say that they exceed the imagination. It was clear from then on that it was only through choice, through the imagination that is, that we could try and say something about it.

We think we know the camps because we have seen, or think we have seen, the watchtowers, the barbed wire, the gas chambers. Because we think we know the number of dead. But statistics never speak. We make no difference between a thousand dead and a hundred thousand. Photographs, souvenirs, gravestones, tell us nothing. In Munich, tourist signs invite you to visit Dachau. But the huts are empty and clean, the grass is growing.

We think we know what the terrible is: a 'terrible' event, a 'terrible' story. It has a beginning, a culminating moment, an end. But we understand nothing. We don't understand the unendingness of hunger. Emptiness. Absence. The body eating itself away. The word 'nothing'. We don't know the camps.

Facts don't speak for themselves, it's an error to think that they do. Or, if they speak, we have to persuade ourselves that we can't hear them, or, more seriously still, that we aren't hearing them aright. In the main the literature of the camps has made this error. It has succumbed to the temptation characteristic of the naturalistic, historico-social novel (the ambition to paint a 'fresco'), and has piled up facts, has multiplied the exhaustive descriptions of episodes it believed to be intrinsically meaningful. But they weren't so. They weren't so for us. We were not involved. We remained strangers to that world, which was a fragment of history that had unfolded somewhere beyond us.

To get us to respond to the world of the camps – that is, to turn what had affected him into something that might affect us, and exhaust his particular experience by making it ours – Robert Antelme elaborates and transforms the facts, themes and circumstances of his deportation by integrating them into a specific literary framework, whereas the other accounts of the camps had used an elementary framework hardly differing from that of the novel. In the first place, he chose to reject any appeal to spectacle or to the immediately emotive, over which it would be too easy for the reader to pause.

He is aided in this, admittedly, by the circumstances of his particular experience, his detention having been spent for the most part in quite a minor Kommando. But his rejection of anything outsized or apocalyptic is in fact part of a determination that governs the organization of his story right down to its smallest details, and which gives it its specific colouring: a desire for simplicity, for a previously unknown everydayness, which goes so far as to *betray* the 'reality' in order to express it more effectively and prevent us from finding it 'unbearable'. Thus it is that we shall learn almost nothing, and then only very late on in the book, of what it meant for Antelme, himself still unharmed, to discover the walking skeletons that were the deportees of slightly longer standing. In every other work about the camps, this is a privileged episode, but such a sudden, limitless discovery of suffering and terror doesn't reveal the camp as it purports to do, and as it in effect *did* for the new arrivals. In the reader it can only evoke a falsified compassion that barely disguises a refusal, pure and simple.

This refusal of compassion goes further still. The world of the camp is held at a distance. Robert Antelme refuses to treat of his experience as a whole, as given once and for all, as a matter of course, eloquent in itself. He breaks it up. He questions it. It might be enough for him to *evoke*, just as it might be enough to display his sores without commenting on them. But between his experience and ourselves, he interposes the whole grid of a discovery, of a memory, of a consciousness that goes to the limit.

Implicit in the other accounts is the *evidence* of the camp, the horror, the evidence of a whole world, shut in on itself, which is restored en bloc. But in *L'Espèce humaine* ['Humankind'], the camp is never a given. It imposes itself, it emerges gradually. It is the mud, then hunger, then cold, then the beatings, hunger again, fleas. Then all of them at once. The waiting and the solitude. The dereliction. The destitution of the body, the insults. The barbed wire and the brutality. The exhaustion. The faces of the SS, of the Kapo, of the Meister. The whole of Germany, the whole horizon: the universe, eternity.

There are no hangings or crematoria. There are no ready-made images, reassuring in their very violence. There isn't in *L'Espèce humaine* a single 'horror image'. Instead there is time dragging itself out, a chronology that hesitates, a present moment that persists, hours that never end, moments of vacancy and unconsciousness, days without a date, brief instants of an 'individual destiny', hours of abandonment: 'It seemed that midday would never come, that the war would never end . . .'

There are no *explanations*. But nor is there one fact which is not transcended, not transformed, not integrated into a much vaster perspective. Whatever the event, it is always accompanied by a becoming aware, as the world of the camp is broadened and unveiled. There is no fact that does not become exemplary. The account is forever breaking off and awareness infiltrates the anecdote, giving it density: the particular moment in the camp becomes dreadfully heavy, takes on meaning, exhausts the camp for a moment then opens out into another memory.

This continual interplay between memory and awareness, between the experimental and the exemplary, between the anecdotal tissue of an event and its global interpretation, between the description of a phenomenon and the analysis of a mechanism, this constant setting of the memory into perspective, this projection of the particular into the general and the general into the particular, these are methods specific to literary creation inasmuch as they organize the raw material, invent a style, and reveal a certain kind of relationship between the elements of the story: a hierarchization, an integration, a progression. They serve to shatter the immediate, ineffective picture we make for ourselves of the reality of the camps. Here, they appear for the very first time detached from their most conventional meanings, challenged, put to the question, scattered, revealed bit by bit through a series of mediations that go to the very heart of our response, without our being able to escape them.

The essential principle of the concentration camp system was everywhere the same: negation. This might involve instant extermination, but that in the end was the simplest case. More often, it was a slow destruction, an elimination. The deportee had to become faceless, to be nothing but skin stretched over protruding bones. He had to be attacked and worn down by cold, by fatigue, by hunger: to demean himself and to regress. He had to offer the spectacle of a degenerate humanity, searching in dustbins and eating peelings or grass. He had to have fleas, scabies, be covered in vermin. He had to be nothing but vermin himself. Then Germany would have the concrete proof of its superiority.

The SS used all known means of oppression. The commonest and most effective was to put common criminals – swindlers, murderers, sadists – in with the political deportees, so that, once mixed in with the 'bandits', the enemy, too, became 'bandits'.

The lives of a certain number of intermediaries – Lagerältester,

Kapos, Vorarbeiter, etc. – were saved by the bureaucracy of the camps, where hierarchization was carried to an extreme and responsibilities were shared out in such a way as to enable a limited number of SS guards to reign over a mass of detainees. In a certain number of camps – mainly the larger ones – the political deportees were of longer standing and more self-aware and, after months or even years of struggle, they took control of the key posts. They succeeded in establishing a legal system, or form of discipline, within the system of the camp which worked against the jurisdiction of the SS because it involved a total and effective solidarity among the detainees. Directives were either not applied or diverted from their original intentions; the detainees in the greatest danger were protected; the most dangerous were eliminated.

In Buchenwald, a town of 40,000 inhabitants, the undercover international organization controlled all the activities of the camp. In Gandersheim, a Kommando of five hundred men, as in most of the small Kommandos, the common criminals carried the day.

Having common criminals in control of the camp meant that the jurisdiction of the SS was aggravated rather than frustrated. It meant, for example, that discipline was made impossible so that the Kapo could *restore* it with his truncheon, to demonstrate that he was different in essence from whoever he was beating and thereby deserved to live and even to prosper. Or, to give another example, that international solidarity was made impossible, with one nationality being set against others, French against Italians, Russians against Poles; in the ensuing battles any sense of a common enemy was lost, so aiding the manoeuvrings of the Kapos.

'At Gandersheim there was no gas chamber or crematorium,' writes Robert Antelme. 'The horror was not on any huge scale. The horror lay in the obscurity, the complete absence of landmarks, the solitude, the ceaseless oppression, the slow annihilation.' Here we have the definition of the typical camp: this is the mechanism of the camps laid bare. The oppression recognized no limits, the deportee no refuge.

Gandersheim was the least particularized of the camps. The risks there were the most modest, the chances the least great. There were no instruments of death, no hangings, no torture. But there was nothing that might enable them to live. The political organization ensured the safety of a certain percentage of the camp's population. Rule by the criminal element meant any organization was out of the question. 'It became impossible to get a bit more food for those comrades who were sinking too fast. Impossible to hide the ones assigned to work that was too hard for them. Impossible to use the *revier* and the *schonung* as happened in other camps.'*

Solidarity is neither a metaphysical given nor a categorical imperative. It is linked to precise circumstances. It is necessary to the survival of a group because it ensures that group's cohesiveness, and it only has to be outlawed for the world of the camps to appear in all its logic. *L'Espèce humaine*, being an *everyday* description, is also the most general description of a camp. The world of the camps is defined less by an immediate, massive extermination, by 'cullings', than by days, months, years of hunger, cold and terror. The accounts given by David Rousset (*Les Jours de notre mort*) and Jean Laffitte (*Ceux qui vivent*) applied to the metropolises, to the vast sorting offices of Buchenwald, Dachau and Mauthausen, where sometimes all-powerful organizations waged an undercover campaign that was both real and effective. But there the mechanism of the camps appears in a false light. We see it through privileged eyes. We know nothing of its precise effect on an isolated individual, yet it is that effect alone that can concern us, that we can be made to respond to. Jean Laffitte's testimony in particular may remain valid at the level of a political experience – it was indispensable even, in 1947, that he should have restored it to us – but it is constantly being falsified by his populist and nationalistic glorification of the struggle, by the description he gives of the camp, by the simplistic, even mystificatory, view he takes – one chapter is entitled 'Visions of terror' and the one after that 'The good times'.

'Total oppression, total destitution,' writes Robert Antelme, 'risk casting everyone into a quasi-solitude. Class-consciousness and a spirit of solidarity are the expression still of a certain well-being

*These two German terms describe the ways in which camp inmates might be spared some of its rigours on grounds of sickness, etc.

surviving among the oppressed. But although it was occasionally reawakened, there was every chance of the consciousness of the political detainees becoming a solitary one. Yet, even though solitary, that consciousness continued to resist. Deprived of the bodies of others, and progressively of one's own body, there was life still for each of us to will to defend.'

Survival, naturally, was a matter of luck. But luck in the end explains nothing. In Robert Antelme's detention there were moments he was unable to control. That he didn't die then was attributable to good fortune, to some purely automatic reaction, or to someone else's unhoped-for gesture. Of other moments he remained master and then he triumphed over death. *L'Espèce humaine* is the story of that triumph.

'Normal' life ignores death. 'We each of us work and eat, knowing we are mortal, but it isn't the piece of bread in its immediacy that causes death to retreat.' It was precisely in this, however, that the deportee was affected. Because everything is being done to make him die, because that is the objective chosen for him by the SS, his life merges with the effort he makes so as not to die. To survive and to live is all the same, in a single willing of the body not to succumb.

Survival is in the first instance a phenomenon of consciousness. It is an 'almost biological claim to membership of the human species', a becoming aware of your body as an irreducible totality, a discovery of yourself as an indestructible singularity. To the omnipotent, omnipresent necessity of death, must be opposed the necessity of life. Just as, everywhere and always, you must 'watch out for the moment of calm that comes . . . must sit down anywhere at all, settle yourself, if only for an instant,' so, everywhere and always, you must 'provoke', must 'interrogate' space, objects, other people. You must deny the jurisdiction of the SS, show it up for the joke it is, its futility, its immediate and total impossibility, its ultimate demise.

The SS guard, 'a God with the face of an old sweat', lived in a world where he was all-powerful. But that power was a delusion. The SS man couldn't do everything. The deportee soon found that he had real power only over him, the deportee; he remained without power over nature, over things. The railway trucks eluded him, and the tree-bark, and the clouds. The whistle of a locomotive was an order to which he had to submit, *just like everyone else.* He couldn't escape it, couldn't impose his jurisdiction on it.

The SS guard had no power over anything that wasn't a man. But even over men his power soon collapsed:

The SS guard stops, he is weary. The pals are standing there. He goes up to them, stares fixedly at them. He has no desire to make them do anything else, he stares hard at them and doesn't manage to discover any other desire in himself. He has a momentary outburst and finds they are still there, out of breath but intact, in front of him. He hasn't caused them to disappear. To stop them staring at him he would have to bring out his revolver, to kill them. He remains for a moment staring at them. No one moves. The silence has been made by him. He shakes his head. He is the stronger, but they are there, and in order for him to be the stronger they have to be there; he can't get away from that.

Everything gives the SS guard away. His powerlessness is glaring. Unable to do everything, he can no longer do anything. He is possessed. He remains powerless before language, and before memory. He has no power over Sundays, or over sleep. He can't cancel the nights altogether. He can do nothing against the west wind, against the West, against the planes flying over Germany, against the sound of the guns. He can't halt History.

The 'burning frontier' of barbed wire that divides the camp from the innocent space of the German countryside is supposed to separate two worlds. There is the normal world, normal life, the life of houses, chairs, shops, the life in which whoever says 'I'm going out' actually does so. And the other one, the forbidden world, the world of death, ruled over by the skull and crossbones of the SS badge and inhabited by abject beings, vermin, the enemies of Germany, 'bandits', shit.

But these two worlds are a lie; they won't let themselves be separated:

The obvious falsity of everything in the countryside, which we had been so aware of when being brought from Buchenwald, now became a provocation. That man's false respectability, the falsehood of his unctuous face and his civilian house were horrible. The revelation of the SS guards' blind fury, displayed without compunction, aroused less hatred perhaps than the falsehood of the Nazi bourgeoisie, who sustained that fury, and who coddled it, nourishing it with their blood and their 'values'.

There weren't two worlds, but only men trying desperately to deny other men. But it was that above all which was impossible:

Here, animals were a luxury, trees divinities, but we could not become either animals or trees. We couldn't and the guards couldn't bring us to that. And it is at the very moment when the mask has taken on the most hideous features, the moment it is about to become our own face, that it falls ... The worst victim can but acknowledge that, even when exercised at its worst, the power of the executioner can be no more than one of the powers of man in general: the power to murder. He may kill a man but he can't turn him into something else.

It is this claim to membership of the species, this awareness that our fundamental humanity cannot be contested, which gives meaning and direction to the effort to survive, which guides it. It calls for a new sense of solidarity, no longer active, the role of the Kapos being to forbid that, but an implicit solidarity, born of what the deportees undergo *together*. It is the basis for a new relationship between the deportee and his own body, with his singularity, with his individual history (his past and his memory, his present, and his possible future), and with others. It projects the sharp light of a more universal system on to the system of the camps, the system of the exploitation of one man by another, from which can be recovered the meaning of the struggle and of its effectiveness:

The most despised member of the proletariat is offered a rationale. He is less alone than the man who despises him, whose space will become more and more exiguous and who will inexorably become more and more solitary, more and more powerless. Their insults can no longer take hold of us, any more than they can take hold of the nightmare that we are in their heads. We are constantly denied, but we are still there.

... The experience of the man who eats peelings is one of the ultimate situations of resistance. It is none other than the extreme experience of the proletarian condition. It is all there: the contempt first of all on the part of those constraining him to that state, who do all they can to maintain it, in such a way that this state appears to account for the whole person of the oppressed man and thereby justifies the oppressor. On the other hand, the determination to eat in order to live is to lay claim to the highest human values . . . Many have eaten peelings. They certainly weren't aware for the most part of the greatness it is possible to discover in that act. Rather they responded to it as to a crowning degradation. But to gather up peelings was not to be degraded, any more than the member of the proletariat is degraded, the 'sordid materialist' who is determined to stake his claim and will not rest from the struggle to bring about his own liberation and the liberation of all.

It was in this unity, this awareness, that the SS guards were to become lost. This it was that they were unable to understand: in a world given over to degradation, degradation became a human value. The man who still has a face, who has muscles, who eats his fill, is and can only be a murderer. Never has the *human form* of the man who has succeeded in keeping a truthful face concealed so gigantic a lie. Never have boils, sores or grey skulls concealed so great a strength: 'We were alive, we were so much detritus, but it was now that our reason triumphed. True, it didn't show. But we have all the more reason when you have less chance of seeing any trace of it . . . Make no mistake: you have succeeded in turning reason into consciousness. You have remade the unity of man. You have manufactured an irreducible consciousness.'

L'Espèce humaine restores to us the trace of the road that Robert Antelme travelled, and which enabled him to survive, by questioning and contesting the world of the camps. Events occurred, facts, which were ground up by time and submerged by memory. Days and nights went by, grew blurred. These were weeks and months when they walked in their sleep.

When he came back, Robert Antelme undertook to write. For his return to have a meaning, and his survival to become a victory, a coherence needed to emerge from this confused, undifferentiated, unapproachable mass, which was by turns a vast machine and a lamentable everyday experience, a coherence that might unify and rank his memories, and endow what he had lived through with its necessity.

This turning of an experience into language, and the possible relationship between our sensibility and a world that annihilates it, appear today as the most perfect example of what literature is capable of being out of all that is currently being produced in France. Writing today seems to believe, increasingly, that its true object is to mask, not to unveil. We are invited on all sides to have a sense of mystery, of the inexplicable. The inexpressible is a value. The unsayable is a dogma. No sooner are everyday gestures described than they become lies. Words are traitors. Between the lines we are invited to read that inaccessible end towards which every genuine writer owes it to himself to tend: silence. No one seeks to disentangle reality, to advance, be it only step by step, to understand. The proliferation of the world is a trap in which we allow ourselves to be snared. Its accumulated sensations exhaust reality: neither the world nor words have any meaning. Literature has lost its authority. It searches in the world for the signs of its defeat: angst oozes out from bare walls, from moorlands, from corridors, from petrified palaces, from impossible memories, from vacant stares. The world is congealed, placed between parentheses.

But it isn't possible to avoid the world. History is not, as Joyce said, 'a nightmare I am trying to wake up from'. We have no other life to live. Even if this life was, for Robert Antelme, that of the camps. It is more immediate to see the camps as a horrible world the possibility of whose existence we can never succeed fully in understanding. But it did exist. It is more immediate and reassuring to see in the world of today something that we cannot be master of. But this world exists. And the famous so-called 'Kafkaesque' world, in which we are overquick to see a brilliant prefiguration of our great modern 'cataclysms', takes no account of it, inferring from it instead an everlasting malediction, a metaphysical angst, a prohibition bearing down on the human 'condition'. But that's not the point.

We don't have to disengage from the world or want it to elude us simply because, in given circumstances, in a history that is ours, we may happen to think we will never be able to grasp it. A relatively privileged portion of our planet knows, or thinks it knows, the angst of history, of the times that stubbornly refuse to resemble the image we persist in forming of them, the angst of a monstrous technology ('will it kill off mankind?'), of memory and of time passing. But we don't put the questions that need to be put in the right way.

We are mistaken. We can dominate the world. Robert Antelme provides us with an irrefutable example of that. This man who recounts and who questions, who fights with the means that have been left to him, who extirpates their secrets from events, and refuses their silence, who defines and opposes, who restores and rewards, has given literature back a direction it had lost. At the heart of *L'Espèce humaine*, the wish to speak and to be heard, the wish to explore and to know, opens out into that unbounded confidence in language and writing that is the basis of all literature, even if, given its intentions, and because of the fate our culture reserves for what is known as 'testimony', *L'Espèce humaine* does not wholly succeed in becoming part of 'literature'. For it is language that throws a bridge between the world and ourselves, language that transcends the world by expressing the inexpressible, and establishes that fundamental relation between the individual and History out of which comes our freedom.

At this level, language and signs become decipherable once again. The world is no longer that chaos which words void of meaning despair of describing. It is a living, difficult reality that the power of words gradually overcomes. This is how literature begins, when, in and through language, the transformation begins – which is far from self-evident and far from immediate – that enables an individual to become aware, by expressing the world and by addressing others. By its movement, its method and finally by its content, *L'Espèce humaine* defines the truth of literature and the truth of the world.

from *Cantatrix Sopranica L.* (1991)

A Scientific and Literary Friendship: Léon Burp and Marcel Gotlib

followed by

*Further Reflections on the Life and Work of Romuald Saint-Sohaint**

The recent award of the Nobel Prize for Experimental Botany to Marcel Gotlib, his triumphant election to the Lille-Roubaix-Tourcoing Academy of Sciences and his appointment as Plenipotentiary Counsellor for Social, Scientific and Cultural Affairs to the European Assembly, are concrete proof of the unanimously high esteem in which, for a number of years, the life's work of this indefatigable researcher has been held, who in the course of his dazzling career has, with an equal genius, blown wide open the major problem areas of contemporary science in most of the key disciplines, from group dynamics to quantum theory, from rural sociology to prehistoric musicology and from cellular anthropology to combinatory physiology. Receiving him last Friday beneath the Cupola,† Leprince-Ringuet was right when he said:

> You have been able to give a decisive impulsion to researches which had previously been wallowing in error and mediocrity. You have been able to resolve, with a matchless elegance and virtuosity, the greater number of those painful enigmas in which generations of researchers had continued to be ensnared. You have been able to clear the way that will soon lead us to the kingdom of Knowledge, to the knowledge of the Great Whole, to Man's decisive domination of an opaque and darkling

*This seems not to have been published commercially in Perec's lifetime. It is one of several pieces deriving from the years he spent working as archivist in a laboratory.

†i.e. into the Académie Française, meeting in its domed chamber.

Universe. Like a Democritus, a Newton, a Pasteur, a Valéry, a Radot, you have caused Science to accomplish the Great Leap Forward that will bring it out from the abyss on the brink of which it had been teetering.[1]

However, although the work of Marcel Gotlib is today universally known and acknowledged, and although most of his contributions have been amply disseminated and vulgarized by his historiographers and exegetes, one of the sectors in which his prodigious spirit of analysis and synthesis has shown itself with the greatest éclat has remained oddly in the shadows. Whereas the precious commentaries of Bouldu,[2] Lévi-Strauss,[3] Reiser,[4] Glützenbaum,[5] Ladding,[6] Oumboulélé,[7] Cloutier,[8] Slowburn,[9] Howland,[10] Druillet,[11] and Paul[12] have brought out once and for all the primordial role played by Gotlib in the fields of comparative criminology, structural anthropology, analytical musicology,

1. Leprince-Ringuet, L., *Comic Rays*, Paris, PUF, 1979.

2. Bouldu, I., 'On the Use of Close Combat in the Detection of Deafness', *Arch. Criminol. Didact.*, 1972, 36, 47–58.

3. Lévi-Strauss, C., 'The Myth of the Fish in Breton Folklore from Saint-Goménolé', *Rev. Fr. Ethnol. Compar.*, 1973, 143, 221–347.

4. Reiser, J.M., 'Untersuchen über Gotlib's Unterschrift des Ludwig Van's Pastorale', *Z.F. Musikol. u. Akustik*, 1971, 63, 48–57.

5. Glützenbaum, O., 'Gotlib's Methods in Acupunctural Treatment of Aerophagia', *Canad. J. Allergol.*, 1979, 3, 367–369.

6. Ladding, A., 'Gotlib's Contribution to the Problem of Street Sanitation and Garbage-can Cleaning', *Brit. J. Soc. Hygiene*, 1976, 327, 1–45.

7. Oumboulélé, M., 'Ng'otlib ng'ifé m'purien ng'kadé m'siné m'dézizi', *Nx. Ng'Cah. Ng'Folk. Afr.*, 1977, 48, 123–456.

8. Cloutier, R., 'Gotlib's Equations Applied to the Calculation of Prespherical Volumes', *Arch. Inst. Mat. Transcend.*, 1976, 66, 34–36.

9. Slowburn, J.L., 'Varietti effetti della rigoladda nelle duellisti', *Arch. Ital. Rigol. Zigomatol.*, 1975, 99, 198–246.

10. Howland, D., 'Gotlibian Measurements in Bantu Statuary. Theory and Methods', *Bull. Archeol. Quantit.*, 1969, 3, 56–80.

11. Druillet, P., 'Capitalist Economy and Tax Credits', *Sem. Zézet.*, 1978, 45, 1165–1167.

12. Paul, P., 'On the Presence of Cannabinol in Lyophilized Broccoli', *Quart. Bull. Police Lab.*, 1979, 158, 975–1007.

clinical stomatology, urban sociology, African ethnology, descriptive geometry, genetic epistemology, integral statistics, political economy and molecular chemistry, nothing, or next to nothing, has been said concerning the prodigious series of experiments realized by Gotlib in the laboratory of Professor Burp between 1957 and 1963, which were so profoundly to overturn our knowledge in the fields of dynamic ethology and animal physiology. No doubt the tragic departure of Léon Burp and the painful silence which Marcel Gotlib imposed on himself for almost fifteen years explain why, out of all his researches, it is these that should have been the most reluctantly given to be known by the public at large. But the time has come today to lift the veil on this unique and exemplary collaboration which will forever remain a model for all researchers. The publication of the correspondence which the two men kept up between 1954 and 1963,[13] finally authorized by Marcel Gotlib, shows very clearly that it is now time to reveal to the scientific world the extraordinary results that they achieved.

Léon Burp and Marcel Gotlib had been friends from the very start. They were both born in Vaudouhé-lès-Gonesse and Léon's uncle's godmother's son was the second cousin of Marcel's sister, Liliane's, husband's nephew. They were fellow pupils at the Great Swiss Seminary in Roubaix, as well as fellow members of the choral group, the 'Joyful Nightingales of the Côtes-du-Rhône'. Then their destinies grew apart. While Marcel Gotlib, with the talents of which we already know, launched himself on a career as a theatre director (these were the days of *Tragic Picnic*, *Stockbreeding in Burgundy*, *Five Foot Six* and *The Gendarme Goes into Retirement*), Léon Burp, after having worked for a while as an expert in macaronic spaghettology in the laboratories of Félix Potin,* left for Austria to sit at the feet of Von Glütenschtummelhimdörf.

For a number of years, the two men met only on special occasions, such as the wedding of Ferdinand Gotlib, one of Marcel's

13. Gotlib, M. and Burp, L., *Correspondence*, Louvain: Desclée de Brouwer, 1980, 17 vols.

*A chain of food shops in France.

cousins, in Vaudouhé (where he married Mlle F. Lacruche), or his uncle Philibert's reception into the Académie Française.[14]

It was now that Marcel Gotlib, discouraged by the commercial failure of his most ambitious work, *2002 Space Odyssey*,[15] finally renounced the Seventh Art, symbolically setting fire in front of the terrace at Fouquet's to the scripts of the three films he was then planning, the titles alone of which have come down to us: *The Things of the Life Ahead*, *Two Englishwomen and the Lost Continent* and *Balzac 001 versus Doctor No.* In fact it was at this time that Marcel Gotlib was to discover Leonardo da Vintchi and to realize that his true vocation was not the cinema but music.

Appointed the following week to be the head of the Metropolitan Opera in New York, he was to create there, in the course of the months that followed, some of the most notable works of those years: *The Bloodred Radiator Plug*, with Kurt Schtimmel, Hans Trüden, Klaus Ziegel, Wolfgang Gröbz and Magda Schweinhund, *Gault and Millau in the Far West*,* *Who is that Son of a Bitch Who Put Some Soap in my Scotch?*, magisterially interpreted by Ephraim Zimbalist Jr, and *The Law of Gravitation*, a monumental saga retracing the prodigious life of Isaac Newton, which was to have a decisive influence on his subsequent changes of direction. But here too, the cabals and machinations hatched by the timorous spirits exasperated by the extent of his ambitions got the better of his tenacity. When he had the brilliant idea of having the eureka-style apple played by the young Zurich tenor Hans Spatenberg, the SPITIM (Society for the Protection of Individuals of a

14. . . . where he was appointed porter in replacement of M. Norbert Leglandu, who was allowed to exercise his right to retirement and took advantage of it to set up, along with his two great grandsons, a group of tapdancers, the Three Klaps.

15. The film was on the way to completion when there appeared on Parisian screens the gross forgery which Stanley Kubrick had knocked up in a few weeks. Gotlib's distributors and producers immediately broke off the filming, preferring to lose the six million dollars they had already invested rather than incur a certain catastrophe.

*Gault and Millau are the compilers of a highly regarded guide to French restaurants.

Tallness Inferior to the Mean) launched a series of demonstrations which led to the Opera House being closed.

Marcel Gotlib returned to France and went through a spiritual crisis in the course of which, assailed by doubts, he contemplated for a while going home to work in his father's coal merchant's business. But his appetite for knowledge, his intellectual curiosity and his unquenchable love of risk soon became uppermost again. It was now that, through the agency of the Chaprot family, of which they had both been long-standing intimates, he met up with Léon Burp once more, who, after having been the head accountant with Aristides, the butcher and poulterer, had just started as head of research in the Laboratory of Comparative Animalology in the Department of Tropical Biology at Malaga-Saint-Ouen.

The rest we know. Within six years the collaboration of Burp and Gotlib had given rise to a series of articles in which all the problems that the specialists in animal physiology had been trying in vain for decades to resolve were elucidated one by one. It would be tedious to draw up the list of all these discoveries, so we shall content ourselves with recalling the most celebrated:

demonstration of the mimetic and ventriloquial faculties of the sloth[16]

discovery of neurotic behaviour patterns in certain animals disturbed by the human environment[17]

elucidation of the mysteries of pigmentation in the zebra[18]

explanation of dehydration in the camel[19]

16. Burp, L. and Gotlib, M., 'Observations on the Mimetic Behaviour of the Bradypus', *J. Physiol. Paris*, 1958, 47, 222.

17. Gotlib, M. and Burp, L., 'On the Degradation of the Ego in Domestic Animals', *Arch. Psychiat. Animal.*, 1958, 66, 35–58.

18. Gotlib, M., Nioutonne, I. and Burp, L., 'Topological Remarks on the Spatio-Temporal Modifications of the Zebra's Stripes (*Zebra zebra L.*)', *Bull. Physiopathol. Tropic.*, 1959, 47, 128–149.

19. Burp, L. and Gotlib, M., 'Fluid Dynamics in *Chamelopsis sahariensis*', in *The Fauna and Flora of Desert or Near Desert Climates*, H. Quatre ed., Presses Universitaires de Brie et Touraine, 1959, 236pp.

analysis of the influence of the aquatic behaviour of the hippopotamus on river levels[20]

study of the speed of propagation of the nervous influx in the giraffe[21]

discovery of sub-tension in the pig[22]

experimental demonstration of stiffness in the pointer[23]

analysis of certain sexual behaviour patterns in the rabbit[24]

demonstration of ticklish zones in a normal human being[25]

and finally, their last two pieces of work, which turned the still primitive discipline of prehistoric anatomo-physiology upside down: one on the evolution of species and the appearance of the crocodile,[26] the other on the adhesive properties of the fossil snail.[27]

Léon Burp's departure, in the dramatic circumstances that we all know of, put a brutal stop to this collaboration, unique in the annals of science. Marcel Gotlib was approached by the Ministry for Scientific Research as Applied to Industry to replace his friend as head of the Laboratory of Comparative Animalology, but he

20. Gotlib, M., Oumboulélé, M. and Burp, L., 'Note on the Use of *Porcinus artiodactylis hippopotamus* for Irrigation on the Banks of the Nile', *Z. f. Nilpferd. Wiss.*, 1959, 99, 375–387.

21. Burp, L., Gotlib, M. and Burp, L., 'Latency of the Reflex Arc in *Girafus girafo*', *Animal Studies*, 1960, 55, 356–387.

22. Gotlib, M. and Burp, L., 'Ladespannung beim Schweine', *Arch. Wurstwar. u. Delikatess.*, 1960, 21, 635–723.

23. Burp, L. and Gotlib, M., 'Stiffness and Ankylosis in Ground-game Dogs', *Science*, 1961, 145, 89–93.

24. Gotlib, M. and Burp, L., 'Sexual Anomalies in the Rabbit', *Science*, 1961, 145, 93–97.

25. Burp, L., Blondeaux, G.J.B., Raffray, X. and Gotlib, M., 'Zygomatic Reflexes and Ticklish Zones', in *International Colloquium on Desopilating Characters and their Effects on Humans*, M. Greg, J. Bonessian, A. Glützenbaum and M. Gotlib eds., Oxford, 1961, pp. 345–576.

26. Gotlib, M. and Burp, L., 'Phylo-genetic Considerations on the Crocodile. Facts and Hypotheses', *J. Palaeontol. Embryol.*, 1962, 1, 23–89.

27. Burp, L. and Gotlib, M., 'Vorgeschichtliche Biologie des Schneckes', in *Studies in Palaeophysiology* Vol. 1, Heidelberg, 1963.

refused, preferring to resume once more the arduous path of creation in grief, solitude and doubt.

Postscript: New Reflections on the Life and Work of Romuald Saint-Sohaint

On several occasions in his works, Marcel Gotlib makes reference to an obscure man of science of whom history has not even retained the name but to whom we owe the paper-clip, the press-stud and the edible boomerang. Our own researches having led us into neighbouring domains, we became keen to learn more about this unacknowledged inventor, whose name at least it seems inconceivable has not been somewhere preserved; and everything gives us to think that the man in question can only be Romuald Saint-Sohaint.

Romuald Saint-Sohaint was born in 1802 in Besançon. His father, Nicolas Saint-Sohaint, was the orderly of General the Count Hugo, who much esteemed his great valour and great size and, very often, on the evening after a battle, took him with him to ride on horseback across the field strewn with the dead on whom the darkness was falling. Everything gives us to suppose that the young Romuald had for the companion of his childhood games the young Victor Hugo, but nothing authorizes us to assert that this left any particular mark on him. We know on the other hand that he revealed very early on an aptitude for algebra, geometry and physics. He entered the Ecole Polytechnique at the age of twenty and left it at the age of twenty-four as a lieutenant of artillery. But garrison life no doubt failed to live up to his deepest aspirations for he resigned three years later. In 1830, in the salon of Mme Récamier at L'Abbaye-aux-Bois, he met a wealthy Spanish widow, the Countess d'Aguda, whom he married the following year. Freed henceforth from all financial worries, Saint-Sohaint was now able to devote himself entirely to his researches. In addition to the metal attachment known as the paper-clip (patented in 1847), the press-stud (patented in 1852 and recognized as being of public utility posthumously, in 1871), Saint-Sohaint discovered the principle of the liquefaction of methane, gamma particles, the origin of Hercynian folds, and the proof by nine,* which was rapidly disseminated among schools of every denomination and earned him the Academic Palms† in 1863. To him we also owe an automatic corkscrew based on guncotton, the sale of which was banned after the blaze in the canteen of the French Legation in Bucharest, a process for making paper at once softer and more resistant which was later taken up by Wolfgang Amadeus Quincampoix, a tricycle that could be completely dismantled, of which the postal authorities ordered 4,000, a system for holding up socks which was all the rage up until the beginning of this century, and a treatise in four volumes devoted to the surfacing and upkeep of local roads, for which he received the Prix Cabrisseau. But his most popular inventions, still in common use today, remain the screwdriver, the serving trolley, the rocking-chair, the nutcracker and the twist drill. And it was because he spent the last years of his life, from 1864 to 1868, in the Charenton Asylum, that the expressions 'to have a screw loose', 'to be off his trolley', 'to be off his rocker', 'to be crackers', and 'to be round the twist' have for us the sense they do.

Nowhere in Saint-Sohaint's works have we found any trace of researches concerning a so-called 'boomerang' custard-pie capable of returning to its starting-point once it has missed its target. On the other hand, Saint-Sohaint appears to have devoted his last moments of lucidity to perfecting a pie that would never miss its target and which, for reasons that remain obscure, he called the 'tarte des Demoiselles'. It was no part of our purpose to ask ourselves what the reasons may have been which led Marcel Gotlib, whose erudition was customarily impeccable and without flaw, not to cite this man of science, unrecognized it is true but not truly unknown, since a street in the 13th arrondissement still bears his name. It was in any case of interest, we thought, to dwell for a moment on this personage, nearly all of whose inventions and discoveries continue to play a part in our everyday lives.

*A method taught in French schools of checking multiplication and division sums.

†A decoration dating back to 1808 and given for meritorious contributions to teaching and to the arts. Holders are entitled to wear a violet ribbon in their buttonhole.

The Winter Journey / Le Voyage d'hiver (1993)*

*First published as a gift volume sent out in December 1979 to friends and employees by the Hachette publishing company; it was republished in *Hachette-Informations* in 1980 and then in *Le Magazine littéraire* in 1983.

In the last week of August 1939, as the talk of war invaded Paris, a young literature teacher, Vincent Degraël, was invited to spend a few days at the place outside Le Havre belonging to the parents of one of his colleagues, Denis Borrade. The day before his departure, while exploring his hosts' shelves in search of one of those books one has always promised oneself one will read, but that one will generally only have time to leaf inattentively through beside the fire before going to make up a fourth at bridge, Degraël lit upon a slim volume entitled *The Winter Journey*, whose author, Hugo Vernier, was quite unknown to him but whose opening pages made so strong an impression on him that he barely found time to make his excuses to his friend and his parents before going up to his room to read it.

The Winter Journey was a sort of narrative written in the first person, and set in a semi-imaginary country whose heavy skies, gloomy forests, mild hills and canals transected by greenish locks evoked with an insidious insistence the landscapes of Flanders and the Ardennes. The book was divided into two parts. The first, shorter part retraced in sybilline terms a journey which had all the appearances of an initiation, whose every stage seemed certainly to have been marked by a failure, and at the end of which the anonymous hero, a man whom everything gave one to suppose was young, arrived beside a lake that was submerged in a thick mist; there, a ferryman was waiting for him, who took him to a steep-sided, small island in the middle of which there rose a tall, gloomy building; hardly had the young man set foot on the narrow pontoon that afforded the only access to the island when a strange-looking couple appeared: an old man and an old woman, both clad in long black capes, who seemed to rise up out of the fog and who came and placed themselves on either side of him, took him by the elbows and pressed themselves as tightly as they could against his sides; welded together almost, they scaled a rock-strewn path, entered the house, climbed a wooden staircase and came to a chamber. There, as inexplicably as they had appeared, the old people vanished, leaving the young man alone in the middle of the room. It was perfunctorily furnished: a bed covered with a flowery cretonne, a table, a chair. A fire was blazing in the fireplace. On the table a meal had been laid: bean soup, a shoulder of beef. Through the tall window of the room, the young man watched the full moon emerging from the clouds; then he sat down at the table and began to eat. This solitary supper brought the first part to an end.

The second part alone formed nearly four-fifths of the book and it quickly appeared that the brief narrative preceding it was merely an anecdotal pretext. It was a long confession of an exacerbated lyricism, mixed in with poems, with enigmatic maxims, with blasphemous incantations. Hardly had he begun reading it before Vincent Degraël felt a sense of unease that he found it impossible to define exactly, but which only grew more pronounced as he turned the pages of the volume with an increasingly shaky hand; it was as if the phrases he had in front of him had become suddenly familiar, were starting irresistibly to remind him of *something*, as if on to each one that he read there had been imposed, or rather superimposed, the at once precise yet blurred memory of a phrase almost identical to it that he had perhaps already read somewhere else; as if these words, more tender than a caress or more treacherous than a poison, words that were alternately limpid and hermetic, obscene and cordial, dazzling, labyrinthine, endlessly swinging like the frantic needle of a compass between a hallucinated violence and a fabulous serenity, formed the outline of a vague configuration in which could be found, jumbled together, Germain Nouveau and Tristan Corbière, Rimbaud and Verhaeren, Charles Cros and Léon Bloy.

These were the very authors with whom Vincent Degraël was concerned – for several years he had been working on a thesis on 'the evolution of French poetry from the Parnassians to the Symbolists' – and his first thought was that he might well have chanced to read this book as part of his researches, then, more likely, that he was the victim of an illusory *déjà vu* in which, as when the simple taste of a sip of tea suddenly carries you back thirty years to England, a mere trifle had succeeded, a sound, a smell, a gesture – perhaps the moment's hesitation he had noticed before taking the book from the shelf where it had been arranged between Verhaeren and Viélé-Griffin, or else the eager way in which he had perused the opening pages – for the false memory of a previous reading to superimpose itself and so to disturb his present reading as to render it impossible. Soon, however, doubt was no longer possible and Degraël had to yield to the evidence. Perhaps his memory was playing tricks on him, perhaps it was only by chance that Vernier seemed to have borrowed his 'solitary jackal haunting stone sepulchres' from Catulle Mendès, perhaps it should be put down to a fortuitous convergence, to a parading of influence, a deliberate homage, unconscious copying, wilful pastiche, a liking for quotation, a fortunate coincidence, perhaps expressions such as 'the flight of time', 'winter fogs', 'dim horizon', 'deep caves', 'vaporous fountains', 'uncertain light of the wild undergrowth' should be seen as belonging by right to all poets so that it was just as normal to meet with them in a paragraph by Hugo Vernier as in the stanzas of Jean Moréas, but it was quite impossible not to recognize, word for word, or almost, reading at random, in one place a fragment from Rimbaud ('I readily could see a mosque in place of a factory, a drum school built by angels') or Mallarmé ('the lucid winter, the season of serene art'), in another Lautréamont ('I gazed in a mirror at that mouth bruised by my own volition'), Gustave Kahn ('Let the song expire . . . my heart weeps/A bistre crawls around the brightness. The solemn/silence has risen slowly, it frightens/ The familiar sounds of the shadowy staff') or, only slightly modified, Verlaine ('in the interminable tedium of the plain, the snow gleamed like sand. The sky was the colour of copper. The train slid without a murmur . . .'), etc.

It was four o'clock in the morning when Degraël finished reading *The Winter Journey*. He had pinpointed some thirty borrowings. There were certainly others. Hugo Vernier's book seemed to be nothing more than a prodigious compilation from the poets of the end of the nineteenth century, a disproportionate cento, a mosaic almost every piece of which was the work of someone else. But at the same time as he was struggling to imagine this unknown author who had wanted to extract the very substance of his own text from the books of others, when he was attempting to picture this admirable and senseless project to himself in its entirety, Degraël felt a wild suspicion arise in him: he had just remembered that in taking the book from the shelf he had automatically made a note of the date, impelled by that reflex of the young researcher who never consults a work without remarking the bibliographical details. Perhaps he had made a mistake, but he certainly thought he had read 1864. He checked it, his heart pounding. He had read it correctly. That would mean Vernier had 'quoted' a line of Mallarmé two years in advance, had plagiarized Verlaine ten years before his 'Forgotten Ariettas', had written some Gustave Kahn nearly a quarter of a century before Kahn did! It would mean that Lautréamont, Germain Nouveau, Rimbaud, Corbière and quite a few others were merely the copyists of an unrecognized poet of genius who, in a single work, had been able to bring together the very substance off which three or four generations would be feeding after him!

Unless, obviously, the printer's date that appeared on the book were wrong. But Degraël refused to entertain that hypothesis: his discovery was too beautiful, too obvious, too necessary not to be true, and he was already imagining the vertiginous consequences it would provoke: the prodigious scandal that the public revelation of this 'premonitory anthology' would occasion, the extent of the fallout, the enormous doubt that would be cast on all that the critics and literary historians had been imperturbably teaching for years and years. Such was his impatience that, abandoning sleep once and for all, he dashed down to the library to try and find out a little more about this Vernier and his work.

He found nothing. The few dictionaries and directories to be found in the Borrades' library knew nothing of the existence of Hugo Vernier. Neither Denis nor his parents were able to tell him anything further; the book had been bought at an auction, ten years before, in Honfleur; they had looked through it without paying it much attention.

All through the day, with Denis's help, Degraël proceeded to make a systematic examination of the book, going to look up its splintered shards in dozens of anthologies and collections. They found almost three hundred and fifty, shared among almost thirty authors; the most celebrated along with the most obscure poets of the *fin de siècle*, and sometimes even a few prose writers (Léon Bloy, Ernest Hello) seemed to have used *The Winter Journey* as a bible from which they had extracted the best of themselves: Banville, Richepin, Huysmans, Charles Cros, Léon Valade rubbed shoulders with Mallarmé and Verlaine and others now fallen into oblivion whose names were Charles de Pomairols, Hippolyte Vaillant, Maurice Rollinat (the godson of George Sand), Laprade, Albert Mérat, Charles Morice or Antony Valabrègue.

Degraël made a careful note of the list of authors and the source of their borrowings and returned to Paris, fully determined to continue his researches the very next day in the Bibliothèque Nationale. But events did not allow him to. In Paris his call-up papers were waiting for him. Joining his unit in Compiègne, he found himself, without really having had the time to understand why, in Saint-Jean-de-Luz, passed over into Spain and from there to England, and only came back to France in 1945. Throughout the war he had carried his notebook with him and had miraculously succeeded in not losing it. His researches had obviously not progressed much, but he had made one, for him capital, discovery all the same. In the British Museum he had been able to consult the *Catalogue général de la librairie française* and the *Bibliographie de la France* and had been able to confirm his tremendous hypothesis: *The Winter Journey*, by Vernier (Hugo) had indeed been published in 1864, at Valenciennes, by Hervé Frères, Publishers and Booksellers, had been registered legally like all books published in France, and had been deposited in the Bibliothèque Nationale, where it had been given the shelfmark Z87912.

Appointed to a teaching post in Beauvais, Vincent Degraël henceforth devoted all his free time to *The Winter Journey*.

Going thoroughly into the private journals and correspondence of most of the poets of the end of the nineteenth century quickly convinced him that, in his day, Hugo Vernier had known the celebrity he deserved: notes such as 'received a letter from Hugo today', or 'wrote Hugo a long letter', 'read V.H. all night', or even Valentin Havercamp's celebrated 'Hugo, Hugo alone' definitely did not refer to 'Victor' Hugo, but to this doomed poet whose brief oeuvre had apparently inflamed all those who had held it in their hands. Glaring contradictions which criticism and literary history had never been able to explain thus found their one logical solution: it was obviously with Hugo Vernier in mind and what they owed to his *Winter Journey* that Rimbaud had written 'I is another' and Lautréamont 'Poetry should be made by all and not by one.'

But the more he established the preponderant place that Hugo Vernier was going to have to occupy in the literary history of late ninteenth-century France, the less was he in a position to furnish tangible proof, for he was never able again to lay his hands on a copy of *The Winter Journey*. The one that he had consulted had been destroyed – along with the villa – during the bombing of Le Havre; the copy deposited in the Bibliothèque Nationale wasn't there when he asked for it and it was only after long enquiries that he was able to learn that, in 1926, the book had been sent to a binder who had never received it. All the researches that he caused to be undertaken by dozens, by hundreds of librarians, archivists and booksellers proved fruitless, and Degraël soon persuaded himself that the edition of five hundred copies had been deliberately destroyed by the very people who had been so directly inspired by it.

Of Hugo Vernier's life, Vincent Degraël learnt nothing, or next to nothing. An unlooked-for brief mention, unearthed in an obscure *Biographie des hommes remarquables de la France du Nord et de la Belgique* (Verviers, 1882) informed him that he had been born in Vimy (Pas-de-Calais) on 3 September 1836. But the records of the Vimy registry office had been burned in 1916, along with duplicate copies lodged in the prefecture in Arras. No death certificate seemed ever to have been made out.

For close on thirty years, Vincent Degraël strove in vain to assemble proof of the existence of this poet and of his work. When he died, in the psychiatric hospital in Verrières, a few of his former pupils undertook to sort the vast pile of documents and manuscripts he had left behind. Among them figured a thick register bound in black cloth whose label bore, carefully and ornamentally inscribed, *The Winter Journey*. The first eight pages retraced the history of his fruitless researches; the other 392 pages were blank.

from *Voeux* (1989)

New Year's Greetings

At each New Year, Georges Perec liked to send his friends a small 'album' by way of wishing them well. Each album contained a new series of word puzzles, of a generally daunting if not impenetrable ingenuity. This kind of puzzle can't by its nature be translated, or only (as here) if it is translated and explained at the same time. Because it would be a pity to publish an anthology of Perec's occasional writings without including an item or two from these charming handsels, I have translated and explained a few of the more manageable examples here. And because, again, I have myself always found games like these very good to play, I have added to Perec's a few examples of my own, composed needless to say in English, in the hope that existing or potential addicts of such pastimes may be encouraged to try the same for themselves. I know of no more loyal or enjoyable way of saluting the genial expertise of Georges Perec.

First, one or two examples from the 'album' for 1974–5. This was entitled 'Les adventures de Dixion Harry' and was composed as it happens on a visit to England, at Griffydam in Leicestershire (a curious village name I at first thought Perec must have made up, until I learnt it was real). The series is Anglo-French in inspiration, as its overall title shows: it has *adventure* where French would have *aventure*, and in the vaguely English name of Dixion Harry we can but hear the English word *dictionary* (not the French *dictionnaire*).

What Perec does is to take a number of English proverbs or sayings and distort them phonetically so as to produce French sentences (of a kind) from them. He then writes a very short 'narrative', of a few lines only, which is both an expanded version of the French sentence and an 'explanation' of it. This explanation is then printed along with the original English saying, the puzzle being to work out if you can how it might have been derived from it without knowing the key (i.e. the distorted French version of the saying), which remains in the possession of the puzzle-setter.

Thus:

1. *All's well that ends well*

The narrative for this goes, in a literal English translation: 'In homage to Lewis Carroll, I have christened my cow Alice. She gives birth to her calf while the devil, completely drunk, calls her.'

The key for which lies in the telegraphic French sentence: '*Alice vêle; Satan, soûl, hèle*' (= Alice calves; Satan, drunk, calls out). The point is not to translate these words, of course, but to *say* them, in French (slurring somewhat where necessary), and so produce a rough phonetic representation of the English saying (as it sounds to a French ear!).

2. *Many hands make light work*

The narrative: 'In order to comply with the desires of his lady, this man rubbed the whole of his body with garlic. This was to fail to recognize the virulence of this plant which, running counter to what he had been seeking, completely ate away his penis!'

The key: '*Mais niant de ce mec, l'ail dévore queue*' (= 'But denying this guy, the garlic devours prick).

3. Working by these same principles, the other way round, I take a familiar French saying: '*Plus ça change, plus c'est la même chose*'.

The narrative: In a judo competition M. is fighting against a Japanese known to be at his most dangerous on the mat when his belt comes undone.

The key: Blue sash on Jap loose eh? Alarm, M. shows.

In his 'Album' for 1976–7 Perec made similar play by distorting the names of twenty-five classical composers.

4. The narrative for one of them goes, in translation: 'It has frequently been asked why Indians shut themselves up in their tents and form a tight circle around their fires. It comes from the fact that they have a superstitious fear of a carnivore which, like a vampire, would leap without fail at their carotids and suck out all their blood!'

The key: '*Loup de wigwam: bête aux veines*' (= wigwam wolf: animal of the veins). Which words, spoken quickly and in a reasonable French accent, supply the name of Ludwig van Beethoven.

5. A second example, this time in dialogue form:

– Where shall I lie down to die?
– Observe what colour your farts are. When you see one turn green, lie down and die, for that's where your place is.

The key: '*Gis où ce pet verdit*' (= lie where that fart turns green), which can be slightly mispronounced to give Giuseppe Verdi.

6. An English composer, finally, not called on by Perec. (The key to this, and the two remaining puzzles of my own composition, I withhold until p. 288).

PC Plodd was telling the Inspector that he and his notoriously left-wing colleague, 'Red' Foster, would split up in order to stay on the trail of the gang they were watching. Plodd would follow the gangsters who were on foot, Foster those who were motorized.

For 1978–9, Perec switched from classical composers to the names of American jazz musicians.

7. The narrative, again in translation: 'Under threat from the terrible flies that cause sleeping sickness, a donkey saved itself by a clever stratagem. It began to perform somersaults which amused the flies so much they forgot to bite it.'

The key: '*Cet âne égaie tsé-tsé*' (= This donkey cheers up tse-tse), yielding the name of Stan Getz.

8. Another narrative: 'The story of William Tell is very different from that recounted in the legend. In actual fact, William Tell missed the apple and killed his son. Despised by everyone and driven out from everywhere, William Tell sought at all costs to redeem himself. One day some villagers, mocking but compassionate, stuck an old dustsheet up on a stake and challenged him to hit it. Tell aimed and fired, but he was decidedly out of luck and missed even this ample target!'

The key: '*Tell honni housse manque*' (= Tell despised dustsheet misses), or Thelonius Monk.

9. And for a jazz musician whom Perec, scandalously, left off his list: 'The missus 'as just gorn off for the evening to a theatre where they put on stage versions of 'er favourite almanac.'

In 1979–80, it was the turn of the names of English and American crime or thriller writers.

10. The narrative: 'Don't talk to me about Knoll, Thonet or Charles Eames. When I sit down what I prefer is an ugly chair.'

The key: '*J'aime ça, les laides chaises*' (= I like them, ugly chairs), or James Hadley Chase.

11. The narrative: 'All the emperors of the Ming dynasty were, as we know, exceptionally corpulent. But the fattest of all was Hi.'

The key: '*Hi, enflé Ming*' (= Hi, bloated Ming), or Ian Fleming.

12. To which I will add a fine American crime writer not done by Perec: '"Don't let that computer freak anywhere near the cage," said the cockney zookeeper. "That tiger 'ates 'em, 'e'll tear 'im apart."'

Key:

6. Sir, Red would tail car (Sir Edward Elgar)
9. She'll 'ear ol' Moore done (Jelly Roll Morton)
12. 'e'll maul a nerd (Elmore Leonard)

IAM ONLINE

Read all about the latest iam projects and news

read about your favourite authors

•

investigate over 40 titles

•

browse our online portfolio

•

enter our Man Booker Prize Quiz

•

learn to read differently

•

e-mail us with your comments and book reviews

•

instantly order any iam book

'More than before, and more easily than before, writers can (to use the name of a fine British Conceptualist website) treat 'information as material', making new forms from new constraints.'

— Stephen Burt, 'Must poets write?', *London Review of Books*, Vol.34, no.9, 10 May 2012

www.informationasmaterial.org

READ LIKE A PIGEON

In every corner of the world, on every subject under the sun, iam represents quality and variety — the very best in publishing today.

For complete information about books available from information as material — including acts of appropriation, copying and plagiarism — and how to order them, write to us at the appropriate address below. Please note that for copyleft reasons the selection of books are unlikely to vary from country to country.

In Middlesbrough, in the United Kingdom: Please write to *information as material, appt 1, Harrow Court, Harrow Road, Acklam TS5 5NY, UK*

In Manchester, in the United Kingdom: Please write to *Cornerhouse Publications, 70 Oxford Street, Manchester M1 5NH, UK*

In London, in the United Kingdom: Please write to *bookartbookshop, 17 Pitfield Street London, Greater London N1 6HB, UK*

In New York City, in the United States: Please write to *Printed Matter Inc., 195 10th Avenue New York, NY 10011, United States*

In Chicago, in the United States: Please write to *Joan Flasch Artists' Book Collection, 37 S. Wabash Avenue, Suite 508, Chicago, IL 60603, United States*

In Toronto, in Canada: Please write to *Art Metropole, 1490 Dundas Street West Toronto, ON M6K 1T5, Canada*

In Amsterdam, in the Netherlands: Please write to *The Johan Deumens Gallery, Gabriel Metsustraat 8, 1st Floor, 1071 EA Amsterdam, the Netherlands*

In Paris, in France: Please write to *Florence Loewy, 9/11 rue de Thorigny, 75003 Paris, France*

In Toulouse, in France: Please write to *les Abattoirs Museum of Modern and Contemporary Art, 76 allées Charles-de-Fitte 31300 Toulouse, France*

In Kitakyushu, in Japan: Please write to *Center for Contemporary Art Kitakyushu, 2-6-1 3F Ogura Yahata-Higashi-ku, Kitakyushu 805-0059, Japan*

READ LIKE A PIGEON

information as material Twenty-First Century Classics offer a selection of the finest works of conceptual writing published this century. Spanning the globe from Calgary to Utah, from New York City to Middlesbrough, the progenitors of uncreativity as a creative practice are represented by iam.

If you would like a catalogue of the Twenty-First Century Classics library, please write to:

iam, appt 1, Harrow Court, Harrow Road, Acklam TS5 5NY, UK

(Available while stocks last)

READ LIKE A PIGEON

A CHOICE OF TWENTY-FIRST CENTURY CLASSICS

Reading the Remove of Literature Nick Thurston

Reading the Remove of Literature is a reading of the English translation of Maurice Blanchot's seminal book *L'Espace littéraire* (1955), performed on the page as an annotative writing that encircles the should-be space of print. Through the progressive appropriation and then erasure of Blanchot's text, and through a processual transposition of hand-writing into formal typography, Thurston has conceptualised and produced an astounding new book.

The Royal Road to the Unconscious Simon Morris

The Royal Road to the Unconscious was conceived by the artist Simon Morris in order to conduct an experiment on Sigmund Freud's writing. Utilising Ed Ruscha's book *Royal Road Test* as a readymade set of instructions, seventy-eight students cut out every single word from Sigmund Freud's *Interpretation of Dreams*. On Sunday, June 1st, 2003, the artist, Simon Morris (thrower) threw the words out of the window of a Renault Clio Sport on Redbridge Road, Crossways, Dorset, travelling at a speed of 90mph, approximately 122 miles southwest of Freud's psychoanalytical couch in London. The action freed the words from the structural unity of Freud's text as it subjected them to an 'aleatory moment' – a seemingly random act of utter madness.

The Answer to the Question Pavel Büchler

Pavel Büchler, with his exacting standards, worked closely with the publisher to determine every detail of this title. He insisted that we used the cheapest pulp paper available and that the book was professionally printed as an offset litho production. We have followed his instructions to the letter, printing to the highest possible standard on the worst possible paper. This small pocket-size volume contains some very big ideas.

The Persons Peter Jaeger

In 2010 the Canadian poet Peter Jaeger celebrated his fiftieth birthday. *The Persons* is a scrapbook of found texts that have been clipped, archived, and sorted for their parallel grammatical structure, with the proper name and verb always preceding their complimentary parts. Those fragments are then rearranged so that no two consecutive sentences come from the same source. Jaeger's life, here, is thus written through the words of others: those protagonists who animated his imagination and left their traces in the newspapers, emails, diaries, books (from literature to philosophy), and all the countless ephemera with which the externalized inner drama of our lives plays out.

Thesaurus Scienta Lancastriae Robert Williams & Jack Aylward-Williams

Thesaurus Scienta Lancastriae is a collaborative work between six-year old Jack Aylward-Williams and his father, Robert Williams. In this book, Jack explains the world to his father, who in turn translates its cosmology to the reader. Their project uses Williamson's Public Park in Lancaster as a microcosm of the world – for an engagement that encompasses the disciplines of geology, botany, zoology, physics, arboriculture, anthropology and many others – as well as providing a site and specific context for the stunning installationary component of their research, which is also documented in this book.

READ LIKE A PIGEON

A CHOICE OF TWENTY-FIRST CENTURY CLASSICS

An Exercise in Pathetic Criticism Kate Briggs

'Rare enough is literary criticism that allows a book to live, opens it up and invites its readers to set their own compass. Kate Briggs's *Exercise in Pathetic Criticism*, inspired by her work on Roland Barthes' last lectures, does just that, and the wealth of possibility contained in Dumas' Count of Monte Cristo unfolds before us in a mosaic of fragments, which, in their very slightness, shimmer with meaning.'—Anna-Louise Milne, Cultural Historian, University of London Institute in Paris

Do or DIY Craig Dworkin, Simon Morris, Nick Thurston

Mixing anecdote and advocacy, the first section of this two-part polemical essay offers an introduction to the concealed history of do-it-yourself publishing—as undertaken by some of the most revered writers in the modern Western literary canon, from Laurence Sterne to Irma Rombauer via Virginia Woolf and Derek Walcott. Having looked back at some of the monuments of literary history, the second section takes its charge from the epigraph, 'Institutions cannot prevent what they cannot imagine', and looks forward to the political praxis of the 21st-century's digital future.

Flatland: A Romance of Many Dimensions Derek Beaulieu

Edwin A. Abbot's famed science fiction novella from 1884, *Flatland: A Romance of Many Dimensions*, is spatially and conceptually appropriated by Beaulieu in his acclaimed book-as-poetic-diagram of the same name. 'As the Greenbergian modernists proclaimed the flatness of the canvas, so Derek Beaulieu reduces the page to a flat plane. The result is a new kind of flatness—call it non-illusionistic literature—a depthless fiction, one where image and narrative is reduced to line and shadow. In the great tradition of Picabia, Beaulieu creates a perfect work of mechanical writing with one foot in the concrete poetic past and another in the flat screen future.'—Kenneth Goldsmith, poet & Founding Editor of UBUweb

The Perverse Library Craig Dworkin

The Perverse Library is the latest poetic bookwork from scholar, critic, and iam co-editor Craig Dworkin. The book comprises of a bibliography of Dworkin's book shelves at home, a supplementary bibliography of absent and imagined books, and an accompanying essay arguing that libraries are in fact defined not by what they contain, but by what books they exclude or fail to include. The essay also investigates the histories of libraries, makes a theoretical argument about the relation of canons to architectural space, and explores the psychology of collecting — including the pathology of bibliomania.

Re-Writing Freud Simon Morris

For this book work, *Re-Writing Freud* the artist Simon Morris has re-written Sigmund Freud's *The Interpretation of Dreams*. A computer programme (designed by Christine Morris) randomly selects words, one at a time from Freud's 222,704 word text and begins to reconstruct the entire book, word by word, making a new book with the same words in a different order.